Volunteers

People and organizations
Series editor: Sheldon Zedeck
Department of Psychology, University of California, Berkeley

The study of organizations has increased significantly in recent years. In recognition of the growing importance of behavioural science research to our understanding of organizations, *People and Organizations* is a new series devoted to advanced research in industrial and organizational psychology, and organizational behaviour.

The books in the series are derived from empirical programmatic research on topics related to organizations and the ways in which people interact, respond to, and cope with the organization. Topics of special interest include: organizational culture, work and family, high technology, organizational commitment, careers, and studies of organizations in international markets. Books in the series are theoretically grounded and include specific guidelines for future research.

Already available:

Leadership and Information Processing
Linking Perceptions and Performance
Robert G. Lord and Karen J. Maher

Role Motivation Theories
John B. Miner

Volunteers

The organizational behavior of unpaid workers

Jone L. Pearce

London and New York

First published in 1993
by Routledge
11 New Fetter Lane, London EC4P 4EE

Simultaneously published in the USA and Canada
by Routledge
29 West 35th Street, New York, NY 10001

© 1993 Jone L. Pearce

Phototypeset in Garamond by
Intype, London
Printed and bound in Great Britain by
Mackays of Chatham PLC, Chatham, Kent

British Library Cataloguing in Publication Data

A catalogue record for this book is available from the British Library.

Library of Congress Cataloging in Publication Data

Pearce, Jone L.
 Volunteers : the organizational behavior of unpaid workers / Jone
L. Pearce.
 p. cm.—(People and organizations)
 Includes bibliographical references and index.
 1. Voluntarism. 2. Volunteers. I. Title. II. Series: People
and organizations (London, England)
 HN49.V64P43 1993
 361.3'7—dc20   92–36057
                                                    CIP

ISBN 0–415–09427–5

Contents

List of tables   vi
Acknowledgements   viii

Part I The context of volunteer organizational behavior

1 Volunteers at work   3

2 The structural uncertainty of volunteers' settings   15

3 Volunteers' jobs   33

Part II Why volunteer?

4 Volunteer motivation   61

5 Volunteers' attitudes: an exploration of their commitment   85

Part III Member reliability and independence

6 The organizational control of volunteers   111

7 The management of interpersonal influence   131

Part IV Toward inclusive organizational studies

8 Implications for theories of organizational behavior   151

9 Implications for volunteer management and research   169

Appendix: study methods   184
References   207
Name index   216
Subject index   220

Tables

2.1 Mean of self-reported reasons for organizational involvement   22

3.1 "How types differ" responses categorized by type   36

3.2 Differences in mean job perceptions between core and peripheral members   49

4.1 Percentage self-reported reasons for volunteering in nationwide surveys   73

5.1 Volunteers' and employees' mean job satisfaction and standard deviations   91

5.2 Mean tenure and extent to which incumbents reevaluate their participation in volunteer-staffed organizations   99

6.1 Means and intercorrelations among power and influence variables   121

6.2 Mean self-reports for core and peripheral volunteers   123

7.1 Employees in volunteer-staffed organizations   142

8.1 Contradictory roles propositions   152

8.2 Uncertain boundaries propositions   154

8.3 Decision-making propositions   156

8.4 Part-time workforce propositions   157

8.5 Effects of compensation on work design propositions   158

8.6 Social network recruiting propositions   160

8.7 Leadership of nondependent workers propositions   161

8.8 Commitment propositions   163

8.9 Devalued effort propositions   165

8.10 Symbolic role of compensation propositions   165

9.1   Effective management of volunteers propositions   170

A.1 (Group of tables)
      A.1(a) Comparison of volunteer- and employee-staffed day care
              centers   194

      A.1(b) Comparison of volunteer- and employee-staffed weekly
              newspapers   194

      A.1(c) Comparison of volunteer- and employee-staffed poverty
              relief agencies   194

      A.1(d) Comparison of volunteer- and employee-staffed
              symphonic orchestras   194

      A.1(e) Comparison of volunteer- and employee-staffed family
              planning clinics   194

      A.1(f) Comparison of volunteer- and employee-staffed gift
              shops   195

      A.1(g) Comparison of volunteer- and employee-staffed fire
              departments   195

      A.1(h) Mean differences between organization types on the
              descriptive characteristics   195

A.2 Means, standard deviations, and intercorrelations among the
     organizational-level variables   201

A.3 Means, standard deviations, and intercorrelations among the
     organization-sample interview scales   201

A.4 Means, standard deviations, and intercorrelations among the pay
     status and questionnaire scales   202

Acknowledgements

I have received generous support from others throughout this project. The research participants and their organizations have been promised anonymity and cannot be personally acknowledged, yet the spirit with which they shared their time and insights made this work possible.

I received financial assistance in support of data collection from Yale University's Beach Fund and from the exceedingly generous J. Richard Hackman, for whom I worked for several months during data collection as a research assistant on his Office of Naval Research Contract NOO14–75C–0269, NR 17–744, to Yale University. Certainly, his assistance in every facet of the data collection and initial interpretations cannot be measured in money. Others who provided particularly important insights during that period were Carol Tropp Schreiber, Madeline Heilman, and Clay Alderfer.

This work has benefited from the critiques and suggestions of Steve Sommer, Anne Tsui, Candace Widmer, Nancy McDuff, Angela Tripoli, Daniel McAllister, Gregory Stephens, and Alan Morris. I particularly want to thank Daniel Feldman, Greta Brooks, and Sheldon Zedeck, whose penetrating analyses of earlier versions have contributed in significant ways to this work and have saved me from many embarrassments.

Finally I would like to thank my family – John, David, and Maggie Lara. Although they haven't read a word of it (yet), they provided the solace and joy that made it possible for me to complete this work. It is dedicated to them.

Part I

The context of volunteer organizational behavior

This work seeks to explore the mystery of why and how volunteers organize their work; it is about the organizational behavior of volunteers. That is, it seeks to present the results of the author's search to understand why volunteers seek organizational work, how they conduct that work once they are members, and how these efforts can best be managed so the participants can meet their objectives for themselves and their organizations. Its purpose is to present a scholarly investigation of what we know about volunteers as organizational participants. It draws upon original research and a broad-ranging review of scholarship about organizational volunteers to learn about their experiences.

The work begins with a description of its scope and an introduction to the theoretical perspective and empirical study in Chapter 1. The two chapters that follow contain analyses of the context in which volunteers work. This is because volunteers' organizational settings are often substantially more complex than may be realized and because these contexts usually differ in significant ways from those employees face. For the present work, the features of the context which are most relevant to individual and interpersonal behavior are those of (1) society's evaluation of the meaning of volunteer work, since volunteers, their clients, and others carry these presumptions into their organizations; (2) the nature and kinds of organizations in which volunteers work and their goals; and (3) the nature of the jobs they perform in their organizations. The first two of these are analyzed in Chapter 2, "The structural uncertainty of volunteers' settings," and the latter is analyzed – primarily using data from the studied organizations – in Chapter 3, "Volunteers' jobs."

Chapter 1

Volunteers at work

It's hard to say exactly why, they [volunteers] probably decide they are doing it for a good reason so they assume a positive attitude about it. If you are paid you probably don't question it, you just assume you are doing it for a living. Volunteers don't know why they are working; they don't know the answer. I guess they assume they do it because they want to do good. These assumptions lead to different ways of doing things. Not that paid people aren't cheerful; it's just that it's not needed.

(Volunteer in a non-sectarian food distribution program)

I see myself as a volunteer and do not feel that my work is judged in accordance with employee standards. As a volunteer, I tend to hand in my work when "my own free will" dictates that I should do so. If I felt that I were an employee of this organization then I would perform to the best of my ability. I believe that any organization, whether it is based on volunteer relationships or employee relationships, should be arranged in a manner whereby the volunteers felt their positions were as credible as working for an employee-based organization. . . . As a volunteer I accomplish assignments at my own free will, or I don't. It doesn't seem to matter to anyone whether the assignments are completed or not. The attitude is "do what you want" or "you're just a volunteer." I like to believe I am more than a volunteer, but it is hard to convince myself otherwise. As a volunteer I feel as though I am "one of the millions" instead of an individual. If this organization wants to keep this staff it needs more rules, regulations, procedures and incentives. Nothing can exist with "your own free will" as an objective or standard. It's not logical or ethical or rational.

(Volunteer reporter, college newspaper, written by respondent in space provided for open-ended comments, questionnaire)

We know very little about how and why individuals volunteer to work in organizations, and we know even less about how their efforts are organized and directed once they are at work. As these quotations suggest, this uncertainty is experienced by the participants as well as outside observers.

We have all heard stories about (or have experienced) the acute frustrations of volunteering to help on a worthy project but finding either disorganization, frayed nerves, or situations in which good people somehow seem to exploit and insult one another. Yet there are millions of volunteer-staffed organizations which quietly and effectively provide invaluable services and promote significant societal change. Why such wide variation in organizational behavior?

This exploration begins by suggesting that a central theme to understanding volunteers' organizational behavior is uncertainty. This uncertainty is reflected in the efforts of the above volunteers to understand their own roles in their organizations, and their responses suggest the variety of understandings and potential frustration that this uncertainty elicits.

The study of uncertainty and of the related concept of ambiguity has long been prominent in organizational behavior; research in role ambiguity and task uncertainty continue to hold a prominent place in its theories (Dess and Beard 1984). Yet the uncertainty experienced by organizational volunteers is inherently more extensive and more central to their experiences than is the case for employees. Volunteers simply face less crystallized expectations about their behavior, purposes, and affective reactions than do paid workers. This stems from the uncertain role of voluntary organizational work in society and from the conflicting or vague purposes of many of these organizations.

The uncertainty individual volunteers face originates, in part, with the societal role of volunteers' organizations. Their organizations vary widely – including self-help groups, political parties, large social welfare institutions, advocacy associations, youth clubs, and so forth. These organized bodies have always fascinated social philosophers and students of social institutions, since they seem to hold great symbolic power to represent freedom from coercion, whether it be from the constraints of family and tradition, the state, or the economic pressures of employment. The "free" character of volunteer-staffed organizations seems to invite social theorists to see them as reflections of the true nature of a society. Thus, volunteers' associations have been praised and condemned, held as examples of virtually every moral or ideological position. Tocqueville's (1968, pp. 1835–40) observation that voluntary associations represent a fundamental characteristic of Americans is one of the earliest and most widely known. This view of associations as representatives of societal character persists (as is reflected, for example, in McPherson and Smith-Lovin 1986).

Thus, volunteer organizational effort is not as constrained as paid work. Volunteers are free to adopt objectives and to organize themselves in any way that suits the participants. Yet, while this may be ideologically attractive, it poses serious practical problems for the participants. Guiding constraints from other settings, such as "efficiency" for business or "voters' preferences" in governmental organizations, simply do not apply. If volunteers are going to work in an integrated and organized fashion to achieve their goals, they need to find procedures by which they can insure that sufficient and appropriate individual behavior is harnessed. This work reports how this is accomplished in a particular set of organizations.

In addition to the question of the integration of volunteers' actions into organized behavior, we also know very little about volunteers' experience of work life. We do not know why they are attracted to such work or their reactions to their organizations once they have joined. The work life of employees has drawn extensive attention, yet research and theory concerning the psychological and social experiences of volunteers in organizations have been modest and fragmented. Social theorists have assumed that experiences as a volunteer have powerful effects on the volunteers and their larger society, but exactly how this influence occurs is rarely addressed.

Furthermore, a thoughtful study of organizational volunteers raises questions that are central to theories concerning organizational behavior of employees. Volunteers, as organizational members, differ from employees in several fundamental respects, and, as will be detailed below, the traditional focus on employees as representatives of all organizational workers has occasionally resulted in misleading interpretations. In brief, in organizational behavior, employees' status as "organizational workers" and "wage/salary earners" has been confounded. It will be suggested that many features of the organizational behavior of employees and their work which we have assumed to be universal are influenced in important ways by their status as "employees." For example, volunteers provide a valuable opportunity to study the advantages and disadvantages of harnessing nonmonetary controls for organizational reward systems. A thoughtful examination of the organizational behavior of volunteers can help extend our understanding of such concepts as organizational design, the role of individual motives and attitudes, the exercise of interpersonal influence, and the role of pay in organizational behavior. Thus, an understanding of volunteer organizational behavior can serve as a mirror that provides a reflection on and, it is hoped, a contribution to general theories of organization behavior.

A clearer understanding of the organizational behavior of volunteers is also important because volunteer workers are a force in their own right. That much organizational work in western industrial society is accomplished by volunteers is self-evident, but their broad presence can be illustrated by the following efforts to quantify it. The most recent national American survey, conducted by the Gallup Organization for Independent Sector in 1987, found that 52 percent of adults reported volunteering. The form of the question does not allow us to know what percentage report volunteering in formal organizations, but it can probably be assumed to be a substantial proportion (see Schram 1985, for review). Although the forms of the survey questions vary, similarly high levels of volunteer membership are found in Canada (Curtis 1971) and France (Rose 1954), with higher levels reported in Denmark (Svalastoga 1957) and Sweden (Heckscher 1948). Smaller scale community studies have found that participation rates in Mexico are similar to those in the United States (Dotson 1953) and that in tropical Africa "a high proportion of individuals in the cities" belong to voluntary associations (Wallerstein 1965). Independent Sector (1986) estimated that the time-value of American volunteer labor in one year totaled over $84 billion. Virtually all of the readers of this book and most of the people they know have worked as organizational volunteers at some time in their lives.

Certainly, all members of society benefit from the unpaid labor of many volunteers. A clearer understanding of how volunteers can more successfully organize themselves in the face of uncertainty has both practical and theoretical import.

STUDY METHODOLOGY

This work addresses the actions, social and psychological experiences – that is, the organizational behavior – of volunteers in formal organizations. It is not an account of voluntary associations or organizations as such, although some acquaintance with these entities will be necessary to an understanding of the context in which organizational volunteers work. Concomitantly, it is not involved in the debate over the "functions" of voluntary associations in modern societies, in the role of citizen participation in pluralism, nor is it concerned with volunteers as "owners" or members of cooperatives. It addresses the face-to-face experiences, intentions, and actions of volunteer (that is, unpaid) workers in organizations. Of course, this still leaves a wide range of material, and some focus is necessary. As will be detailed below, this study of volunteers' organizational behavior is organized into sections addressing the major practical problems volunteers confront in managing their uncertainty.

The focus is on only those volunteers in formal organizations. The distinction between associations and organizations will be developed in the next chapter. For the present discussion, it is noted that organizations are usually seen as instruments – in effect, "tools" – for performing some work or providing a type of service or product. It is precisely this combination of absence of pay *and* the need to behave in a disciplined manner that is of theoretical interest. Organizational volunteers present an interesting "problem" to students of organizational behavior, and insights into the "why" and "how" of their organizational behavior can provide a more complete understanding of the universal features of behavior in an organizational context.

The information presented in this book is based on data collected by the author as well as available published accounts reflecting on volunteer organizational behavior. The author has conducted a program of empirical research that included systematic data collection in seven employee-staffed organizations that were matched by tasks to seven volunteer-staffed organizations. The study was designed to systematically compare the organizational behavior of volunteers doing work comparable to that of employees. Thus the sample consists of a volunteer-staffed day care center matched with an employee-staffed day care center, matched volunteer- and employee-staffed newspapers, matched poverty relief agencies, volunteer- and employee-staffed symphonic orchestras, matched family planning clinics, gift shops, and fire departments. Measures included questionnaires, structured interviews, observation, and the collection of archival documents. The reader is advised to review the detailed descriptions of samples, procedures, and measures for this study in the Appendix before examining the study results reported in the remaining chapters.

However, this book is intended to move beyond the systematic data to include information from two additional sources. First, a comprehensive review of any social science literature that has addressed – however briefly – the organizational behavior of volunteers is provided. This is intended to be a collection of empirical and theoretical knowledge about the organizational behavior of volunteers. Second, this author's empirical studies were designed to address relatively narrow questions of volunteer motivation and control, while the focus of this book is on development of theory concerning the implications of the organizational behavior of volunteers for the field of organizational behavior as a whole. Much of this book moves broadly beyond the available systematic empirical data; it is speculative and theoretical, drawing upon relevant evidence and arguments when they are available, but the emphasis is on the development of a theoretically coherent understanding rather than on the reporting of an incremental contribution to the empirical literature.

It is important to note the prominent impediments to a scholarly treatment of volunteer organizational behavior. First, most volunteers work in nonprofit organizations, and this is a very loose and heterogeneous category. At their most formal, they provide work experiences virtually identical to profit-making or governmental entities providing similar services (e.g. hospitals, universities). At the other extreme, they are more properly characterized as informal associations or collectivities rather than as organizations. Certainly, the work experiences of volunteers in these very divergent organizations will be quite different (Billis 1987).

This problem of heterogeneity has been addressed in the first instance by focusing solely on volunteers working in formal organizations producing some product or service for those outside of the organization. That is, attention is directed to the local volunteer fire department and the poverty relief agency, not to the bridge club or farmers' grain cooperative. This eliminates that vast array of clubs, societies, parties, and cooperatives from the direct focus of this study (although some of this analysis may apply to features of these associational volunteers). This focus serves two purposes. First, the pressures on organizational volunteers are intensified when some-one outside the organizational membership must be reliably served – for example, the different effects of the absenteeism of firefighters at a fire and of chess players at the club's most recent tournament. In addition, since one of the primary purposes of this effort is the further development of our theories of general organizational behavior, it would seem to be most profitable to focus on those organizations that are most similar to the traditional focus of the field. Second, the problem of heterogeneity of settings for volunteer work will be addressed by a careful attempt to describe the particular kind of studied organization in detail. Even restrict-ing the focus to volunteers in formal work settings leaves a broad array of organizations and environments, expectations and experiences. Thus, any salient differences among the seven particular study settings are described in full.

In addition to the wide variety of volunteer work settings, an additional impediment to the systematic study of volunteer organizational behavior is the isolating of what is unique about being a volunteer or an employee. As noted above, there are many quite fundamental differences between volunteers and employees. These differences are so strong for the workers that volunteers and employees appear to occupy fundamentally different social categories, and comparisons can be seen as insulting or "crazy" by both volunteers and employees. Volunteer organizational workers are different – and this book is an attempt to provide a sufficiently rich charac-terization of these differences. However, a major premise supporting this undertaking is that working for organizations provides similar constraints and opportunities for both paid and unpaid workers, and that theory can usefully incorporate volunteer as well as employee organizational members.

THEORETICAL OVERVIEW

The fundamental difference between volunteers and employees is that vol-unteers receive no financial remuneration for their organizational work. This is a simple difference and may initially seem to be relatively small, given the very significant differences in the roles of members within a single organization and the great variety of tasks and environments facing organizations. Further, many in the human relations tradition have argued that money really is not a very significant force affecting workers' actions in organizations. For example, Herzberg, Mausner, and Snyderman (1959) argued that pay was a mere "hygiene" and not a "motivator" of work performance. Yet, it will be suggested here that this difference in mode of compensation appears to have quite profound effects on how the work is structured for these different kinds of workers, on their own and others' expectations concerning their actions in the workplace, and even on how they are expected to think and feel about their organization and its work. This absence of pay for organizational work seems to remove a psychologically important rationale and, therefore, creates uncomfortable dissonance for participants and observers. The dissonance is resolved through explanations that do not depend on money, but the indeterminacy and ideological character of these explanations do not fully resolve the uncertainty. The reasons for these pronounced defining features of pay are interesting and will be explored in depth in Chapter 8. Here the theoretical arguments developed in this book are introduced by a brief outline of some of the psychological, social, and structural effects of working without wages.

The uncertainty volunteers face can be framed by drawing on Barker's (Barker 1968; Barker and Gump 1964) concept of "behavior setting." Such settings are "time–place–thing" milieus with their own attendant social meanings. Barker and his colleagues hold that behavior settings "coerce" behavior, that is, they provide more uniformity and predictability in a set of individuals than do the differing characteristics of the individuals. This work is an attempt to discover and to articulate the particular situational demands upon organizational volunteers and to reflect, indirectly, on the distinct demands upon employees. The features of organizational volunteers' settings that seem to be most important are introduced below.

The meaning of volunteer work

Volunteers are seen as occupying a fundamentally uncertain societal position. In contrast to volunteers, employees have very visible incentives, and so society tends to believe that it knows what they are. (That employees cannot, in practice, be reduced to simple "economic individuals" is virtually the defining characteristic of organizational behavior as a field.) However, organizational volunteering is *inherently* contradictory in nature. It is "work" – working within a formal structure to provide a service to others – and it is a "leisure activity" – something done whenever convenient because it is personally rewarding. The problems caused by facile assumptions about the motives of employees have been well documented, but the difficulties for volunteers are in many respects more basic.

The problems of volunteers' limited time, uncertain motives, and a high degree of individual independence can result in debilitating levels of uncertainty for organizational volunteers. Volunteers need to adopt a shared "definition of the situation" before they can take action. Within a single organization different members may hold conflicting definitions of volunteer work – some that it is something to do when in the mood, others that it is work that must be conducted in a "businesslike" manner – and the ease of exit means that differences of opinion about these assumptions can lead to organizational dissolution.

This lack of clear definition extends to the mixed messages volunteers receive about the value of their work. On the one hand, their efforts are degraded by expressions such as "you get what you pay for," and "if society really wanted it done, it would pay for it." Yet volunteers are also virtuous, self-sacrificial contributors – "givers" not "takers." Without the concrete crutch of "working for a living," volunteers are suspect: they are too autonomous and, therefore, cannot be made reliable; they have no visible "payoff" and, so, are not predictable; they must have hidden, "selfish" reasons for working and, so, are hypocrites. Under these circumstances, it is not surprising that practitioner writings concerned with volunteers take on such normative and crusading tones. This inherent feature of volunteer work sets the context in which volunteer organizational behavior takes place and, therefore, is described in Chapter 2.

Volunteers' jobs

Volunteer work tends to be structured differently than the work of employees. Research evidence presented here suggests that the jobs and relations between jobs are different than the jobs of employees working on the same organizational tasks. For example, volunteer work is usually done part-time, often just a few hours a month. It is a spare-time "leisure activity." Without paying these workers, the organization usually cannot expect more than a few hours per week or month from them. Therefore, work must be broken up into small part-time pieces. This leads to different interaction patterns among workers and to a need for additional coordination positions. Further, volunteers simply do not spend as much time at their work and with their co-workers as most employees do. This leads to a social network structure in which a central person or people (the "core membership") interact(s) with all other individuals (the "periphery"), who interact only with the core members. This division between core and periphery is not based directly on formal organizational authority as are the divisions in bureaucratic organizations, but on personal characteristics, such as level of commitment to the organization. In contrast, linkages among full-time employees tend to be much more extensive (they know more people) and stronger (they know them well).

In addition, volunteers, since they are unpaid, are all "paid" equally and relatively cheaply, and so there is little economic reason to differentiate among them. For many volunteer-staffed organizations, this results, for example, in a less compelling need to keep clear records of who is a worker, a client, or occasional helper, since there is no risk of mistakenly paying a nonworker. Thus, there is little need to make the fine status distinctions characteristic of many employee-staffed organizations. Despite the attractiveness of these egalitarian workplace structures, they occasionally contributed to uncertainty in organizational responsibility in several sampled organizations. This can lead to the "chaotic" character of many organizations that are staffed and run by volunteers.

The particular forms of organizational and job design characteristic of the studied volunteer-staffed organizations are analyzed in Chapter 3.

Unpaid labor

Volunteers have no direct monetary reason for joining or staying with the organization. This creates unique pressures both for volunteers and for organizations that rely on volunteer labor. As noted above, volunteer motives are uncertain; they do not have the clear and compelling "reason" for working that employees can always claim. Why, then, do they work? This central uncertainty of volunteer motivation has led to the largest body of academic research on volunteers, and it has spawned a lively debate among those concerned with the motivation of volunteers. For example, what is the role of altruism in volunteering? Is altruism simply a socially acceptable explanation for a process that often is not subject to careful rational calculation?

Additional insight into volunteer motivation can be gleaned from the fact that substantial numbers of volunteers are recruited through personal contacts, and volunteers are significantly more likely than employees to report that friendly co-workers are important in their decisions to remain with their organizations. That is, social contacts seem to be more important for volunteers than for employees, or at least important in different ways. These ideas concerning volunteer motivation are developed in Chapter 4.

The fact of volunteers' unpaid labor also leads to a different pattern of affective reactions to the workplace. There is also substantial uncertainty about the meaning of one of the most consistently supported empirical findings: that volunteers have significantly more positive workplace attitudes than do employees. Further, there is evidence that volunteers may not engage in an elaborate rational analysis of their options before joining, but "try on" the work and decide later whether or not they want to stay. Thus, volunteering appears to be a less behaviorally committing act than taking a paid job. This tentativeness about the act of volunteering leads to multiple interpretations about volunteers' more positive attitudes. The first interpretation is that, since volunteers receive little extrinsic gain, they must have joined because of their positive feelings about the work itself, the organization, its mission, or the other people involved. Alternatively, volunteers could experience insufficient justification for their work and, therefore, attribute positive attitudes or a high degree of intrinsic motivation to themselves to justify their actions. The role of attributions in employees' attitudes is attracting increasing interest, and volunteers provide a unique opportunity for analyses of the attributional processes in attitude formation. Chapter 5 presents an analysis of volunteer attitudes.

Workplace independence

This lack of concrete committing mechanisms for volunteer workers has wider implications than simple uncertainty about volunteer motivation and attitudes. It creates an additional difficulty for those who are responsible for directing and coordinating their work: volunteers are not as dependent on their organizations as are many employees. Therefore, they are free to work in a much more independent and even idiosyncratic manner. Since there are very few "carrots" and virtually no meaningful "sticks," the control of volunteers' actions is quite uncertain. Yet volunteer workers do perform reliably for many organizations, and they do submit to influence; volunteer workers are very rarely "out of control."

Many have speculated about how such control can be maintained, suggesting that selective recruitment, symbolic rewards, manipulation of social influence, and the ability of organizational leaders to make the values of the organization salient to members predominate. These ideas have all been offered by sociological theorists of voluntary organizations, and so these arguments rarely are accompanied by analyses of the actual social influence at the interpersonal level. Further, available data on interpersonal influence among volunteers suggests that the process is more complex. For example, results reported here suggest that volunteers have significantly more potential influence in their organizations than do comparable employees, but that most volunteers seek to avoid the actual exercise of influence. Therefore, evidence from this study suggests that volunteers are brought into the system of organizational behavior through combinations of formal bureaucratic requirements and direct interpersonal influences. Chapter 6 provides an overview of the control systems used with organizational volunteers. In particular, the dominant role of direct interpersonal influence in these organizations is examined. This is done in Chapter 7 with its focus on the implementation of interpersonal influence through charismatic authority, the special problems of officeholders in these organizations, and employee–volunteer relations.

ORGANIZATION OF THE BOOK

The theoretical organization of this book is based on an integration of two fairly independent approaches to understanding organizational behavior. The practitioner literature written for and about volunteers in organizations appears to address fundamentally different concerns than does the applied management (of employees) literature. Volunteers' own practical literature can be seen as a reflection of the concerns of those who work with organizational volunteers – that is, of the writers' own practical managerial "problems" with them. Further, the preponderance of empirical studies of volunteers have been designed to address these practical questions, and so a review of this literature needs to be accomplished within the framework of the questions addressed. Therefore, chapters of the book are grouped into sections. The sections contain the material addressing the basic practical problems faced by those working with volunteers. Each section introduces practical questions concerning the organizational behavior of volunteers addressed in its chapters.

Within these sections, the individual chapters address topics familiar to those interested in employee organizational behavior. This is because the perspective taken here is decidedly based in the organizational behavior field as it has developed to understand the problems of employee-staffed organizations. Some divergence in these two approaches results from the different management problems that accompany paid and unpaid workers. For example, the presence of alienated employees who remain in their jobs because they have no other job opportunities has led to large volumes of research and theory on the monitoring and management of employee job attitudes. Yet the actions of alienated volunteers are never studied, since unhappy volunteers have been assumed to leave the organization at the very moment they become dissatisfied. Because of this, there has not been a comparable concern with such job attitudes in the practical volunteer litera-ture. Similarly, the largest area of research concerning volunteers addresses the question of what attracts volunteers to particular organizations, with relatively little attention to this question for employees.

Another difference between the volunteer and management literatures, particularly the academic research, stems from the fact that research on the organizational behavior of volunteers is less developed than comparable work with employees. This is most visible in the area of motivation, which has been a central concern of both groups of researchers. This difference in theoretical and research development, in combination with the focus of the book on informing the general organizational behavior audience, has led to an organization of the chapters of this book by traditional organizational behavior topics.

Therefore, Section I is introductory, laying the foundation for the sub-sequent analyses. These chapters help to define the "behavior settings" in which volunteers find themselves. These settings carry expectations that differ in important ways from the settings of employees, and an understand-ing of them is a critical foundation for subsequent discussions of volunteer organizational behavior. Section II addresses the pressing practical problem: why volunteer? Section III is concerned with the other preeminent practical volunteer organizational behavior problem: volunteer reliability. The free-dom of volunteers to act idiosyncratically creates potential organizational performance problems of the most fundamental kind. Their motives are unclear. Often they are associational owners and so cannot be terminated and have a right to contribute to "policy." These settings are usually understaffed, so any contribution is better than none. How, then, can volunteers' actions be brought into a coordinated system of organizational behavior? Section IV, the final section, is an integration of the previous material into a summary of volunteer organizational behavior and a theoretical expansion of general theories of organizational behavior. Chapter 8 provides a summary and implications of the foregoing material on volunteers for the field of organizational behavior. The work concludes with Chapter 9, a summary and extension of the foregoing work for volunteer-focused research, as well as the practical management of volunteer-staffed organizations.

Chapter 2

The structural uncertainty of volunteers' settings

Volunteers are found in a wide variety of organizational settings; in fact, it would be difficult to conceive of more heterogeneous workplaces. Employees at least must have an employer, and all employers must maintain procedures, however informal, for monitoring employees' contributions and paying the wages. In addition, employees depend on a reliable source of revenue (for salaries). Volunteer work entails no such constraints. "Volunteering," in fact, has been viewed as an entirely solitary act – encompassing the good Samaritan who assists a stranger in a public setting, the honest returner of a "lost wallet," and even "free will" (see Smith *et al.* 1980 for a comprehensive review). This study of organizational behavior focuses on volunteers working in formal organizations producing some product or service for nonmembers. However, it is important to be reminded of the wide variety of meanings attached to the word "volunteer," since semantic ambiguity influences the kinds of expectations brought by volunteers and others with whom they come in contact.

In this chapter, the societal and structural forces that bear on volunteers' individual and interpersonal organizational behavior are outlined. This is based on a review of sociological theorists' analyses of the particular kinds of organizations in which volunteers work and a brief discussion of scholarly writings on their "societal role." These ideas are supported throughout by illustrations from the sampled volunteer-staffed organizations. The chapter concludes with a summary of the psychological and social-psychological experiences of volunteers, the contrast between individual and organizational purposes in these organizations, their "value-rational" rather than "legal-rational" character, and their uncertain legitimacy.

THE ORGANIZATIONAL SETTING

By far the largest number of volunteers work in "voluntary organizations." Yet, it is necessary to note at the outset that this section's focus on voluntary organizations *must include employees*, since voluntary organizations also have paid employees. As is discussed in detail below, voluntary organizations can be extremely formal and large, staffed entirely by employees and retaining only a statutorily required unpaid board of directors. Voluntary organizations can also be very informal with all work done by volunteers and producing only an intermittent and variable service. The mixed employee–volunteer workforce composition is itself one of the important features of organizational life for volunteers, and it will be analyzed at length in Chapter 8.

Voluntary organizations complete the organizational work of nonprofit nongovernmental entities. This is a heterogeneous category, including Mount Sinai Hospital, the American Heritage Foundation, and the British Museum, as well as millions of small community organizations that offer social services and assistance and that work to preserve the community's historical and environmental heritage. These diverse settings are analyzed, first by exploring why volunteers are most likely to be found there and next by clarifying the distinction between voluntary organizations and voluntary associations. Thirdly, theorists who have distinguished between voluntary and other organizations are reviewed for insights into the distinctive characteristics of volunteers' organizations. Finally, a few theorists have attempted to group the diverse voluntary organizations, and their work has implications for the generalizability of the data from the sampled volunteers.

The initial problem is that the voluntary sector itself is amorphous. It is a "leftover" sector defined by what it is not – nonprofit nongovernment – rather than by what it is. Further confusion results from the various reasons for scholars' interest. Like the volunteer worker who is seen as an icon of freedom, voluntary organizations have also attracted many social philosophers who see them as exemplars of various good and evil aspects of their societies. In addition, in contrast to the neglect of volunteer workers by organizational psychologists and management theorists, organizational theorists have long been interested in clarifying what voluntary organizations are. This work is useful both to illustrate the theoretical contributions possible from an analysis of this sector and to provide a background in the differences between these organizations and the more formal settings in which employees are usually found.

Volunteers in voluntary organizations

Although volunteers are found primarily in nonprofit nongovernmental organizations, as with all other features of this vast category of workers, this is not a hard and fast rule. For example, there are volunteers assisting in publicly owned and even private for-profit hospitals, although volunteers in government or private profit-making organizations are generally confined to social or health service organizations. These organizations (such as hospitals) grew in the voluntary sector and often retain strong nonprofit nongovernmental counterparts that "pioneered" volunteer programs in that industry. However, the number of volunteers working for government or profit-making organizations is proportionately small. It is easy to understand that volunteers might not frequently donate their time to profit-making organizations, reasoning that if the cause is worthy enough for them to donate their time, the owners should donate their capital. However, with the growth of governmental provision of social services in this century, there has been a concomitant growth in volunteers working for governmental agencies.

Kramer (1981) provided a detailed analysis of the declining presence in the post-war period of volunteers in social welfare service organizations that were shifting from the voluntary to governmental sector in Israel, England, the Netherlands, and the United States. He found that, except in the Netherlands, there was no difference in use of direct service volunteers between governmental and nonprofit agencies performing similar work. With increasing governmental support for these nonprofit agencies, the overall decline came almost completely in "fundraising" volunteers. However, the growth in volunteering has been shifting from these social welfare services to peer self-help and advocacy organizations that serve different roles than those large social welfare service institutions.

Separate attention will not be given to volunteers in governmental social welfare and health services agencies. For the present purposes, these volunteers' settings are not significantly different from the settings of volunteers working in comparable large nonprofit organizations. The volunteer bringing the library cart to hospitalized patients in the government-owned major hospital experiences work in much the same way as does his or her counterpart across town in the large regional hospital that is owned by a religious organization.

That type of governmental volunteer that genuinely has no counterpart in the nonprofit nongovernmental sector – VISTA, Peace Corps, and other governmentally initiated "volunteer" programs – is also excluded from the present analysis. These individuals are financially supported by their labor. They are called "volunteers" because, presumably, they are taking lower wages than they could command elsewhere to do work that contributes to society. But by this definition, we would also need to include many professionals, such as nurses, social workers, or even school teachers, as "volunteers." This appropriation of the term "volunteer" by these governmental agencies suggests that the symbolic and emotional meanings of the word go beyond the technical meaning of unpaid labor.

Thus, organizational volunteers are most commonly found in nonprofit nongovernmental organizations – what have been called "charities." Volunteer labor is a "donation" to a worthwhile or necessary social purpose. This donative character of volunteer labor introduces a symbolic dimension that is explored in detail later in this chapter.

Voluntary organizations and voluntary associations

The terms voluntary organization and voluntary association have often been used interchangeably (e.g. Perrow 1970). However, Thompson (1976) distinguished the two, and his rationale has important implications for the present work. He defined an "association" as a group of people who share an interest and have agreed to pursue it jointly. The association will need a process ("constitution") to determine who is a member and who may speak for the association, that is, how its "will" is to be determined. However, it needs no additional structural features. The confusion between voluntary associations and voluntary organizations arises because often associations will create instruments to achieve their goals. These instruments are organizations. An organization is a "tool" for accomplishing some goal, using human labor rather than physical materials to do its "work" (Thompson 1967). An organization has a goal imposed upon it by its "owner," be that owner an association, shareholders, or the citizens of a state. It is exactly this feature of human beings, who have their own goals in serving as "instruments" in organizations, that creates the unique pressures that make the field of organizational behavior (Argyris 1957; Barnard 1938).

This helps highlight the fact that volunteer organizational workers are subject to the social and psychological pressures experienced by all organizational workers. Volunteers, too, "sell" their labor and must subject themselves to the organizational controls to insure "integrated organizational behavior" among all participants (Simon 1957). Association members are not subject to these controls. Association members come together because they can better achieve their joint or shared goals in this way. For example, bridge enthusiasts can find more opportunities to play if they join a bridge club. Association members are both the "owners" and "consumers" of the association's output and need please no one but themselves. Their constraints are minimal and solely concern maintaining the association (Thompson 1976).

In contrast, organizations – be they employee- or volunteer-staffed – are instruments engaged in "exchanges" with nonmembers. They produce a service or product for outsiders. For example, the sampled volunteer fire-fighters put out all fires in their territory, not just those on member property; the student newspaper was produced for the entire campus community, not just for its reporters and editors. This dependence and "openness" produce additional pressures on workers, whether they be volunteer or salaried.

The performance of an organization is judged by outsiders. Those providing resources and those who use its product or service want to be assured that this instrument is performing its stated "function." If performance is inadequate, the organization will lose vital support. In the case of the firefighters, residents would no longer be able to obtain fire insurance, and in the case of the student newspaper, the student government would no longer pay for materials and production. All of the traditional concerns of organizational managers for performance standards and coordination are as necessary for a volunteer-staffed organization as they are for any organization. The sole difference is that their "human instruments" are not given monetary inducements for their contributions. Thus volunteers performing work for others would be expected to experience a greater degree of performance pressure than purely associational volunteers. This added burden is exacerbated by the fact that the same volunteers often "own" the organization.

The uncertainty fostered when owners and workers are the same individuals performing very distinct roles in voluntary organizations was addressed by Thompson (1976). We often confuse voluntary associations with voluntary organizations, he suggested, because sometimes members of an association fill roles in the association's apparatus or organization – or at least some of them do. They play dual roles as both owners and instruments (Thompson 1976, p. 2). The distinction has significant implications for the organizational behavior of volunteers, since it adds an important uncertainty: when are volunteers acting as association members or owners, and when are they acting as organizational workers?

Of the seven volunteer-staffed organizations studied, four (day care, poverty relief, gift shop, and fire department) were staffed by volunteers who were the legal owners of the organization, and in the remaining three (student newspaper, symphony, and family planning clinic), the studied volunteer workers did not formally own the organization for which they worked. As a practical matter, this meant that the volunteers in the first four organizations elected their board of directors and key officeholders, whereas these positions were filled by an outside association for the latter three (respectively, the college student government, the college president, and the state-wide board of trustees).

In the studied organizations, this ownership–worker confusion usually took the form of officeholders' dissatisfaction with volunteers who would not remain in subordinate roles. The problem was acute in the gift shop in which the paid shop manager was perpetually dissatisfied with the purchase and merchandise display initiatives of the volunteers. The manager saw these activities as within her professional expertise, while the volunteers believed that "running the shop" meant they could participate in the "creative" decisions as well as overall strategy.

However, those volunteers who were not legally owners were also vocal in their criticism of the office-holding managers' decisions. The volunteer musicians were quick with their criticisms of pieces selected for concerts. The "insubordination" of the family planning volunteers and the insurrection of the volunteer reporters and editors receive detailed analyses below.

Thus, despite the legal ownership by working volunteers in only four of the seven sampled organizations, volunteers in each were vocal in expressing their own policy and management preferences. So, although the confusion in associational owner and worker status was present in the sampled organizations, it does not appear to account completely for the relatively greater assertiveness of volunteer workers.

Organizational typologies

If volunteers are usually found in voluntary organizations rather than in governmental or profit-making organizations, is there anything distinctive about these kinds of organizations that would be expected to have an impact on the organizational behavior of their members? Organizational typologies have long interested societal or organizational theorists. Those typologists who have given special attention to voluntary organizations include Clark and Wilson (1961) and Etzioni (1975). Both typologists were centrally concerned with the differing psychological attachments in different kinds of organizations.

Clark and Wilson's (1961) typology has been the basis for several subsequent analyses of individual volunteers' motives. They classified organizations by the incentives which these organizations offered to individuals to become members. The primary types of incentives are material, solidary, and purposive incentives. Material incentives for organizational participation include any material benefit: pay and work experience useful for later employment are examples. Although organizations can provide a mix of incentives, Clark and Wilson divide voluntary organizations into primarily solidary and purposive. Solidary incentives include socializing, congeniality, a sense of group membership, status, and fun. Their common characteristic is their independence of the service ends of the organization, so great flexibility is allowed in the goals the groups pursue. The authors suggest that the goals of these kinds of voluntary organizations tend to be noncontroversial so that they will not divide the membership or impair its prestige. Among the sampled organizations, only the association that ran the gift shop could be considered a primarily solidary organization. It is true that it undertook different activities over time and was seriously considering whether it should disband the gift shop because it led to intolerable strife. In contrast, purposive incentives attract members based on the organization's goals. Members seek some change in the status quo. The remaining six organizations would be seen as purposive, and their goals played an important role in attracting and binding volunteers. This split focus in volunteers' motives, social or goal-oriented, plays an important role in the literature on volunteer motivation and receives detailed empirical analysis in the sampled organizations in Chapter 5.

Etzioni (1975) classified organizations by the three basic compliance mechanisms used to control the behavior of their members: coercive, utilitarian, and normative. Coercive organizations are ones which exert power over their members through the application or threat of physical sanctions; few western volunteer-staffed organizations could be seen as coercive. Utilitarian organizations, such as profit-making corporations, obtain compliance through remuneration and are expected to obtain calculative involvement with mild alienation and mild commitment from their members. These would most frequently characterize lower ranking employees in businesses and government. Finally, normative organizations are those that allocate symbolic rewards and sanctions, such as esteem or acceptance, and can claim the moral and "positive" involvement of high intensity. Etzioni categorized "voluntary associations" as primarily normative, but within this group there may be important variations in whether the organization attempts to build "moral" or "social" commitments.

If employees were unambiguously working for remuneration and volunteers for symbolic rewards alone, Etzioni (1975) suggested specific differences in motivation and management practices associated with these types. However, as Etzioni himself notes, many employees are more appropriately characterized as morally, rather than calculatively, involved.

In the present study, the employees in the employee-staffed organizations were relatively more calculatively involved than were volunteers and the handful of employees working in the volunteer-staffed organizations. Table 2.1 presents results for volunteers' and employees' self-reported reasons for their organizational involvement. Volunteers report significantly less interest in instrumental gain and in the work activities in their own right and relatively more interest in providing service to others. This pattern is also reflected in the informal observations – with substantial alienation particularly among the unionized employees in the poverty relief agency and the fire department. Working for social interaction seems to be complex and variable among volunteers and receives detailed attention later in this work. Finally, it is important to note that there is a substantial overlap between these two sets of workers in their relative calculative (material rewards) and moral involvement (symbolic rewards). Particularly for employees in the voluntary sector – and perhaps in the governmental sectors – high levels of moral involvement are quite common. Yet, despite the comparable availability of symbolic rewards to employee-staffed organizational workers doing the same tasks (recall that these organizations were providing the same services), volunteers were more likely to report working for symbolic reward of service and are less likely to report working for the more material instrumental and intrinsic rewards than are employees. This suggests that Etzioni's typology may provide good general guidance.

Table 2.1 Mean of self-reported reasons for organizational involvement

Reason for working	Volunteers	Employees	F(1,214)	r²
Material rewards				
Instrumental gain	5.39	5.68	2.52*	.03
Intrinsic interest	5.26	5.60	4.37*	.03
Symbolic rewards				
Service	5.56	5.34	6.48**	.05
Social	5.44	5.24	1.67	–
n	151	65		

*$p \leq .05$
**$p \leq .01$

In addition to the above organizational typologists, Knoke and Prensky (1982) and Perrow (1970) have devoted special attention to distinguishing voluntary associations from governmental and profit-making organizations. Knoke and Prensky (1982) provide an insightful comparison between "firms and bureaus" and "voluntary associations." Their analysis is one of the few to integrate individual-level organizational behavior propositions with organizational-level theories. They suggested that normative incentives offered to volunteers are inferior to material or solidary incentives in building member commitment. This is in contrast to the foregoing theorists, such as Etzioni (1975), who suggested that normative compliance elicits higher involvement. Knoke and Prensky (1982) draw on Olson (1965), who argued that "collectivities" working toward broad public benefits would have trouble attracting members, since the benefits of their work will go to all members. Knoke and Prensky suggested that normative inducements tend to be "public goods" in which the organization can seldom achieve monopoly control itself. Individuals motivated by values view the individual organization as less significant than the larger cause and so have no particular incentives to work for this specific organization. Thus these organizations are "weak."

Knoke and Prensky (1982) made other provocative statements about voluntary associations. For example, they suggested that structural features such as division of labor, technology, and size are "totally irrelevant" to associations. Clearly, voluntary organizations (instruments of associations) do have division of labor and, as organizations, do have technologies that can rival the complexity of governmental agencies or businesses. Voluntary organizations can also grow to a large size. The problem is again one of heterogeneity. There are undoubtedly small voluntary organizations that could be accurately characterized as the "peripheral, unstructured, and confused" entities described by Knoke and Prensky (1982); it is just that we cannot assume that volunteers always find themselves working in such settings.

Perrow, the other theorist of voluntary associations, did not attempt to characterize their incentives, but focused instead on what was unique about their exchanges with their environments. Many others (Etzioni 1975; Sills 1968; Smith *et al.* 1980) have noted the vast heterogeneity among associations, but only Perrow (1970) explicitly attempted to develop a theoretical argument for what is distinctive about these entities. He dismissed previous theoretical attempts:

> The category of voluntary associations is one of the grossest and most poorly conceptualized in the field of organizational analysis. The variety and diversity of organizations that can be considered by any one of several definitions to be voluntary associations is enormous. Almost any defining feature, such as goals, runs immediately into the problem that there are many exceptions and there are organizations which are obviously not voluntary which have the same defining characteristics.
>
> (Perrow 1970, p. 94)

Perrow suggested that voluntary associations can be distinguished by the nature of the "raw material" that they transform in order to meet various output expectations. Voluntary associations are distinctive in that most of their raw materials (workers) are also direct consumers of some part of the product. This worker-consumed "output" is generally nonmonetary (e.g. fellowship, feelings that one has contributed to a better society). Perrow (1970) made the interesting point that these voluntary organizations can be uniquely characterized by the fact that volunteer workers, in contrast to other "stake holders," can make no legal claim on the organization. Employees can claim wages that are due for labor contributions, and shareholders can sue management for malpractice in dissipating the company's assets, but volunteers can make no legal claim that they didn't receive sufficient symbolic compensation.

Framing volunteer organizational work in this way suggests some striking organizational behavior implications. Although the voluntary organization may not be serving its volunteer workers as its "primary clients," volunteers are still, in some sense, consumers of their organizations' "services." Organizations that pay their workers are clearly aware of the fact that they must generate sufficient revenue to pay wages, yet the need to generate sufficient "symbolic rewards" to compensate the volunteer workers seems to be inherently less compelling. Since symbolic rewards are necessarily less tangible, they are easier to overlook. Managers may be so occupied with the needs of their "primary clients" that needful "secondary clients" (volunteer workers) can easily be forgotten. In the seven sampled organizations, there is evidence that the secondary clients were often explicitly "served." For example, the musical director of the symphony consciously included some music that appealed more to the volunteer musicians than to the more popular taste of the "nonplaying audience." Thus, even in settings in which volunteers are not formally clients, Perrow's work suggests that they require "service" from the organization.

These typologists have emphasized different defining features of organizations; however, together they contribute three new themes to the present analysis. First, the category of voluntary organizations is not easily characterized theoretically. It contains organizations of numerous different "types" that can range from formal entities, which are virtually identical in every respect except ownership to businesses or governmental organizations, to confused, unstructured, and peripheral collectivities, such as those described by Knoke and Prensky (1982). Clearly, volunteers work in a broad range of organizational settings, and these different settings can have important effects on their organizational behavior. An attempt to organize this heterogeneity is presented in the next section.

Secondly, there is some disagreement about what binds volunteers to their organizations. How do these organizations maintain volunteers' participation and induce their commitment? Is it through solidary or normative inducements? Which results in greater organizational commitment?

Finally, not only do many volunteers face role conflict resulting from their roles as owners and workers, but we must add another: the fundamental role conflict between their roles as clients and workers.

Typologies of voluntary organizations

Since voluntary organizations vary so widely, an examination of their theoretical categorizations may prove useful in developing a taxonomy of settings for volunteers. Taxonomies of voluntary organizations have been predominantly typologies based on the organizations' "functions."

The most widely used typology is that of Babchuk and Gordon (1962). They classified voluntary organizations as (1) "expressive," organizations that act to express or satisfy interests that members have in relation to themselves; (2) "instrumental" organizations, which are means to some goal for societal change or the production of goods or services for nonmembers; and (3) "instrumental–expressive," which have characteristics of both types. These are similar to Clark and Wilson's solidary–purposive distinction. There is empirical support for this typology. Jacoby and Babchuk (1963) found that members of these different organizations could differentiate them consistently with this typology and that these different organizational objectives were seen as important in attracting volunteers.

Although these categories have been widely used by sociologists to categorize voluntary associations, particularly in large-scale "community studies," members' own reports of their personal reasons for joining and remaining do not conform with the type of organization for which they work. Moore (1961) found that middle-class women belonged predominantly to organizations she categorized as expressive, but that the members themselves stressed the importance of the instrumental purposes of their organizations. Similarly, Warner *et al.* (1949) and Minnis (1952) detailed what they believed to be the expressive or social, in contrast to what members characterized as instrumental, character of civic organizations. Smith and Freedman (1972) reviewed this debate over "manifest and latent" organizational functions and concluded that it was inappropriate to dismiss the members' definition as incorrect, since their own definition of the situation can have real consequences for their actions.

Thus for the present focus on organizational behavior we cannot rely on this expressive–instrumental categorization as a reliable guide to individual volunteer motivation. Although *organizations* can be reliably categorized by members and theorists, these categories apparently do not provide clear guidance about members' individual motives for joining. Just because a particular organization is categorized as "instrumental" does not suggest that all members have joined in order to forward the organization's goals; they may volunteer because they enjoy the activities or the social life. Similarly, it seems that expressive organizations may have many instrumental attractions, such as learning new skills and making contributions to social welfare.

One final typology that has implications for volunteer organizational behavior is provided by Sills (1968). Of particular interest is his discussion of the process of organizational "institutionalization." He classified voluntary organizations by the degree to which they exhibited "formal-organization like" characteristics. At the one end are those that are oriented toward the gradual improvement of society and are formal and "matter of fact" (such as, for example, hospitals). At the other end are those that are more radical and ideological whose members bring a high degree of affect to their involvement (such as social movements). The former are like the formal organizational behavior settings in which employees have been traditionally studied, whereas the latter would be expected to offer different social settings for the study of organizational behavior.

Some insight into the interpersonal effects of these more ideological organizational settings is suggested by Rothschild-Whitt's (1979) study of counter-culture collectives. Members of these free clinics and alternative schools worked for them because they believed in the "value" that their organization represented for its own sake, disregarding its prospects of success. Since authority was based on membership consensus, much more self-discipline and capacity for cooperative behavior was required of members than in traditional bureaucracies. These organizations rejected supervision and standardization as forms of social control and instead relied extensively on "personalistic and moralistic appeals." She reported that within these organizations there was minimal division of labor and frequent job rotation – practices designed to reduce expertise-based status differences. The time-consuming processes of building consensus and attempting moral suasion fostered extremely intense relationships, and disagreements were personalized and more psychologically threatening.

Thus these ideological organizations would be expected to be characterized by egalitarian rather than performance- or "merit"-based expectations for the settings. We would expect a great deal of role ambiguity and informal personal relationships rather than the more formal work role relations found in the larger, more formal voluntary organizations. Further, these settings seem to be dependent on a more homogeneous workforce with implications for recruitment and retention. Finally, the emotional intensity is no doubt a powerful element of the worker's setting. Thus, volunteers will find themselves in organizations that range from the more matter-of-fact bureaucracies familiar to those studying employees to small ideological and emotionally intense groupings, as well as mixed settings with varying combinations of these pressures.

Applying the theories of Babchuk and Gordon (1962), Sills (1968), and Rothschild-Whitt (1979) to the sampled organizations will help illuminate them. First, all except the gift shop would be considered to be "instrumental" organizations, which isn't surprising considering that only those who produced some product or service for outsiders were selected. As noted before, the association which ran the gift shop was expressive. Similarly, none could be characterized as extreme ideological or high emotional intensity organizations. For example, the volunteer firemen were quite dispassionate; one said he volunteered "to keep my property tax rates down." The musicians wanted an audience to play for in order to develop their performance skills, and the gift shop volunteers were helping their organization raise revenue. The closest any of these studied organizations came to having ideological value-rational characteristics were the volunteers in the poverty relief agency (although the majority were matter-of-fact, "doing good"). Interestingly, the chapter chairwoman of the family planning clinic relished telling stories of the "old days" in which the local chapter led the fight to legalize birth control. Now that the organization was just another accepted member of the local community's health care delivery system, she clearly missed the excitement of the old ideological battles.

In addition, since all were selected as examples of volunteer-dominated organizations, they were not the large, established bureaucratic institutions in which volunteers often work. Rather, the organizations that form the basis for this analysis range along the middle of this continuum, having neither the intimate emotional intensity nor the formalized and structured involvement of volunteers at the extremes.

THE VALUE OF ORGANIZATIONAL VOLUNTEERS

One final feature of sociological theory related to the organizational behavior of volunteers needs to be addressed: the debate over the value of volunteer work. Sills (1968) suggested that researchers may not have given voluntary organizations extensive attention because they are "not very important" either to society or to their own members, who often see their involvement as a peripheral activity taking a secondary role to job and family. This assumption was often echoed in informal discussions with volunteer leaders who excused absenteeism and poor performance with the expression, "After all, it's only a volunteer job." Even the presumably more dispassionate scholarly writings often are a thinly veiled defense of volunteers' value to society.

Academic interest in the value of volunteers began with the traditional analysis of the "functions" of voluntary organizations for society. Sills (1968) provided the best discussion of these. Accordingly, voluntary organizations serve the functions of (1) mediation between the government and individuals; (2) integration of subgroups into the national society; (3) affirmation of values, as in political parties; (4) governing, or providing such "governmental tasks" as raising money for the library or the licensing of professionals; (5) initiating social change; and (6) distributing power, in which the power of the sovereign state is balanced by the power of dispersed associations. As Sills noted, all of these functions are positive in character and, until recently, most social theorists viewed the presence of voluntary organizations as a positive characteristic of society.

However, several researchers have provided empirical evidence that associations act as barriers to upward social mobility in Great Britain (Morris 1965) and for American women (McPherson and Smith-Lovin 1986). These latter scholars analyzed the socioeconomic and occupational status of members of a random sample of national US voluntary associations. Since the membership of these associations was extremely homogeneous (more so than other institutions such as businesses), they suggested that these groups act to reinforce existing social divisions.

The most prominent critique of the value of volunteer labor was developed by Gold (1971). This social critic inquired why women have come to be the "leading volunteers." She scathingly attacked social service volunteers' motives and the dysfunctions of these activities for the volunteers (maintaining them in low status supportive roles) and society (keeping wages low for paid service workers and blunting pressure for more financial support for social services). Her work initiated a major societal debate during the 1970s on the value of service volunteering. Gold (1979) reported 44 "nonduplicative" newspaper and magazine articles supporting her assertions and didn't even try to count the massive number of articles supporting the value of service volunteers. Although the debate is no longer as topical, the value of volunteer work as an undisputed positive social good can no longer be taken for granted by volunteers or their organizations.

Particularly germane to the present discussion is the suggested negative value of volunteers who "compete" with paid employees for the same work.

In most of the settings in which volunteers work there are also employees. Often volunteers' work is supervised by employees, and occasionally they work alongside employees. In fact, there is a developmental pattern to most large voluntary organizations, with the founders and early workers being all-volunteer, to the hiring of one part-time "coordinator" or "director," and then an increase in the proportion of work done by the paid staff. Levine and Levine (1970) described this historical pattern for the helping services. Ultimately the voluntary organization's work may be done completely by employees. Of course, not all organizations move completely through this cycle, and many (such as the sampled poverty relief agency and family planning clinic) actively resist losing their "volunteer character."

A recent scholar to question the value of volunteer organizational workers, Young (1987), directly addressed volunteers' effects on the behavioral setting of employee co-workers and supervisors. Young suggested that volunteers in nonprofit organizations undermine their executives' abilities to insure good performance by their direct personal connections to the board, by contributing to a "clubby" environment with social rather than service goals, by seeing paid jobs as a source of patronage, and by encouraging the general expectation of altruism that undermines the use of performance-based incentives with paid staff. The management of the potentially strained relationship between volunteer and employee co-workers in the studied organizations is analyzed in Chapter 8.

In summary, the value of the volunteers' organizational work is the subject of widely differing – and often passionately held – opinions. Expressions such as "you get what you pay for" and "if society really wanted it done, it would pay for it" devalue their efforts. Some assume they must have hidden, "selfish," and so hypocritical, reasons for working. Others elevate them as the very embodiment of liberty and guardians of freedom from state coercion: they are virtuous, self-sacrificing contributors. The legitimacy of what employees do is never questioned to this extent; after all, they must work for a living. This debate creates substantial uncertainty for volunteer workers. Are their efforts commendable or self-indulgent? How do others view this work, and how should volunteers view it? Thus, this controversy creates important uncertainties for volunteers. They are aware of the debate and can never be certain on which "side" any new acquaintance will be. It contributes to the obsessive quality of praising and boosterism in many of these organizations and among practitioners writing for them.

THE CONTEXT OF VOLUNTEERS' WORK

This review of social and organizational theorists' conceptions of voluntary organizations and their roles in society helps to provide contextual grounding for the psychological and social experiences of volunteer workers. Several of their implications are developed below.

Role conflict

Volunteers face fundamentally mixed messages about their roles as organizational workers. As volunteer workers they experience multiple roles: they are usually owners and clients, as well as workers. Volunteers are attracted to the organization, in part, by the offer of contribution to important societal goals. Wouldn't they then feel free to voice their own opinions about the ways these goals are being pursued? As Thompson (1976) noted, many of the associational owners of the organization also perform work roles and many volunteer workers elect members to the board or other leadership positions. Many self-help organizations recruit their volunteers from among their clients, and so the distinction between worker and client can also become very blurred. In the sampled organizations, and apparently in others (Billis 1987), even volunteer and employee statuses were exchanged, further contributing to the uncertainty over one another's roles. Volunteers and others in their settings may have difficulty drawing distinct boundaries around these different organizational roles.

Further, the very term "volunteer" carries connotations beyond the narrow technical meaning of unpaid labor. In western societies, the word represents social values of freedom and giving to others. By implication, it is something one contributes when one can; it is not a contract to deliver labor at a known "inducement." Thus it does not suggest the same degree of "contractual obligation" by the volunteer worker. When someone assumes the status of volunteer worker, what actually is owed?

These multiple and vaguely defined roles can create confusion for volunteers and other members of the organization. What are volunteers' relationships with others? Who is allowed to unmake organizational decisions if they don't appear to be sensible? Who is deserving of help, and who is the helper? Employees, at least, have a prototypic set of assumptions (such as who is the boss and who is the client) that volunteers simply cannot assume. Further, this uncertainty leads individuals to adopt different, and possibly contradictory, expectations within the same organization. In some organizations that are more formal and bureaucratic, the uncertainties are removed through clear rules and written contracts with the termination of anyone who cannot or will not follow them. In other volunteer-staffed organizations, like those described by Rothschild-Whitt (1979), this blurring of responsibilities is itself liberating, an important value of the setting.

Organizational vs individual purposes

Although several of the typologies reviewed categorized organizations by their purposes, there is considerable empirical evidence that these organizational purposes do not reflect the dominant individual purposes of their members. Thirty years after Cyert and March's (1963) seminal distinction between individual and organizational goals, it would seem that this point would be rather obvious. However, because of the general theoretical definition of associations as collections of individuals who come together to pursue their joint goals – and the widespread use of "contributions to the organization's goals" in the recruitment of volunteers – it should be reiterated. It is simply incorrect to assume that all volunteers' goals for participation coincide with the organization's goals. Individual reasons for volunteering can vary a great deal, and multiple reasons even for a single volunteer are probably more common than not. This uncertainty of motives is analyzed in detail in Chapter 5.

Legal-rational to value-rational settings

Following from Sills (1968), voluntary organizations can be arrayed along a continuum ranging from extremely "bureaucratic" (Weber's [1968] legal-rational authority) to the value-rational or "peripheral, unstructured, and confused" entities described by Rothschild-Whitt (1979) and Knoke and Prensky (1982). At the one end, they are the formal organizations which have become familiar to students of employees' organizational behavior. In these settings we would expect norms characterized by a concern for task performance, hierarchy of authority, impersonality, contractually delineated duties, and formalism. At the other extreme, we would expect a concern for values rather than for efficiency or effectiveness, with little vertical or horizontal specialization, very personal and emotionally intense relationships, unclear individual responsibilities, and a disdain for rules.

Thus, the behavioral settings in which volunteers work can vary tremendously in normative expectations regarding fundamental procedures and relationships. In some settings, volunteer workers are assumed to be virtually the same as paid employees. The best popular example of this setting is the hospital volunteer, although the sampled fire department, newspaper, and orchestra volunteers of the present study come close to this level of contractual clarity. Certainly, volunteers' experiences in one of these formal organizations would be very different from their experiences in organizations at the other extreme.

Further complications are introduced when it is noted that individuals holding these different assumptions about their organizations may work in the same voluntary organization. Anecdotal examples abound of individuals holding legal-rational ideals volunteering for an organization operating at the other end of the continuum. These volunteers struggle to make the organization more business-like. Committee meetings in which some members attend to express their values among like-minded colleagues are torture to the volunteer who wants to get things done.

Therefore, many of the structural "organizational" features we take for granted in the study of the organizational behavior of employees will apply to some, but not all, volunteers. As will be detailed in Chapter 4, not all volunteers have jobs, and quite a few believe that they do not have supervisors (Chapter 7), yet they do operate in an integrated system of organizational behavior.

Legitimacy of work

Finally, volunteers often face fundamental ambiguity about the value of their work. Are they givers or takers? Volunteering is variously attacked or praised; the very term itself connotes the extremes of positive (free, without fear or favor, altruistic) and negative (nonprofessional, dilettante, pseudo-work, occupational therapy) judgments. In practice, many volunteers are quite clear about their roles and contributions, because they have – or more likely their organization has – taken pains to make sure that it is so. However, this potential questioning never occurs for employees. As the volunteer quoted in Chapter 1 noted, "you just assume you are doing it for a living," and as that volunteer suggested, "These [different] assumptions lead to different ways of doing things." She implies that volunteers must constantly prove themselves valuable ("be cheerful"). Similarly, the usefulness of their activities must be continually demonstrated to volunteers. Thus there often develops a brittle lack of self-assurance in these organizations.

CONCLUSIONS

This chapter has briefly reviewed the sociological and social theory regarding volunteers and their organizations, providing several behavioral implications. Volunteers' societal role and the assumptions attached to "volunteering" are fundamentally different from those attached to "working." Volunteering is a much broader and more multi-faceted role and, therefore, does not carry expectations that are as strong and clear as those for employees. These societal assumptions are exacerbated by the wide range of organizations in which volunteers work. They vary from very formal and bureaucratic to small, unstructured, and confused enterprises. Although employee-staffed organizations certainly vary in their formal properties, the simple presence of "employees" forces some structure and regularity on the organization in order to monitor performance and pay wages (and certain legal protective requirements must be met). Employee-staffed organizations must be sufficiently affluent to pay regular wages; volunteer organizations need only collect a few friends. Thus, the organizations in which volunteers work can be quite unpredictable and unstable, and this provides a more demanding and complex setting in which to work.

Chapter 3

Volunteers' jobs

When volunteers work in organizational settings, the way their jobs are designed and the formal interrelationships with co-workers appear to differ in significant ways from the structures designed for employees. Study data will be presented indicating that not only are there noteworthy differences in the ways work is organized for volunteers and for employees, but that these organizational differences have their own independent effects on the organizational behavior of volunteers. That is, volunteer status not only has direct influences on the organizational behavior of volunteers but has additional indirect effects through differential job structures.

The reasons for these differences in job design in volunteer-staffed and employee-staffed organizations seem to derive from both the part-time nature of volunteer involvement and the fact that all volunteers are paid "equally" and "cheaply." Drawing on the seven volunteer-staffed organizations matched with seven employee-staffed organizations doing comparable organizational work it is suggested that these differences result in (1) contact among interdependent workers that is quantitatively and qualitatively different; (2) less formalization in job responsibilities and membership status for volunteers; (3) different divisions of the same organizational work; (4) dependence on a "core" set of members for control rather than a hierarchy of authority; and (5) lower performance and selection requirements due to understaffing in volunteer-staffed organizations. The chapter concludes with implications both for the management of volunteers and for general organizational theories that emphasize "technology" while neglecting the importance of co-worker proximity and labor costs on organizational design decisions.

IMPORTANCE OF STRUCTURAL DESIGN

The structuring of organizational responsibilities is one of the primary vehicles organizations use to remove ambiguity facing workers about their expected actions. Individual workers are assigned specific "jobs" and placed into a hierarchy of authority that defines who may give them instructions and advice in particular domains. It is this explicit or "formal" structuring of individuals' actions and interrelationships that is the defining feature of organizations as social settings. Certainly, in practice these constraints vary in specificity, even within a single organization; nevertheless the author's own work uncovered consistent patterns of differences between volunteer-staffed and employee-staffed organizations.

Despite the intuitive importance of understanding organizational design, there has been a complete neglect of this topic in studies of organizational volunteers. In contrast, "departmentalization" and "organization design" were one of the earliest topics of interest to management (of employees) scholars (Fayol 1949; Gulick and Urwick 1937). These and subsequent scholars of organization design have emphasized the "nature of the work" or "technology" (who needs to talk to whom to get the job done) as the dominant design variable.

Although theorists studying the design of work for employee-staffed organizations agree on the centrality of technology in the design of efficient organizations, there has been significant theoretical and empirical confusion concerning exactly what these terms mean. Sometimes work has been conceptualized as differences in "information processing requirements" (Galbraith 1977), or as "routinization" (Perrow 1979), or as the "movement of work, authority, information and decisions" (Mintzberg 1979). Many researchers rely on Thompson's (1967) three-part categorization of technology into serially interdependent, mediating, and intensive technologies. However much debated the central concepts of technology have been in organizational behavior, there is widespread agreement that the nature of the work is the dominant consideration in design decisions. Yet despite the care taken in the present study to match volunteers and employees on "technology," systematic differences were found in the jobs and their interrelationships when work was designed either for volunteers or for employees.

This present study provides a unique opportunity to examine the influence of volunteer/employee status with "the nature of the work" held relatively constant. As described in detail in the Appendix, the study of the 14 matched organizations was specifically designed to hold the organization's work constant in comparing volunteer and employed workers. As Perrow (1979) noted, similarities and differences in general identity do not necessarily dictate the nature of the "work" performed, and this was certainly the case in the present study. One of the most interesting features of this study was the amount of discretion these organizations had in defining what tasks to perform under the general umbrella of their identity and purpose. As will be detailed below, these choices were influenced not only by resources and different environmental demands, but also by the nature of their workforces. However, these general categories did provide some control for the nature of the "raw material" and "processes" associated with organizations of the same primary task. In a limited sense, the present study provides an opportunity to contrast the power of the "technological imperative" in organizational design with the effects of volunteer/paid workforce status.

Certainly, primary task was an important defining feature for these organizations. Members of each of the seven primary-task-sets shared job titles (e.g. firefighter, sales clerk, teacher, concert master, and so on), as well as technical jargon and expertise. In several of the task-sets there were natural career progressions connecting volunteer and paid work. For example, several of the paid firefighters had once been volunteers, and one of the interviewed volunteer firefighters stated that his reason for volunteering was to earn the extra civil service "points" on the examination for a paid firefighter's job. Similarly, the chapter chairwoman of the volunteer-staffed family planning clinic and the coordinator of the poverty relief agency were professionals (nurse and social worker, respectively) keeping active in their professions through their volunteer work while raising small children. All interviewees readily identified with their primary task, and most could give detailed descriptions of the similarities and differences between volunteer-staffed and employee-staffed organizations in their task-set. In short, the primary task identity and purpose were very salient to interviewees.

However, despite the importance of the nature of work in the design literature and the diversity of primary tasks in this study, volunteer/employing type did result in striking differences in the design of work in these organizations. This can be seen initially in interviewees' coded responses to an open-ended question asking them to suggest how volunteer-staffed and employee-staffed organizations in their field differed, reported in Table 3.1. As the table indicates, four of the six coded categories were concerned with structural differences in the work – employees work more continuously; volunteers have more (part-time) people to do the same work; volunteers have more autonomy; employing organizations have the power or sanctions to insure performance – and only one was concerned with individual motives and rewards. Thus, even though a difference in monetary rewards is the defining feature of a volunteer/employee difference, the majority of respondents, without prompts, reported structural features of the work setting, rather than the defining "pay status" incentives difference. In the following five sections this type difference is analyzed with attention to differences in contact, formalization, kinds of jobs and roles adopted by members, and staffing needs.

Table 3.1 "How types differ" responses categorized by type

How is [the counterpart type] organization different from this one?	Number of volunteers responding	Number of employees responding	Σ
1. Employees work more continuously	5	5	10
2. Volunteers have more people to do same work	1	3	4
3. Volunteers have more autonomy	9	5	14
4. Employing organizations have the power to insure performance	12	10	22
5. Employees develop better skills	5	3	8
6. Volunteers are more committed to the work	19	3	22
7. Don't know how different	3	10	13
8. Other	7	7	14
Σ	61	46	107

Note: A test of whether the categories differed by respondent produced a $\chi^2 = 16.45$, $p \leq .05$.

DIFFERENTIAL CONTACT

Contact among interdependent workers was quantitatively and qualitatively different in these two types of organizations. This appeared to result primarily because volunteer work was a spare-time activity. Most volunteers worked "part-time" while most of the paid employees worked "full-time" (a mean of 9.09 hours for volunteers and 35.20 for employees, $F(1,214) = 323.51$, $p < .01$). Although there were a handful of volunteers who worked more weekly hours than comparable employees, the vast majority of volunteers worked only a fraction of the time their organization operated.

These overall differences mask some important task differences. For the day care centers, newspapers, poverty relief agencies, family planning clinics, and gift shops, the hours differences were exactly what would be expected – more volunteers working part-time shifts contrasted with fewer employees working full-time shifts. For the orchestras, volunteers and paid professionals had essentially equal requirements: they were all required to appear for all rehearsals and performances. However, the professional orchestra scheduled more rehearsal hours per performance.

The firefighters presented an interesting exception to the general pattern described in this section. Firefighting is an inherently "part-time" activity – firefighters are needed only when there is a fire, and for a certain amount of training, drill, and equipment maintenance. However, the ability to get to a fire quickly (volunteers must go first to the firehouse to get the equipment and then take it to the fire) and the reliability of knowing who will show up to fight a fire provide significant performance improvements when firefighters are paid to remain at the house for a "shift." This means that firefighters must be kept at the firehouse even when there is "no work [firefighting] to do." So in contrast to the other five settings characterized by communication and coordination complexities among volunteers doing "only a small piece of a job," the *volunteer* firefighters' time use was better adapted to their task than was that of the employees. Paid firefighters complained of "boredom," "busy work" (they continuously cleaned the house and equipment), and the personal conflicts that arose, just as if they were "married to one another," all exacerbated by long shifts of 12 hours each.

Therefore, although volunteers actually worked fewer weekly hours than employees in all seven task-sets, the volunteers in the orchestra and fire department were always completing a psychologically "whole job," and thus, the following discussion is more characteristic of the other five volunteer-staffed organizations with the traditional "part-of-a-job" volunteer pattern.

Informal "real time" coordination

As noted in Chapter 2, volunteer work is often considered to be a peripheral activity, taking a secondary role to the primary responsibilities of job and family. Without compensating them, organizations really cannot expect a great deal of time commitment from their volunteer workers, and this need to staff an organization with a part-time workforce results in different modes of interpersonal communication for informal coordination. One of the most important communication impacts is the reduced opportunity to communicate informally and in "real time."

Employees had significantly more face-to-face contact with one another than did volunteers (4.15 vs 3.70, $F(1,115) = 5.27$, $p < .05$). Although there was not a statistically significant difference in reported reliance on phone/written communication (volunteers had .19 vs .6 for employees, $F(1,115) = 2.48$), observation of the day-to-day workings of these organizations suggested that the volunteer-staffed organizations compensated for a lack of opportunities for face-to-face coordination through the use of phones and a central display area for current information.

Volunteers made extensive use of telephones for co-worker information exchange. A member of the poverty relief agency's governing steering committee reported that they would occasionally hold committee meetings via telephone. One or two members checked with a few others and then got back together, pooled information, and made the consensus decision. In all seven volunteer-staffed organizations a list of workers' home (and office where appropriate) phone numbers was prominently tacked to a wall next to the office telephone. The researcher observed the use of these lists dozens of times, and they seemed to be vital to the organizations' day-to-day functioning. In contrast, no home phone lists were ever observed in any of the seven employee-staffed organizations. If these lists were kept, they were not displayed, nor was their use ever observed.

In addition, observation of the day-to-day workings of these organizations suggested that these volunteer-staffed organizations also relied on central display areas for current information. The format differed: in the day care center and poverty relief agency notes were taped to front doors, members of the orchestra found notes on their music stands at each rehearsal and performance, the newspaper had a blackboard for this purpose, while the traditional bulletin board served the family planning clinic, gift shop, and fire department. Volunteers would invariably glance at these areas for new information when they arrived. Alternatively, employees would share important job-relevant information, more or less immediately, or make formal oral announcements at the beginning of the work day or shift. Only the volunteer-staffed fire department ever managed to bring all workers together at the same time (annual election). The bulletin boards in the employing organizations seemed to be reserved for dated announcements; for example, civil service job openings, public relations material, a yellowed copy of health and safety regulations. The researcher never observed an employee reading these boards.

The practices of these volunteers underscore the amount of unnoticed "real time" informal coordination that is accomplished by workers completing larger components of tasks and working in close physical proximity to others doing related work. A more detailed examination of the means by which volunteer-staffed organizations manage to compensate for this absence of informal face-to-face coordination is developed in the section on different jobs below. What follows are observations about the effects of these modes of communication on the social quality of volunteers' workplaces, focusing on the overlapping work/non-work boundaries for interaction in volunteer settings.

A time and a place

An interesting byproduct of these differences in communication was the difference that evolved in distinct settings for types of communication. As is indicated by the above description, volunteers, particularly those in decision-making roles, could not draw clear boundaries separating their volunteer work from the rest of their lives. It appeared to be expected that a volunteer could receive a call any time or place to do organizational business; the most vivid example is that of the volunteer firefighters who were on call 24 hours a day to fight a fire. Even the handful of employees who need to be called at odd hours often shared this duty with colleagues each taking a different "shift" (as in a shared obstetrics practice). There was also less separation of outside interests from the workplace itself in volunteer-staffed organizations. The following description from the researcher's field notes describing an interview with a volunteer is typical:

> [While interviewing the captain of Company "A" at the company fire-house kitchen table.] [The house vice president] sat there with us during the interview. He was pretty quiet, just sitting and listening to the older man's descriptions, and occasionally smiling at one of [the captain's] jokes. While we were in the kitchen a guy would poke his head in every now and then. At one point a group of young men bounded in with a dog. They enveloped us in their general conversation, the dog jumped on us, and in about five minutes they left. Apparently this company house serves as a "hang-out" for its members and their friends. . . . At the end of the interview, it was [the captain] and three younger men left sitting at the table.
>
> (Field notes, 7/31)

Employees were more likely to separate their "work life" from their "personal life." All interviews with employees took place in their offices or in a formally allotted place. Interviews with volunteers took place in the volunteer workplace, in interviewees' homes, at their places of employment, in their friends' homes. Even non-work-related conversations at the employee-staffed workplace tended to be segregated into coffee breaks or the waiting time between patients. The volunteers simply did not separate their volunteer work from the rest of their lives to the same extent as did employees. Volunteers often worked out of their homes (telephone volunteers, and meetings in most of the organizations) and used the volunteer work setting as much as a place to go to socialize as to do work.

Although this blending of work and non-work was pervasive in these volunteer-staffed organizations, the intensity of social contact with fellow volunteers varied enormously. Despite the attractions of the work setting to many of its volunteers as a place to meet friends, volunteer involvement produced a very different kind of social integration for others. Many volunteers worked very few hours in a month, sometimes from their own homes (telephone volunteers in the poverty relief agency) and had only the most minimal contact with others in the organization. Some volunteers had worked for these organizations for years and had met only a few co-workers face-to-face. For every volunteer who built his or her social life around the organization, there were many more whose sole contacts were brief, job-related communications, sometimes only by phone or in writing. This degree of social isolation from the workplace was not possible for full-time employees working in the same office as their co-workers. Note that this is not a statement about differences in general sociability, since many of these isolated volunteers were quite gregarious in other settings, simply that for many their volunteer work was a "small contribution" that they made while remaining more actively involved in other facets of their lives. This variance in the relative involvement of volunteers is discussed in more detail under the section titled "Core and periphery."

LESS FORMALIZED RESPONSIBILITIES

The organizations staffed by volunteers divided work in different ways than did employees. These differences seemed to center both on less formalization for volunteers and on the use of different specialized roles in organizations staffed by employees and volunteers. Both of these structural differences seemed dependent on the fact that all volunteers were paid equally while different employees in the same organization commanded substantial differences in pay. This pay equality is discussed first, then its effects on formalization are analyzed. The next section contains the data on differences in specialization in these organizations.

Equal pay

Volunteers were all paid equally and relatively inexpensively. Labor costs were indirect and informal, often involving the expenditure of resources that were not depleted when spent, such as praise and respect. Arguments can be made about whether or not volunteer labor is "free"; however, what is not disputed is the fact that all volunteers received an equal share of the organization's tangible compensation. If resources must be spent to recruit and thank volunteers, these resources were not awarded differentially to individual volunteers. The most productive hard-working volunteers may have received more tokens of appreciation, but they did not receive additional concrete rewards. Volunteers with valued skills (e.g. nurses in the family planning clinic or experienced firefighters) may have worked in specialized jobs that drew on those skills, but they did not receive any more "compensation" than the unskilled volunteer of one week's seniority. Volunteers received equal pay for decidedly unequal work.

This practice is virtually unknown with employees, with the exception of a few small ideologically based collectives. Even socialist societies, which might have been expected to implement Marx's famous dictum, "From each according to his abilities, to each according to his needs," have found that they must pay differential wages to attract workers to undesirable jobs or to motivate high levels of effort, and even to encourage cooperation with the authorities (Bendix 1974). It is perhaps because differential pay is a constant in employee-staffed organizations that the role of differential labor costs in job design has gone unnoticed by theorists of organizational design.

Informal job duties

Without differential labor costs there is no need to develop precise job duties for compensation purposes. Since there are no labor markets to tie wages to, nor any need to protect internal equity in pay by justifying pay differences by variations in responsibilities, knowledge requirements, and so forth (Mahoney 1979), there is no pressure to be precise about formal responsibilities. All of these volunteer-staffed organizations had "jobs" that defined what workers were to do – sales clerks made sales, editors were responsible for filling their "page" with stories. However, volunteers were much more likely to treat these as mere guidelines, sometimes "helping out" when needed (editors doing composite work) and sometimes being "insubordinate" or ignoring those features of the job they found distasteful. Although these practices certainly occurred among employees, their scope and frequency were much more extensive among the studied volunteers.

Further, many of the jobs in these organizations, especially for new volunteers, consisted of "showing up and watching," despite the formal sounding titles of Assistant Teacher or Sales Clerk. In contrast to traditional employee-staffed organizations where the newer and "lower-level" employees are expected to be the most severely constrained by narrow responsibilities and the higher ranking members expect more discretion in defining and carrying out their jobs (Fox 1974), in these volunteer-staffed organizations the inexperienced members had the open-ended non-jobs. Higher ranking volunteers – captains in the fire departments, editors in the newspaper – usually held responsibility for a concrete "task" with relatively clear standards of performance or non-performance. Often newer members stood around waiting to be "told what to do" or "given an assignment" by these "leading" or office-holding volunteers. So it wasn't surprising that these newcomers, who socialized with their fellows while waiting to be noticed (and sometimes left their shifts at the organization without performing any "work"), would not make sharp distinctions between work and non-work in the volunteer setting.

Only one of the sampled organizations, the volunteer-staffed poverty relief agency, had formal job descriptions, clear job assignments, and a formal orientation and training program for all new volunteers. Since their volunteers worked "off-site," they could not use the informal controls of the other volunteer-staffed organizations but needed a tightly organized and formal procedure for insuring that food was delivered to those who needed it. This had an interesting byproduct in that this poverty relief agency did not have the high turnover among new members that characterized all the other volunteer-staffed organizations (except the fire department with its glamorous and locally prestigious work). In the other five organizations, new volunteers frequently got "fed up" while waiting for an overworked and harassed officeholder to give them something to do. The relief agency had many long-term volunteers who, as one suggested, "like this organization because I can work my few hours a month without being dragged into endless committee work, as I have been in other organizations." Another byproduct, however, was that this organization, with its efficient management systems, also had a higher proportion of social isolates. This feature is explored in depth in the chapters on interpersonal influence.

In addition to their effects on turnover, informal job responsibilities also meant that only the few long-seniority volunteers could feel confident that they "knew what to do." Even relatively low-level full-time employees can build special expertise by observing over time. Thus the informality of responsibilities combined with only part-time involvement also contributes to the weak behavioral coercion (Barker 1968) in these volunteer-staffed organizations.

Membership uncertainty

In addition to uncertainty in job responsibilities for many volunteers, members of these volunteer-staffed organizations also had astonishing degrees of uncertainty about who was or was not a worker in the organization. Except for the fire department, which had to submit its list of members to a state agency, these organizations did not have clear markers for member entrance or exit. The organizational size figures reported in the Appendix for these six volunteer-staffed organizations were all "estimates." In contrast, an employee must be "hired," and all of the employee-staffed organizations required that applicants demonstrate qualifications before they were accepted. The employee-staffed day care center director reported that she received hundreds of unsolicited résumés a year, and none of these organizations had any difficulty in immediately replacing an employee who had left. Entry was a difficult and anxious time for prospective employees. Entry into the volunteer-staffed organizations was easy, with current members recruiting new members. Prospective volunteers were accepted unconditionally, with no application forms and no tests.

This membership uncertainty in volunteer-staffed organizations is reflected in the differences in reported time to be "socialized" into the organization. In response to the organization-sample interview question, "How long did it take you to feel like a regular member of this organization?", volunteers reported a mean of 6.77 months compared to 4.17 months for employees ($F(1,115) = 2.91$, $p < .10$). Although part of this difference may reflect the greater number of hours the employees spend doing organizational work, the longer and more rigorous process of entry probably provides additional anticipatory socialization for employees (Van Maanen and Schein 1979).

Organizational exit followed a similar pattern. Exit from the paid jobs, while not theoretically difficult, had been traumatic in practice. Stories of the flamboyant or quiet departure of ex-employees were told and retold to the researcher, even by employees who had been hired after the incident. In these employee-staffed organizations, there were procedures (e.g. probationary periods) and state laws governing the termination of a member.

In contrast, in the volunteer organizations, it wasn't clear who was in or out. Just because an individual hadn't worked in a while didn't necessarily mean that he or she had left. In all of these volunteer-staffed organizations, family members or friends of a volunteer would occasionally help out; should they be listed as members? For many tasks, such as calling someone with a message or typing the newsletter, the "organization" may not even have known that a "nonmember" was doing its work. It was impossible to get a precise count of the size of these volunteer-staffed organizations, while, in contrast, the question received an immediate confident response in employee-staffed ones. These uncertainties were exacerbated by the multiple roles volunteers often served in these organizations (see Chapter 2). Day care teachers' aides were often parents, all volunteer firefighters were also clients of the organization, and board members of the six volunteer-owned organizations usually worked at "low level" jobs.

This uncertainty concerning the responsibilities of volunteers and about who is or who is not working for the organization creates important differences in the context of organizational behavior. First, volunteers continuously find that they are working alongside "strangers." They don't know the individual and therefore face the awkwardness of introductions. But, perhaps more important, they do not know what level of expertise or what up-to-the-minute information a co-worker may possess. In full-time settings with more stable relationships, workers have opportunities to build up trust (or distrust) in the other individuals with whom they work.

Finally, authority evaporates when the organization is unsure who is and who is not subject to its direction. Organizations all have means for insuring coordinated action, and the volunteer-staffed organizations had formal procedures for setting policies, and roles assigned to communicate and enforce the policies. In practice, however, "enforcement" was a more delicate affair than in the employee-staffed organizations. These fundamental questions of volunteer control in organizations are explored in Chapters 6 and 7.

DIFFERENT KINDS OF JOBS

The fact of equal and inexpensive pay for volunteers working at a fragment of a full-time job leads to different formal jobs in volunteer-staffed organizations. When compared to the sampled employee-staffed organizations, the volunteer organizations were "missing" one kind of position that was present in the employee-staffed organizations – support staff – and had added one that the full-time employees did not seem to need – coordinators. Each of these is analyzed below.

Support staff

The employee-staffed organizations all had support staff members, while none of the comparable volunteer-staffed organizations did. Some of these support positions resulted from the addition of more complex support tasks in the employee-staffed organizations. For example, the employee-staffed day care center provided food for their children and so employed a kitchen staff, while the parents of the volunteer-staffed day care center provided their own children's meals for the day. This cannot, however, account for the more prevalent use of lesser-paid para-professionals (such as intake social workers, account clerks, nurse's aides), nor for the fact that all seven employee-staffed organizations had secretaries while only the sole paid employee of the volunteer-staffed family planning clinic had this job title.

This different use of formal support roles seems to result from two pressures. First, the volunteer-staffed organizations may need to "share" the less prestigious or uninteresting support and maintenance activities in order to maintain volunteer participation. Therefore, these tasks are divided and shared among those with more interesting decision-making responsibility (e.g. the day care treasurer typed his own financial report) or direct client contact.

Similarly, in the employee-staffed organizations, it may be more cost efficient to use the more expensive workers (e.g. physicians) sparingly, while assigning as many less skilled tasks as possible to lower wage support workers. This division of labor by cost was most apparent in the task-set with the greatest salary differential between low and high wage workers: the family planning clinic. In this case, the advantage provided by full-time workers completing a psychologically "whole job" (Hackman and Oldham 1980) was sacrificed to the financial considerations of dispensing differential wages to different categories of employees.

However, these differential labor costs do not completely capture the differences in use of support workers. Two additional features seemed to influence job specialization. First, the employing organizations appeared to "build career ladders" by breaking their jobs down into fine gradations with increasing responsibility. This offered additional "incentives" and "goals" for career-oriented employees in pyramidal hierarchies with few opportunities for upward movement. No studies of organization design could be located that discussed this use of design for motivational rather than simple technical efficiency or external signaling.

Second, the case of secretaries is particularly interesting. Benet (1972) argued that secretaries are employed, not so much because they allow efficient use of more expensive workers, but because they are the accepted symbols of prestige. This was echoed by the interview description from the secretary in the employee-staffed fire department:

> [Could you describe a typical day?] Depends. I should be here between 8:00 and 8:15. I'm here by 8:30. I take the fire reports and type them up. I look in the grey file for correspondence; if there are letters there I type them. [Do you always get the letters from the file?] Sometimes he puts them in the file, sometimes he gives them to me . . . . Things for the city . . . [Could you describe exactly what you did yesterday, in detail?] . . . . No . . . there was nothing yesterday . . . . The workmen were here putting paneling in the office. The phone didn't ring once all afternoon. But I have to be here, I'd catch a lot of flak if I wasn't here and it rang. It's so frustrating . . . . They really don't need a secretary in this office.
>
> (Organization-sample interview)

All of the employee-staffed organizations had "offices" and offices have secretaries. Society simply does not expect the director of an agency to type his or her own letters. However, the normative expectations regarding the proper activities for volunteer workers are not as precise. Those expectations that do exist seemed to focus more on "pitching in," downplaying rank differences, and demonstrating the spirit of cooperation and dedication characteristic of "good volunteers."

Coordinators

Working on parts-of-a-job increased the need for explicit coordination. If jobs that otherwise would have been done by one person are now done by two or even two dozen others, there is an increased need to coordinate across individuals. Single individuals can remember what they did in the morning and adjust their own activities in the afternoon with no need to consult anyone else.

Despite the fact that theories of organizational coordination have always been prominent in organization theory, their analyses, assuming employees, did not capture these volunteers' solutions to their coordination problems. According to Thompson (1967), explicit coordination may take the form of increased standardization of tasks (reduced worker discretion) which would reduce the need to exchange information. This is one of the governing principles of "scientific management" which seeks to gain the maximum possible efficiencies from division of labor (Taylor 1967). However, there were real limits in the use of this approach in these volunteer-staffed organizations. To attract and retain unpaid workers, these organizations had to insure that the tasks and workplace were attractive to their workers. Extreme standardization is notoriously unattractive to most workers. Similarly, standardization requires a great deal of reliability and predictability in the workforce, and most of these organizations had to rely on untrained workers who did not feel themselves particularly subject to the organization's authority. Therefore, all seven of the sampled volunteer-staffed organizations developed an alternative role that was not present in any of the sampled employee-staffed organizations: the coordinator.

The coordinator scheduled workers and tasks. Much as a production scheduler in a factory, the coordinator was responsible for making sure that sufficient resources (workers) were available for any given task. The coordination task could be relatively straightforward, as in the day care center in which the teachers' assistants would sign up for their shifts for the following semester in the last week of the previous one. In the fire department and newspaper, coordination was decentralized to the company and "page" levels, respectively. The individual fire companies scheduled volunteers into maintenance duties and drills, and page editors coordinated their own volunteer reporters. In the family planning clinic and newspaper, the scheduling of new unskilled volunteers was haphazard, contributing to stresses in both organizations.

In all cases, coordination of volunteers was central to these volunteer-staffed organizations and virtually absent in the comparable employee-staffed organizations. The personal abilities of these organizations' coordinators – promptness, responsiveness to individual requests, and the quality of their "backup lists" – was central to the continuation of these organizations. Its importance can be seen in the collapse of the newspaper during data collection.

Unlike many other college newspapers that are run out of a journalism department with de facto faculty control, this newspaper was a genuinely student-run organization. Other than the editor-in-chief, the newspaper was not staffed by career-oriented journalism majors. For example, the sports editor was a campus athlete who simply wanted to insure campus sports coverage, and the entertainment page editor enjoyed the free records and movie tickets. There was no formal mechanism for keeping track of reporters; all scheduling was the responsibility of the editors, a responsibility most did not faithfully perform.

This neglect was seen by reporters as indifference to the importance of their contribution. The quotation at the beginning of Chapter 1 provides a flavor of the way reporters responded. This reporter's bitterness about an editor's indifference to whether or not her assignments were completed is palpable. Thus volunteers became more frequently "unreliable," and the editors had to do more of their own reporting. They became overburdened and, in turn, felt unappreciated, leading to the following incident.

During data collection, there was a rebellion among the page editors:

> During the interview [the former editor-in-chief] related the details of the story about the strike. On this week's issue the feature and campus

editors are not on the masthead. It seems that, according to [the former editor-in-chief], [the editor-in-chief] was *thinking* about using surplus ad revenue for scholarships next year. The feature and campus editors wanted the $200 now, so they "went on strike." My informant said he thought it was a joke. He, personally, did not like the idea of paying them and particularly didn't like their walking out. He noted bitterly that the campus editor said at the beginning of the year that they should put out their paper "whenever they feel like it" and had quit several times before. He noted with pride that they were able to get out the eight pages without them and could carry on for the last few issues. He stated that he was against paying them because "they were volunteers."

(Field notes, 4/20)

These volunteer-staffed organizations simply could not function without competent coordinators. The importance – and unattractiveness – of this work is probably the reason the first paid positions are usually the voluntary organizations' coordinators.

CORE AND PERIPHERY

Although all of these seven volunteer-staffed organizations had formal policy-making structures, in practice they depended on a "core" set of members or activists for coordination and control rather than a hierarchy of authority as such. In organization theory, hierarchy is the principal means by which organizations insure that their divided roles complement each other, that "the left hand knows what the right hand is doing" (Simon 1957). In what has been called "vertical specialization," some workers specialize in collecting information, and then give directives to those who "report to them" to insure that actions are coordinated and the organization remains in control (see Galbraith 1977).

Most of these volunteer-staffed organizations had formal and clear lines of authority for particular settings – for the fighting of a fire, the treatment of a patient in the clinic examining room, the display of stories on a newspaper page, and certainly there was no uncertainty about who was conducting the orchestra. Aside from these narrowly circumscribed tasks, there were no "bosses." Volunteers would take direction from anyone or no one. This potentially chaotic situation was, in practice, kept in check by the reliance on what will here be called "the core members."

The observation that volunteers in organizations divide into two groups – the minority who "rule" and the inactive or "apathetic" majority – dates from the earliest organizational theories (Michels 1959). This "iron law of oligarchy" has had many explanations: large organizational size, task specialization, time availability of members, and the nature of organizational activities (see Sills 1968, for a review). It has another parallel in Thompson's

(1967) identification of the evolution of an "inner circle" when decision-making is dispersed. Certainly, this bifurcation of the membership was present in all of these volunteer-staffed organizations. However, since the focus of this work is on the organizational behavior of volunteer workers (rather than on the policy-making processes) and since the metaphor of an apathetic peasantry ruled by an aristocratic clique does not do justice to the character of these volunteers' working relationships, the terms "core" and "peripheral" volunteers will be used to describe the two groups.

Members of the core were those who "took an interest in the organization." They hung around the workplace, volunteered to help out, showed up when they said they would, and generally made themselves useful and informed. Core volunteers usually, but not always, held a formal office (formal position of authority). However, their influence came from their membership in the core, not their office.

Members of the periphery were less involved. They spent less time on the organization's activities and were less informed about them. In contrast to members of the core, this organization was not a "central life interest" (Dubin *et al.* 1976) to peripheral members. Some members of the periphery were reliable steady contributors, simply not wanting to "get further involved" than they were. Others were occasional contributors or those who "tried out" the organization for a brief time, found that it didn't suit them, and left. Members of the periphery were not necessarily "apathetic," some were just busy and felt that the core members (what was usually called "the leadership") were doing a fine job. It was at the periphery that volunteer and nonworker status blurred. Core members were clearly "in" the organizations; not all members of the periphery were.

Of course, no organization had formal roles designating core from peripheral members, and the boundaries between these two groups were fluid. It was common to find "new board members" who were in the periphery, despite their formal offices. For example, a newly arrived local clergyman had just joined the board of the poverty relief agency during the research. These individuals were comparable to Sills' (1957) "Joiners" who were involved in many community activities. Similarly, some members of the periphery were former core members, who wanted to reduce their involvement and no longer held any office, but retained their expertise and status, if not an extensive current time commitment.

What is most important for the present study of organizational behavior, the influence of members of the core was based primarily not on office or formal authority but on their personal qualities. Since members of the core spent more of their time on the organization's business and they conferred among themselves, they usually "knew what was going on." Similarly, they had often built substantial technical expertise over the years. The volunteer fire departments' companies elected their captains, but since the captains were the ones who directed activities at the scene of a fire, firefighters would not entrust their lives to a "popular" man who had no expertise. Similarly, the coordinator of the poverty relief agency was a credentialed social worker, the chapter chairwoman of the family planning clinic was a registered nurse, the newspaper's editor-in-chief intended a professional journalism career, and they all had seniority that was many times the "average" for their organizations. Table 3.2 indicates that they did, in fact, contribute significantly more time to the organization and felt that their work was more demanding.

Table 3.2 Differences in mean job perceptions between core and peripheral members

Analysis of variance	df	SS	MS	F(1,115)	r^2
Hours worked per week (respondent report)					
Core/periphery	1	782.95	782.95	8.55**	.05
Error	149	14426.70	91.57		
Changing procedures					
Core/periphery	1	8.13	8.13	7.54**	.05
Error	149	160.62	1.08		
Work demands					
Core/periphery	1	15.41	15.41	7.85**	.05
Error	149	292.64	1.96		
Work praiseworthiness					
Core/periphery	1	1.17	1.17	0.83	–
Error	149	208.63	1.40		

Variable	Core	Periphery
Hours worked per week	13.24	7.85
Changing procedures	4.20	3.65
Work demands	3.94	3.19
Work praiseworthiness	6.01	5.81
n	35	116

** $p \leq .01$

Virtually all volunteers could name the central members of their organization's core (while often being unable to report their titles and responsibilities accurately). These members were simply "the leadership," and they "ran things." If a volunteer wanted information or to make a change, he or she would call "the office," speak with one of the several core members who would be expected to be there, and usually be satisfied with the transaction. For those task-sets that required on-site coordinated action, the peripheral members would simply look to that member of the core who gave them instructions.

Thus, organizational control was informal and personal; volunteers accepted influence because of who a particular person was, not because of the authority of an office. Very new volunteers, who didn't know anyone yet, accepted influence from anyone who seemed to know what to do. In neither case were these volunteers governed by Weber's (1968) legal-rational authority (obedience to the office rather than the person). Only in the volunteer fire department did offices, as such, have prestige – and in this organization, with its life-threatening tasks and yearly elections, office and expertise were tightly bound. In the other six organizations, titles and offices were referred to jokingly, and no one was foolish enough to expect that a command would be obeyed because it was given by an officeholder.

It is perhaps because offices held so little prestige that movement from the periphery to the core was not difficult in any of these volunteer-staffed organizations. In none did core members fight to retain their "elite status." They were not subject to the "goal displacement" in which core members subvert the institution's interests in order to retain their positions (see Sills 1957, for review). In some of the organizations, it took relatively more persistence and commitment to move into the core, yet, in every case, core members welcomed those who took the trouble to get involved in their organizations.

In summary, the core members provided the time and commitment that was necessary for the coordination of these organizations. These small volunteer-staffed organizations could not rely on specialization and formalization or on formal authority to control their workers. Yet the informal mechanisms that substituted for these formal coordination mechanisms required personal contact and relationships of trust that were hard to develop with a limited involvement, hence the core membership. Unfortunately, this solution to the organizational control problem was fragile and incomplete, as is discussed in subsequent chapters. Finally, it is important to note for subsequent discussions that the experiences of volunteers in their organizations were quite different depending on whether they were members of the core or periphery.

UNDERSTAFFING

Finally, an additional insight into the structural effects of volunteer staffing of organizations can be provided by the work of Barker and Gump (Barker 1968; Barker and Gump 1964). Barker's (1968) analysis of "behavior settings" provides a useful framework for contrasting volunteer-staffed organizations with employee-staffed ones. Particularly useful has been Barker and Gump's (1964) observation that some settings have more power to "coerce" uniformity and predictability than do others. Volunteer work settings were observed to be less powerful for their workers than were employee-staffed ones. Because volunteer-staffed organizations require organizational work from members whom they do not pay, they are settings that frequently face problems of "undermanning," to use Barker's term.

Drawing on their studies of small and large high schools, Barker and

Gump argued that each setting is viewed as having an optimal number of occupants. When the settings have fewer occupants than they need to fulfill their demands, a condition of understaffing exists. In understaffed settings, (1) there is more pressure on individuals to participate, to become functionaries rather than spectators; (2) there are decreased barriers to entering the settings, including lowered standards of performance; and (3) there is greater interest in the outcomes of the setting, when compared with over- or optimally staffed settings. These three features appear to provide an apt characterization of the volunteer-staffed organizations in this study, with the exception of the fire department. Fighting fires is an attractive occupation, providing opportunities for heroism and glamour without the necessity of leaving your steady job and family. The volunteer fire department had a waiting list and did not share the characteristics of understaffed systems noted above.

There were heavy pressures on individuals to participate in all of the other volunteer-staffed organizations. Family and friends were continually being pressed into service. The poverty relief agency, newspaper, and orchestra all had formal recruitment programs.

In addition, there can be no doubt that the barriers to participation in the volunteer-staffed organizations were substantially lower than the comparable employee-staffed organizations. The entrance requirements for the two types of organizations have been described above. It was also true that the performance standards for individuals, as well as the goals the organizations set for themselves, were significantly lower for these volunteer-staffed organizations. The volunteer-staffed organizations always served fewer clients (see Appendix, Table A.1). Furthermore, these employee-staffed organizations invariably performed more services for the clients. For example, the volunteer-staffed poverty relief agency confined itself to delivering food and transportation to the poor, while the employee-staffed agency tried to raise its clients out of poverty. The employee-staffed fire department fought more difficult industrial fires and had a large fire prevention program. All would agree that the quality of the professional musicians' concerts was superior to that of the volunteer community orchestra.

Individuals could retain their volunteer jobs as long as they did not directly damage the effort; poor task performance and even minimal participation were tolerated. These low levels of performance were accepted because poor performance was better than the alternative of no performance, and sometimes because the organization made an explicit commitment to include all who were interested in its goals even if they could not really contribute much to the organization.

Finally, McGrath suggested that Barker's analysis of under- and overstaffing has implications for the participants' motives:

persons who participate when undermanning prevails must be those who value the consequences of the setting "coming off," relative to its failing to come off, sufficiently to assume the overload. Under conditions of overmanning, persons who "apply for" and enter the setting must value the consequences of their participating in the setting – presumably in terms of payoffs from successful performance – if they are willing to strive for the high standards.

(McGrath 1976, p. 1383)

This quotation sounds like the classic distinction between volunteers and employees: that volunteers work to further the goals of the organization while employees are in it for the money. However, this sweeping generalization will be analyzed and found wanting in the next two chapters.

CONCLUSIONS

In summary, the design of work, and structural relationships among volunteer organizational workers, differ from those found in the comparable employee-staffed organizations. Apparently, because volunteers tend to work parts-of-jobs and to receive undifferentiated low compensation, we find that they (1) use less "real time" informal coordination among workers, (2) have less clear internal and external boundaries, (3) have different specializations, (4) are bifurcated into a core and peripheral membership, and (5) work in understaffed behavioral settings. These structural distinctions have implications both for general theories of organizational design and for the continuing analysis of the organizational behavior of volunteers.

ORGANIZATIONAL DESIGN

Three broad features of organizational design that seemed to be important factors in accounting for the observed volunteer/employee organizational structural differences, but which have not been emphasized in organization design, are suggested. These are (1) the informal coordination completed by individuals working long hours side by side, (2) the role of differential labor costs in design, and (3) the institutional or symbolic use of design (Meyer and Rowan 1977; Meyer 1979). Although these design effects have been made more visible by the matching of volunteer-staffed organizations with employee-staffed ones, they are not confined to volunteer work.

Co-worker proximity and coordination

Proximity has been implicit as a design variable since the earliest analyses of organizational design. Thompson (1967) suggested that departmentalization should be based on creating groups that minimize coordination costs by grouping interdependent workers into teams. However, Thompson and his successors have not addressed the coordination that occurs among those who may not be completely task interdependent (as in a surgical team) but share other, less compelling, interdependencies.

The importance of this more subtle role of proximity in task coordination is implicitly recognized in job rotation programs – most commonly found among management trainees. These programs reflect the assumption that coordination is facilitated when someone has worked directly with ("knows") someone else. Finally, the commonly noted problem of control loss in large hierarchies seems to reflect "proximity loss." Williamson (1967) argued that the documented inefficiencies of larger organizational size result from the fact that workers with necessary information are less proximate to one another, making coordination more difficult. This analysis of volunteers' work confirms these scattered suggestions that direct face-to-face contact may be much more important to coordination than has been recognized in organization design research and theory. Proximity itself should be the direct subject of study in design.

Differential labor costs

The relative costs of different labor "inputs" also have been neglected in formal theories of design. They have, of course, received extensive attention in industrial engineering and labor economics but have not been addressed in the organization design literature. With all of the attention directed to potential efficiency gains in the grouping of workers, omission of the fact that the cost savings of a design which may be "inefficient" in coordination but reduces total labor costs is surprising. The most striking example of this process is the growing use of subcontracting and overseas production facilities. In both cases we would expect increased information processing demands or "transaction costs" (Williamson 1975). However, these are apparently more than compensated by the significantly lower wages the subcontractors or overseas facilities pay.

Similarly, the present analysis suggests that part-time volunteers are usually more "inefficient" than employees. Volunteers increase coordination costs with their part-time commitment, and they are often unwilling to submit to authoritative direction, which can decrease the organization's performance levels. Yet, paradoxically, they also are more "efficient" than employees, as in each task-set the volunteer-staffed organization was able to deliver its (reduced) service at a significantly lower cost than the employee-staffed organization. In all of these labor-intensive services, the budgets of the volunteer-staffed organizations were a fraction of those of the matched employee-staffed ones.

Even a cursory examination of employee-staffed organizations reveals ample evidence of the important role played by differential labor costs in the design of jobs and their interrelationships. The total labor costs for an organization are central to any consideration of efficiency, and yet the only recognition of differential labor costs in design theories seems to be the recognition that supervisors are paid more than subordinates (e.g. Galbraith 1977). This would appear to be an obvious area for future research in organizational design.

Use of structure to reward

Finally, the present analysis supports the arguments of Meyer and Rowan (1977) and Meyer (1979) that many organizations are as likely to use organizational structure for non-technical purposes as for technical ones. Although these theorists focused on the value of signals to outside groups, this analysis suggests that design signals are also targeted to an organization's own workers. The employee-staffed organizations developed elaborate job specializations and comparatively tall hierarchies, apparently to provide the perception of career mobility for their employees. They hired secretaries who, in at least one case, had very little "real work" to do, seemingly to signal that the agency and its director were important. The volunteer-staffed organizations also used design to signal, but they sent different "messages." They were careful to use job titles that did not imply status differences. There were no volunteer "secretaries" or "directors" which imply hierarchy and subservience. Instead, they had "chairpersons" and "coordinators," signifying more democracy and egalitarianism. These (different) symbolic uses of titles and design in both employee-staffed and volunteer-staffed organizations were often at the expense of efficiency. Secretaries are expensive. In organizations like the voluntary family planning clinic with its numerous chairpersons (of the "chapter," of the "volunteers," and of the "board of directors"), it was difficult to know who was responsible for what.

This emphasis on the symbolic role of formal structure is consistent with the theoretical work of Meyer and Rowan (1977). They posited that a logic of building "confidence and trust" among important environmental supporters sometimes took precedence over concerns for coordination and surveillance. Eisenhardt (1988) found that accepted "rules of thumb" or patterns of action were important explanatory factors in sales compensation policy. The differing design patterns in these volunteer- and employee-staffed organizations are consistent with this "institutional perspective" on organizational practices.

ORGANIZATIONAL BEHAVIOR OF VOLUNTEERS

Such structural features as described above influence the organizational behavior of volunteers. To summarize, these design effects include (1) exacerbation of the weakness of the setting's behavioral demands, (2) egalitarian values about workplace relations, (3) groupings with either strong co-worker social ties or weak co-worker ties, and (4) difficulty in maintaining pride in what may be genuinely mediocre organizational performance.

Weak behavioral demands

In their analysis, Barker and his associates mentioned "ambiguous demands" as one of the characteristics that settings can have, but did not focus on this feature. There is substantial uncertainty about who is a volunteer and who is not, about role expectations, tasks and performance levels, and about unknown co-workers' skills and congeniality. This problem is more severe for peripheral members, but even core volunteers face frequent changes in staff and uncertainty about the involvement of many peripheral members. (Table 3.2 indicates that they also complain more about organizational changes.) Thus, in addition to all of the societal uncertainty about volunteers' organizations and of the value of volunteer work described in the previous chapter, uncertainty is compounded by substantially more structural uncertainty in volunteer-staffed organizations.

There can be little doubt that this uncertainty leads to stress and discomfort. There is a large body of research supporting the association between organizational role conflict and ambiguity and stress in employee-staffed organizations (Pearce 1981). Granted the stress a volunteer faces may be different than that faced by an employee threatened with job loss; however, managing and controlling this uncertainty becomes the central management task facing volunteer-staffed organizations. Even modest discomfort can lead volunteers to leave their spare-time involvements, thus threatening the continued existence of their organizations. Those who cannot impose some order on their volunteer-staffed organization's activities may not survive.

Egalitarian practices

The studied volunteer-staffed organizations were egalitarian in character. In contrast to employee-staffed organizations in which hierarchical level conveys strong social status implications, no real status attached to office in these organizations. Officeholders had no power to command obedience and no more tangible rewards for their efforts. Status came from dedication to the organization, skill, and reliability, which were not dependent on organizational office. Further, even when these laudable personal traits were present, they were often unknown to substantial numbers of fellow volunteers. Thus egalitarian practices were fostered, not only by ideology, but also by the isolation from co-workers experienced by many peripheral volunteers.

This egalitarianism has significant implications for the differential use of rewards (even intangible ones). Differential rewards are the very cornerstone of employee-based theories of motivation (Vroom 1964; Pinder 1984), and this analysis would imply that volunteer-staffed organizations may not be able to draw on these approaches for fostering volunteer motivation to perform. How do we design a motivational system in organizations based on egalitarian principles? These ideas are explored in the remaining chapters.

Bifurcated membership

Volunteers tend to be divided into two kinds of workers: the core and the periphery. Members of the core are knowledgeable, and the organization is often central to their self- and social identities. For peripheral volunteers, their membership is rarely thought of at all. It is a civic contribution, a diversion, or something they do because a family member dragged them into it. For most employees, their work is an important, even if possibly disliked, part of their lives. Events at work can have a serious influence on them, and they often take a strong interest in what happens. This may characterize some core volunteers, but very few peripheral ones. As Dubin *et al.* (1976) have stated, much of our analysis of the organizational behavior of workers assumes that the workers do take an interest in their workplaces.

Following Dubin *et al.*, volunteer work seems to be a "central life interest" for a few volunteers but a very peripheral interest for the majority. This difference has important implications for analyses of motivation and influence in these organizations. For example, Clark and Wilson (1961), reviewed in the previous chapter, suggested that solidary or positive social interactions are the primary incentives for volunteers. Yet how can such incentives operate on socially disengaged members of the periphery? Clark and Wilson apparently envisioned a small dedicated band with few peripheral members. Yet these volunteer-staffed organizations and, no doubt, many others also rely on volunteers who are not activists but who, nevertheless, make an important contribution to the organization. In subsequent chapters, evidence is presented suggesting that solidary incentives also operate for peripheral volunteers, but in different ways than for the core.

Low performance expectations

Finally, volunteer-staffed organizations are likely to face relatively low performance expectations for workers. Because they do not pay their workers they cannot make stringent demands on them either in selection or in job performance. Continually training unskilled workers often adds even more burdens to the already overworked core membership. This, in and of itself, can create tremendous morale and motivation problems. If the quality of their organization's service is low, it becomes difficult for members to take pride in their work. It is hard to rally workers for "professional standards" if their everyday experience gives lie to this appeal. A vicious circle can develop in which poor work leads to expectations of poor work and the subsequent departure of volunteers who do not want to be a part of poor performance, which results in even poorer work, and so on. This is not a characterization of all volunteer-staffed organizations, but it can happen and did so in the studied volunteer-staffed newspaper. The struggle against this kind of decline is the paramount problem of motivation and control in these settings.

Part II

Why volunteer?

Volunteers are not paid for their labor, and so are assumed to have no monetary reasons for working. Employees work for money and volunteers for love. Of course, as with any stereotype, there are many exceptions among volunteers and employees. Medical school aspirants may volunteer in the local hospital in order to "build a good application," and many employees choose a profession because they love the work or can contribute to society, rather than because it provides the highest possible financial gain. Yet these general assumptions are reflected in the scholarly and practical writings on employees and volunteers.

Volunteers' reasons for volunteering are a mystery. They do not have the comfort of an easy answer. Sometimes their motives are straightforward – as employees' motives are often complex. However, they lack the clear and compelling reason that employees may claim – money. Further, attracting inexpensive voluntary labor is of substantial practical importance to those organizations that depend on them.

Because of this mystery, one of the most comprehensive areas of empirical research concerning organizational volunteers is the study of the "reasons" for volunteering. This effort includes the search for volunteers' needs or motives, their demographic and social characteristics, and their attitudes or values – concern with the individual characteristics of volunteers. This is, by far, the largest body of empirical research on organizational volunteers. It has led to a lively debate on the meaning of "altruism," to which this volume will add. This material is reviewed and summarized in Chapter 4, "Volunteer motivation."

The study of the motives and attitudes of volunteers provides a fruitful arena in which to investigate the causal status of motives and attitudes in organizational behavior. Because volunteers have no visible and compelling financial reason for working and because there are such potentially powerful forces of post-decision justification operating, they can provide a clearer picture of these processes than employees can. These ideas are explored in Chapter 5, "Volunteers' attitudes: an exploration of their commitment."

Chapter 4

Volunteer motivation

Motivation has long been a central focus of those interested in the organizational behavior of volunteers as well as employees. Yet students of volunteer and employee behavior have focused on differing facets of motivation. This seems to reflect the wide variety of philosophical perspectives about human nature (see Levine 1975) represented by the concept of motivation itself, centering as it does on the direction and intensity of individual exertions. Since the present work focuses on work motivation, Pinder's (1984) definition is adopted: motivation is a set of forces, either weak or strong, to initiate, direct, and sustain work-related behavior. It encompasses motivations to join an organization, to reject a supervisor's orders, and to choose activities at work, as well as how "hard" to work.

This chapter begins with a review and theoretical integration of the rather voluminous literature on volunteer motivation, or, as it is usually termed, motivation to join or to volunteer. In contrast to the subjects covered in the other chapters, volunteer motivation has received widespread empirical and theoretical attention. The present study provides information that helps to integrate and clarify previous research. This discussion of an integrative framework of volunteers' motivation to join the organization is followed by implications for within-organization volunteer motivation. Before proceeding, the widely disparate literature on the motivation to volunteer requires a few comments.

LITERATURE ON VOLUNTEER MOTIVATION

There are substantial differences in focus in the employee and volunteer work motivation literatures. Questions about employee motivation have centered on understanding direction and persistence, primarily of those behaviors leading to high levels of job performance, with some interest in attendance and turnover. Pinder (1984) provides a comprehensive review of employee motivation.

In the employee motivation literature there has been only modest concern for the reasons why employees join particular organizations. Over thirty years ago March and Simon (1958) outlined a model of the "decision to participate," although it provides little beyond the recognition that joiners see some advantage in joining. The best reviews of employee motivation to join are provided by Wanous (1980) and Schwab, Rynes, and Aldag (1987). Wanous distinguished "rational" from "non-rational" perspectives on organizational choice. In the rational approach the prospective entrants evaluate the attractiveness of the organization by weighting their beliefs about expected outcomes by the importance of those beliefs. Although there is some empirical evidence to support these assertions about organizational choice, the results were not conclusive (Wanous 1980). The nonrational perspective holds that individuals do not systematically evaluate the possible outcomes of a choice and weight them by their importance. Rather, prospective entrants make an implicit choice based on only a few unweighted factors and then search for information to confirm and justify their initial decision (Soelberg 1967). Again, empirical data that could confirm this model of choice are scarce: Soelberg (1967) reported that 74 percent of his subjects could identify an "acceptable choice" two weeks before ending their job search, while Sheridan, Richards, and Slocum (1975) did not find evidence of early implicit choices. This difference in theories about how job choices are made has implications for the study of volunteer motivation that are developed below.

Although research on job choice is a small component of research on employee motivation, interest in volunteer motivation is dominated by attempts to understand the volunteers' choice to join organizations – with a virtual absence of concern for what motivates volunteers' actions once they are working. Motivational concerns about organizational volunteers are dominated by incredulity as to why volunteers volunteer and a focus on methods to "meet volunteers' needs." As an illustration, Moore (1985) subtitled his book on volunteer motivation, *How the Rewards of Unpaid Work Can Meet People's Needs*.

Despite the differences in the target behaviors of interest to scholars of volunteer and employee motivation, inquiries from both perspectives began by focusing on differences in individual needs or motives. Yet, while students of employee motivation have shifted their attention from differences in individuals' wants to include structural constraints and opportunities (e.g. Hackman and Oldham 1980; Luthans and Kreitner 1975), the study of volunteers' motivation has remained preoccupied with motives. Updated lists of "reasons for volunteering" are compiled, and ever more erudite arguments for or against the importance of altruism in volunteering are developed. Thus, one of the purposes of the present work is to move the study of volunteers' motives beyond its limiting focus on individual differences to a broader concern with both the structural factors in the decision to volunteer and volunteers' motivation to exert effort once they have joined organizations.

The largest body of volunteer empirical research seeks to differentiate individuals by their motives, demographic or socioeconomic characteristics, and is of two types. The first, and smallest, group of studies attempts to identify the benefits volunteers "receive" for their work. This area has become dominated by a debate. Much organizational volunteering seems altruistic; however, many scholars have insisted that volunteers do receive something for their efforts, and this perspective has guided most who have addressed the question in the practitioner literature. For example, Schindler-Rainman and Lippitt (1971) conceptualize the volunteer's decision to commit time and energy as forces pushing toward a yes decision (e.g. "chance to learn new skills") opposed by forces pushing toward a no decision. As this illustration suggests, virtually all of the approaches to volunteers' motivation to join assume volunteers rationally weigh alternatives. This debate is examined in detail.

The alternative and more voluminous type of research seeks to know the type of person who volunteers. These efforts have primarily been "community studies" from the fields of sociology and anthropology and have sought to identify the demographic or attitudinal differences between volunteers and nonvolunteers. In the present chapter, knowledge from this second body of research (who is the volunteer?) is interpreted and refocused to address this chapter's primary question: why volunteer? Simple distinctions between volunteers and nonvolunteers need to be complemented by theory specifying why volunteering is appealing to certain people and not to others. For example, the fact that homeowners (Babchuk and Gordon 1962) and individuals who are more optimistic (Hausknecht 1962) are more likely to volunteer is an interesting, but relatively useless, fact. In this chapter, both these literatures on the individual characteristics of volunteers will be integrated into a coherent perspective of individuals' motives to volunteer, then it will conclude with a reflection on the utility of studying individual characteristics in developing an understanding of volunteer motivation.

Before beginning the literature review, three general limitations merit discussion. First, research and theory in much of this work have proceeded independently of one another. The majority of both speculative observations and empirical studies consists of the production of lists of benefits ("reasons") or lists of demographic or social characteristics, with only the barest efforts to use the data to develop an integrated understanding of volunteering. Therefore, this chapter will concentrate on this integration, referring the reader for the details of these numerous studies to previous reviews (e.g. Smith *et al.* 1972; and Smith 1973).

Second, the study of the motivations of individual volunteers is plagued by a particularly difficult methodological problem. It seems that the most obvious way to begin is to ask the volunteers themselves why they do it. However, as is indicated by the quotation at the beginning of Chapter 1 in which the volunteer indicated that "Volunteers don't know why they are working," this is not necessarily a question that volunteers are able or willing to answer. As will be detailed below, their motives are quite complex. Furthermore, society praises altruism and condemns "using" charitable activities for the pursuit of selfish goals such as social position, diversion, and socializing, and thus there is a social-desirability bias in stated reasons for volunteering (Smith 1981).

Thus, if volunteers' own self-reports are not reliable, the benefits of volunteering need to be inferred from volunteers' actions. Yet, this approach is also less than satisfactory. An example will help indicate the difficulties involved. Does the fact that social interaction occurs and friendships are formed among volunteers necessarily imply that these are the salient rewards to these volunteers? Controlled tests of these inferences, in which opportunities for social interaction or other rewards might be removed in a systematic fashion and the responses observed, are rarely feasible. These problems are not unique to the study of volunteers' motives; unfortunately, they are infrequently recognized in that literature.

Finally, since most of those interested in understanding volunteer motivation have not distinguished between volunteers in organizational or in less formal settings, this chapter includes research on volunteers in diverse settings. To restrict our attention solely to organizational volunteers would leave only a handful of studies. Where the distinction is relevant to interpretations of the findings, the institutional composition of the sample will be discussed.

THE PERSON WHO VOLUNTEERS

A clearer understanding of the individual who volunteers should help us to understand volunteer motivation better. This is by far the largest body of empirical research on volunteering, and although this effort suffers the theoretical fragmentation mentioned earlier, it is an excellent data base for theory-building. (Smith *et al.* 1972 and Smith and Freedman 1972 provide comprehensive reviews.) It has two major strengths. First, there have been numerous replications, over time and across different populations. For example, Payne, Payne, and Reddy (in Smith *et al.* 1972) listed 24 studies demonstrating a positive association between income and volunteering, and recent surveys continue to report this association (cf ACTION 1975; Edwards and White 1980). Such consistent empirical results should be mined for insights into volunteer motivation. Second, the work on economic, social, and demographic characteristics is useful precisely because the measures are reliable. Measures of income, education, property ownership, sex, and political affiliation are not without measurement error, but this error is miniscule when compared to the error in such variables as self-reports of reasons for volunteering. In addition, virtually all such variables are clearly antecedents of volunteering, so the problem of separating the effects of volunteering from the factors that lead to the initial decision to volunteer can be avoided. (See Chapter 5 for extended discussion of this problem.) In other words, we do know a lot about who volunteers, and this evidence provides a solid foundation for learning more about why individuals volunteer.

The results of this research will be grouped into four categories: socio-economic status, interpersonal networks, demographic characteristics, and personality traits.

Socioeconomic status

Those with higher income, educational level, occupational status, and family/lineage status and those who own more property are more likely to volunteer, to volunteer for multiple associations and organizations, and to assume leadership roles in their organizations than are those who have fewer of these advantages. There is overwhelming support for these con-clusions; the relationships are found in every decade and in every country in which they have been examined (including the sampled organizations). The following studies are illustrative of the breadth of the support for these conclusions. Wright and Hyman (1958) and Hyman and Wright (1971) found these relationships in their secondary analysis of the 1952 and 1955 nation-wide United States National Opinion Research Corporation surveys, as did a more recent US survey (Gallup Organization 1987). Income and education are associated with participation in Australia (Hardee 1961), Canada (Curtis 1971), and Denmark (Svalastoga 1957) and this association was found by Almond and Verba (1963) in their classic comparative study of the civic cultures of Britain, Germany, Mexico, and the United States.

There have been attempts to identify the particular component of socio-economic status that leads to volunteering – that is, "What is the particular causal factor?" Edwards and White (1980) analyzed which of the socio-economic predictors of volunteering (e.g. income, education, or occupa-tional status) explained the most variance in a sophisticated multivariate model of volunteering. Since the independent variables were more strongly correlated with each other than with volunteering, they were not able to identify which one predominated. Finally, McPherson and Lockwood (1980) completed an excellent re-analysis of Babchuk and Booth's (1969) community study data using multivariate techniques. Using multiple regression, in which they systematically controlled for alternative explana-tory variables, they reported that education was the better predictor of volunteering.

Furthermore, socioeconomic status is consistently associated with the kinds of organizations joined: blue-collar volunteers are more likely to join churches, unions, fraternal societies, and sports clubs, with the middle and upper classes concentrated in general interest, business and professional, service, cultural, educational, and political pressure groups (Cousens 1964).

In summary, there simply is overwhelming evidence that those of higher socioeconomic status are more likely to volunteer, with education apparently the leading cause. Furthermore, members of different social groups appear to be attracted to different kinds of organizations. Yet, what these findings tell us about volunteer motivation is more difficult to judge. The traditional argument was that those (at least women) of higher socioeconomic status had more leisure time (Lundberg *et al.* 1934). However, this explanation appears to be too simplistic, since other groups with ample leisure time (youth, those over 60, the unemployed) have markedly lower levels of volunteering. Rather, it seems more likely to result from (1) the greater attractiveness of those of higher status, (2) differing definitions of role-appropriate activities, and (3) differences in networks of interpersonal relationships.

First, those of high socioeconomic status may simply be more attractive recruits. Volunteers are often used extensively for fundraising, and there is evidence from numerous studies that charitable giving and volunteer work are positively associated (e.g. Gallup Organization 1987). Therefore, recruiters may target those who can contribute the most to their voluntary organizations. Additionally, many organizations exist to maintain and foster social hierarchy (Clark and Wilson 1961; Minnis 1952). Clearly, the higher the socioeconomic status of an individual, then the greater his or her attractions for status-oriented organizations.

Second, many voluntary organizations in western society are either directly or indirectly related to one's business or professional roles. Members of professions join their professional associations, and those owning small businesses join clubs and sit on boards to increase their business contacts. As an illustration, executives' firms will often pay their country club dues, and, if they do not, dues can be deducted from taxes as a business expense. Voluntary associations and organizations are simply a part of the job for many high socioeconomic status individuals, which is undoubtedly a factor in the greater number of memberships for these individuals.

Third, volunteers recruit those they already know into their organizations, and high socioeconomic status volunteers are more likely to know more members of their class. The role of interpersonal networks in volunteer joining is so important that it is explored in depth.

Interpersonal networks

There is substantial evidence that those who come into contact with volunteers are more likely to volunteer (an early example is Anderson 1943). For example, the spouses of volunteers are more likely to also be volunteers (Babchuk 1965; Adams and Mogey 1967). In addition, newcomers to a region show lower rates of volunteering than long-time residents. Zimmer (1955, 1956) interviewed a random sample of residents of a small midwestern town to discover how recent rural immigrants differed from long-time town dwellers in their patterns of volunteering, and other characteristics. He found that immigrants were initially less likely to volunteer, but that they soon approximated the volunteering levels of the native population. His research suggested familiarity, rather than some inherent differences in propensity to volunteer, was the most important factor. There is additional evidence that recruitment into religious groups depends heavily on social networks (Stark and Bainbridge 1980; Snow *et al.* 1980; Heinrich 1977). Further support for the importance of personal networks in the recruitment of volunteers is found in the positive correlation between volunteering and having a large number of friends (Scott 1957) and between volunteering and being involved with fellow workers (Spinard 1960).

In addition, there is substantial research demonstrating that most organizational volunteers are recruited through personal contact. Sills (1957) found that only 10 percent of the volunteers in his sample volunteered on their own initiative; the rest were recruited by a friend (52 percent), another member of the community (20 percent), or by an occupational colleague (18 percent). These proportions are surprisingly stable. A Gallup Report found that 44 percent volunteered because they were asked by someone, 29 percent because a family member was involved, and 31 percent through participation in a group, with only 25 percent seeking the volunteer activity on their own and a tiny 6 percent responding to an advertisement or news media information (Independent Sector 1981). In September 1987 the Gallup Organization (1987) reported that 59 percent reported volunteering because they were "asked by someone in the organization," 22 percent because they were "asked by a friend or neighbor," and 14 percent had been "asked by a customer/employer," with only 4 percent reporting responding to mass media approaches.

As would be expected, these broader patterns were also evident in the seven volunteer-staffed organizations. Personal contact brought 64 percent of the volunteers into the organization, with 29 percent taking the initiative in response to an ad, and 11 percent through personal knowledge of the organization; the remaining 7 percent of the interviewees were founders of their organizations.

The evidence is strong and consistent: most volunteers are recruited by their friends, relatives, or associates. Thus, those with more extensive personal contacts are more likely to be recruited. The more people you know, the more likely you are to know a volunteer eager to recruit a co-worker. This also is reflected in the theories of social movements and collective action, which have consistently emphasized interpersonal bonds (Wilson and Orum 1976; Knoke and Wright-Isak 1982). No doubt, there are important organizational variations. For example, large, visible, matter-of-fact institutions, such as hospitals and museums, probably attract more volunteers "on their own initiative" while less prominent value-rational organizations may rely completely on personal contact.

Demographic characteristics

The following studies reporting relationships between volunteering and demographic characteristics are more difficult to summarize neatly. For example, the relationship between age and volunteering is complex: volunteering among teenagers increases until about 18 years, then decreases, remaining low until the late twenties, when it rises, reaching a peak from age 40 to 55, from which it gradually decreases. Mayo (1950) studied the participation rates for each person over 10 years of age in a rural South Carolina county. He noted an increase in participation during teenage years but found a sharp decline, to the lowest rates for any group, during the twenties. Other researchers have recorded a peak in volunteering when individuals are in their forties and fifties (ACTION 1975; Gallup Organization 1987). These age-group results find support in national US surveys (Wright and Hyman 1958; Hausknecht 1962), as well as in the more in-depth community studies (e.g. Babchuk and Booth 1969).

Contrary to the stereotyped vision of the volunteer as a white matron, when socioeconomic status is controlled, American blacks are more likely to volunteer than are whites (Orum 1966; Olsen 1970); and men are more likely to be volunteers than are women. Wright and Hyman (1958) and Komarovsky (1946) found that men were more likely to be volunteers than women in the United States, and Almond and Verba (1963) reported that the imbalance is even more extreme in Mexico and in Great Britain. However, Hausknecht (1962), Lundberg et al. (1934), Mayo (1950), ACTION (1975), and the Gallup Organization (1987) have reported that American women are at least as likely to volunteer as men. The conflicts are resolved when the types of organizations are examined, since women and men consistently belong to different types of groups. Argyle (1959) and ACTION (1975) reported that women were more likely to join religious or service organizations, while men joined professional associations and lodges that are functional for their careers (Hausknecht 1962).

Finally, the relative participation rates in various countries has been a source of controversy. Rose (1958), relying on national survey data, observation, and a "systematic commentary study," concluded that volunteering was negligible in France. Supporting evidence was provided by Anderson and Anderson's (1965) anthropological study of a French village. However, Gallagher (1957) argued that voluntary organizations in France were numerous but that there were proportionately fewer of the reform and welfare type when compared to the United States.

These demographic studies support the importance of interpersonal ties noted in the previous section. For example, cohesive subpopulations (e.g. immigrant groups) have denser interpersonal networks and, therefore, higher rates of volunteering. Further, the low rates of volunteering among young adults can be explained by their greater mobility in pursuit of education and careers. Similarly, the elderly lose their interpersonal contacts through retirement, widowhood, departure of their children, and deaths of friends.

Personality

This review of studies of who volunteers is completed with studies seeking to discover the personality differences between volunteers and nonvolunteers. Unfortunately, this literature is not as useful as the previous research. First, the personality scales themselves were often of suspect reliability and validity. Furthermore, investigators used, more often than not, an instrument developed for other purposes, such as clinical diagnosis, and neglected to report its item content (what questions actually were asked) or its reliability for their sample. Finally, as is the case with other cross-sectional studies of volunteers, it is difficult to know if personality differences lead to different rates of volunteering or are the *result* of voluntary work.

Most of the personality traits described in studies seeking to differentiate volunteers from nonvolunteers can be summarized as follows: those reporting more confidence and gregariousness are more likely to be volunteers. Using national survey data, Hausknecht (1962) found a positive relationship between how interviewees rated "optimism concerning the future" and their number of volunteer memberships. Smith (1966) reported that volunteers had more "social confidence," were more "dominant," and more "sociable" than matched nonvolunteers in his study of volunteer activity in Chile. Brown (1953) found volunteers in three rural Pennsylvania communities had relatively more positive self-images. Almond and Verba (1963) reported that a "subjective sense of political competence" was associated with membership in multiple voluntary organizations in their cross-national study. (See Smith *et al.* 1972 for a comprehensive review.) Gough (1952) administered the MMPI personality test to four high school senior classes in Minnesota to identify the personality profiles distinguishing those students with extensive participation in voluntary extracurricular activities from those with low levels of volunteering. He found that the personality items indicating liking social interaction, self-confidence, a sense of poise and assurance were significantly more characteristic of students involved in volunteering activities. Unfortunately, this cross-sectional study (no longitudinal studies of personality and volunteering could be located) cannot rule out the effects that voluntary participation may have on these personality characteristics.

Thus, correlations between membership in voluntary organizations and various measures related to confidence and gregariousness are found in these diverse samples. They are consistent with the common sense assumption that those with more self-confidence are more likely to "volunteer" for a new experience. They provide indirect support for the importance of interpersonal networks, since those who are more gregarious are more likely to know more people.

VOLUNTEERS' MOTIVES

Unlike employees, volunteers' motives for joining cannot easily be reduced to a simple and reassuring assumption. This is probably the major reason why the topic has held such fascination for social theorists.

Conjectural approaches

The rewards of volunteering are an enduring topic for speculation. Previously reviewed organizational theorists, such as Etzioni (1975) and Clark and Wilson (1961), based their analyses on participants' motives. The theme suggested earlier by Barker and Gump (1964) – that organizational volunteers must greatly value the "outcomes of the setting" (i.e. the organization's goals or mission) in order to justify their low personal payoffs – has been stressed repeatedly. The practitioner literature has stressed altruistic motives such as "concern for others" and a "service focus" (Schindler-Rainman and Lippitt 1971; Ellis and Noyes 1978). Other writers have emphasized volunteers' self-interested motives, such as "opportunities to learn" and "to attain higher status" (Naylor 1967). Among the more complex of these observations was one made by Leat (1977), who suggested that people who feel they are viewed as "recipients" (e.g. housewives and the retired) may volunteer in the hope that their own giving will lead to increased esteem. Gordon Allport (1945, 1952) argued that individuals volunteer in order to conform, for ego defense, for feelings of security and superiority, or for ego-extending reasons such as personal growth.

Unfortunately, these speculations are of limited usefulness. Each observer is content simply to develop a list with little attempt to explain the circumstances under which particular rewards become salient. That is, which of the many rewards available to a given volunteer were the dominant or necessary attractions? These lists usually include anything that might appeal to anyone and so are not subject to empirical rejection. All these lists are limited by the author's insight and often are dominated by the writer's own training and unique experiences. For example, Allport was a psychologist who studied personality theory, hence his emphasis on concepts from psychoanalytic theory.

Empirically based lists

Many sociologists have concluded their surveys of participation, who volunteers in a community, with speculations about motives. Among the first lists of rewards developed from systematic empirical observation was that of Lundberg *et al.* (1934). In their study of leisure activities in a suburban county, they employed interviews, questionnaires, and diaries. They observed that the wealthier the community, the greater the percentage of participants in leisure-oriented groups. Furthermore, they found that women dominated in these organizations and concluded that these women joined in order to find "outlets for the great amount of leisure which technological and economic changes have bestowed" (p. 131). After examining organization membership lists in Boulder, Colorado, Bushee (1945) argued that individuals in his sample volunteered for individual recognition, social relations, self-improvement, and community improvement. Babchuk and Gordon (1962) interviewed slum residents in Rochester, New York, who had joined organizer-created community groups, and a comparison sample of members of traditional voluntary organizations. They concluded that many volunteers were using these groups for personal upward mobility.

Similarly, lists of the motives of certain kinds of volunteers working in a particular organization have been created. For example, Chapman (1985) found that, in addition to traditional service reasons, university student volunteers were also interested in career-related work experience. Gottlieb (1974) found that female volunteers in VISTA (a government-sponsored program in which individuals work for two years at nominal wages in community and indigent service in the USA) tended to "be more altruistic" than their male counterparts, who were more likely to want to "get away from doing what I was doing." The present review will focus on the more comprehensive or more theoretically developed of these kinds of studies.

Nationwide surveys

Four nationwide surveys of volunteers' motives have been conducted. Anderson and Moore (1978) conducted one such survey (mailed questionnaire) through Canada's 49 volunteer bureaus (community "placement centers" for those who want to volunteer). They found that the "desire to help others" and "feel useful" consistently dominated other responses in these volunteers' reports. However, they also detected differences among certain demographic subgroups: men and women working full-time reported that they worked more for self-fulfillment and personal development; those over 60 and unemployed women were more likely to volunteer to feel useful and to occupy their spare time.

Schram (1985) compared national surveys of Americans in the 1965 and 1974 Current Population Surveys conducted by the United States Bureau of Census (mailed questionnaires) with the 1981 Gallup telephone poll sponsored by Independent Sector. These have the advantage of being broad samplings across all types of volunteer activities as well as covering a 16-year period. The questions were not strictly comparable in the three surveys. In 1965, respondents were asked, "What are your main reasons for doing volunteer work?" with coded, open-ended answers. In 1974 and in 1981, interviewees were asked, "Please think back to the first nonreligious volunteer work you ever did. What were your reasons for doing volunteer work at that time?" and they were given a list of possible reasons. Despite these methodological differences, Schram (1985) found little change in the reasons for doing volunteer work: 35 to 45 percent "to help people," about 30 percent because they "enjoy volunteer work," and (for 1981 only) 35 percent "had an interest in activity or work." All other reasons together were suggested by less than 10 percent of respondents. There were some differences among types of volunteers. Using 1974 responses, the elderly emphasized to a greater extent the desire to help others, a sense of duty, and enjoyment of the volunteer activity itself. Not surprisingly, "having a child in the program" dominated among those in the age-group likely to have young children at home (25 to 44 years), and young adults (18 to 24 years) were significantly more likely to report that they volunteered with the hope that the work would lead to a paying job.

More recently, the Gallup Organization conducted personal in-home interviews with a representative sample of 1,033 Americans (Gallup Organization 1987). Their self-reported reasons were somewhat more inclusive: 50 percent "to help others," 35 percent had an interest in "the program," 30 percent "enjoy the work," 28 percent "religious concerns," 27 percent "personal involvement," with the other responses less than 10 percent. Interestingly, 4 percent reported volunteering to "keep taxes down" – the first time this response has appeared on a national survey of volunteers' motives.

The Anderson and Moore (1978), Schram (1985), and Gallup (1987) reports of volunteers' self-reported reasons for volunteering are summarized in Table 4.1. Although "service to others" – what some writers have referred to as the altruistic motives – continue to predominate, it is interesting to note the increased mention of work and co-worker interestingness and instrumental gain in the nearly 25–year period between the first and most recent US nationwide surveys. Whether this reflects differences in the surveys, in the societal acceptance of nonaltruistic self-reports of reasons for volunteering, or even some large-scale shift in volunteers' actual motives over these two decades is difficult to know.

The sampled volunteers' self-reported reasons for volunteering are similar to those found in these nationwide surveys (Table 2.1). We find a wide variety of reasons listed, with all of them being near or greater than "5" (for "somewhat important") in each of the scales. There were interesting

Table 4.1 Percentage self-reported reasons for volunteering in nationwide surveys

Reason	Anderson & Moore (Canada) 1978	United States Bureau of Census		Independent Sector (US) 1981	Gallup (US) 1987
		1965	1974		
Service to others[1]	75[2]	70[2]	85[2]	45[2]	50[2]
Work and co-workers interesting	39	31	36	64	65
Instrumental gain	21	–	25	39	27
Asked to volunteer/Nothing else to do	31	4	19	6	–
Other (Σ)	13	4	–	22	32

[1] Author's categorization of reported reasons.
[2] Lists percentage mentioning; respondent may have mentioned more than one reason.

statistically significant differences across organizations. There was less service motivation among newspaper volunteers (as well as newspaper employees), reflecting the fact that their task was comparatively less purely a service to others. Similarly, the relatively more isolated telephone volunteers reported less rewarding social interaction. The interviews revealed a wide variety of self-reported motives: the firefighter who earned additional "points" on his civil service exam (for a paid firefighter position); the volunteer driver who had been pressed into service because his mother was an active "core" member of the poverty relief agency; one of his relief agency colleagues who saw herself as making a small contribution to alleviate poverty; the family planning volunteers who had been clients of the organization; the musicians who loved to make music; and an alienated shop volunteer who hated working there but found it the most convenient way to earn required "community service credits" for her voluntary association.

However, all of these research efforts, as comprehensive and consistent as they are, suffer from the social desirability problem identified earlier. The format of these surveys provides few options for complex or hesitant answers. As noted in Chapter 2, many have not accepted the immediate reasons given by the volunteers in their studies (e.g. Minnis 1952). Such inferences are seconded by Smith (1981), who presented persuasive evidence that volunteers' self-reports "at most, tell us about socioculturally accepted 'reasons' people tend to give. Not surprisingly, the giving of altruistic reasons for involvement is fairly popular" (p. 25). Smith cautioned that he does not mean that volunteers are uninterested in helping others, only that this motive may not be as dominant as it appears to be if self-reports are taken at face value.

Grounded theories

Two studies of the motives for volunteering are noteworthy because the researchers were not content merely to list the reasons various groups of volunteers gave for their participation, but they actually used these reasons to develop testable hypotheses about volunteer organizational behavior. In his classic study of the National Foundation for Infantile Paralysis, Sills (1957) classified its volunteers by their motives for joining: (1) Polio Veterans (those having prior experience with polio); (2) Humanitarians (those whose fundamental consideration was the welfare of others); and (3) Good Citizens and Joiners (those fulfilling an obligation to the community, job obligations, or enhancing personal status). He found that these types of volunteers had different initial images of the organization and that they tended to join through different channels. For example, Polio Veterans were most likely to have joined on their own initiative, Humanitarians and Joiners to have been asked by an organizational or occupational colleague, and Good Citizens were more likely to have been approached by a community member they did not personally know. The following quotations from Sills' work help provide a flavor of the differences among these types of volunteers:

> [Humanitarians] I always figured you have to do something outside yourself. It's the same as Sunday School where I teach. If you can't branch out and do for others, you don't deserve to prosper yourself.

> [Good Citizens] I started my program in 1949. They called and asked for some publicity and, of course, I was very interested in doing something for it . . . . I have two children myself, so I was interested in the whole polio problem. So I told them, "Anything at all, I'll do it."

> [Joiners] I came in on this seven years ago. I belong to the Lions Club. They were asked to sponsor the March of Dimes, and they asked me to head it as Payday Town County Chairman.

> (Sills 1957, pp. 106–9)

Sills further makes a distinction between two types of "service": those serving generalized "humanitarian" goals for which the particular organization is just one of many, and those (in this case, Polio Veterans) who have a particular personal interest in the mission of this organization. Sills found that recruitment and retention followed very different paths with those holding different service motives. In addition, like Clark and Wilson, Sills placed much more emphasis on social processes, both as motives ("joiners") and in the actual recruitment of volunteers.

Sharp (1978) studied the relative effectiveness of various formal block associations that introduced urban neighbors and provided training in identifying potential criminals. Using Clark and Wilson's (1961) typology, she categorized these associations by the primary incentives offered to members: (1) material incentives – such as summer employment, (2) solidary incentives, and (3) purposive incentives. She discovered that actual block-watching activity (e.g. "People here are not likely to call the police when they see something suspicious in your neighborhood," negatively scored) was significantly greater in those associations relying on solidary incentives than in either the material or purposive groups. She noted that the solidary groups were more common in the upper-income neighborhoods, and she presented convincing arguments that material incentives may attract a membership with only a limited commitment, while the purposive associations may have difficulties in sustaining a "crisis orientation" over extended periods of time.

Sharp's empirical research echoes the theoretical arguments of Etzioni (1975), who suggested that remunerative involvement leads to lower levels of commitment than does normative involvement, and Knoke and Prensky (1982), who suggested that expressive incentives would not be binding. Note that the importance of solidary incentives discovered by both Sills and Sharp (and Minnis and Smith) are in sharp contrast to their relatively weaker role in the self-reports of volunteers (see Table 4.1).

This research on the reasons for volunteering can be briefly summarized as follows. First, individuals volunteer to satisfy a wide diversity of personal needs, such as job-training among youths and personal contacts for some business people. However, three attractions of volunteering appear across divergent studies – volunteering to serve, for social contact, and to promote the goals of the particular organization. Each of these three dominant motives are discussed at length below.

VOLUNTEER TO SERVE: THE ALTRUISM DEBATE

The humanitarian motives of volunteers elicit a great deal of controversy, exacerbated by the fact that volunteers themselves consistently list "service to others" as their most important reason for volunteering. Smith's (1981) rather modest suggestions that there is a social-desirability bias in favor of altruistic reasons for volunteering and that volunteers' motives may be more selfish than would be suggested by many self-report surveys of volunteers have generated a lively dispute in the literature on volunteer motivation. He suggested that it is the "voluntariness of volunteer work (that is, the absence of coercion or direct remuneration), which is distinctive, rather than an absence of selfishness" (p. 33). Olson (1965) and Gidron (1977) make similar arguments against an altruistic motive.

Olson (1965) describes the presumption that members of developed societies have some undefined "instinct" to join associations. He suggested that this is a label for their actions, not an explanation. Rather, he argued that volunteers derive some benefit themselves, personally, from joining (although he does not suggest exactly what this benefit might be). Similar conclusions were drawn by Gidron (1977), who suggested that volunteers report numerous nonaltruistic reasons for volunteering. He noted that, since volunteers also state that they work for self-oriented reasons and often give no clear reasons at all, the suggestion that altruism is the essence of volunteering is more romance than a description of reality.

Alternatively, others have sought to defend the central role of selfless motives in organizational volunteering. Allen and Rushton (1983) reviewed the available research on the altruism of volunteers and concluded that many community volunteers do have an "altruistic personality." Flashman and Quick (1985) countered Smith (1981) with evidence from social psychology (Batson and Coke 1978) which suggested that subjects will help others (take their electric shocks for them) when there is no expectation of personal gain. Like Van Til (1985), they emphasized the multiplicity of volunteers' motives.

In some senses, this debate derives from the use of the (more common) term "altruism" rather than the more accurate term, "prosocial." To be altruistic implies "self-sacrifice" or actions that are *contrary* to the actor's best interest. In contrast, "prosocial" acts are those designed to produce and maintain the well-being of others without the restriction in other kinds of potential "payoffs" for the actors (Rushton and Sorrentino 1981). A theoretical discussion of prosocial acts among employees has recently been introduced to organizational behavior researchers by Dozier and Miceli (1985) and Brief and Motowidlo (1986). These theorists used this social psychological concept as an explanatory variable for a wide variety of employee actions.

Volunteering clearly is prosocial, and for some individuals these generalized service goals may be the dominant motives. With prosocial volunteers no longer required to be self-sacrificial, the discovery of social or other "self-"interested motives no longer serves to destroy the assertion that service motives also play a role. Prosocial motives must retain some role in understanding organizational volunteers, since volunteering for organizational work is clearly only one of the many leisure activities that provide opportunities for rewards such as personal growth and conviviality. As a type of leisure activity, organizational volunteering's unique feature is that it provides a service to others and the opportunity for volunteers to feel that they are contributing something of value – that they are givers as well as takers. This reasoning seems to dominate for those volunteers (Sills' Good Citizens) for whom any good works will suffice.

The strength of service motives has noteworthy implications for the organizational behavior of volunteers once they are working. First, there is some evidence that service motives appear to recede in importance after volunteers begin to work. Clark and Wilson (1961) suggested that new associations and organizations were dominated by members with purposive interests (goal achievement) but that for many mature ones solidary motives had more importance.

Pearce (1983b) reported that volunteers themselves reported a decline in the importance of service motives after joining their organizations. Volunteers from three different organizations reported a statistically significant decline in the importance of their service reasons for working ("chance to further the goals of the organization" and "chance to make a real contribution") with a corresponding increase in social motives ("associating with a good group of people" and "enjoyment of the company of my co-workers").

Additional evidence for the decline in importance of generalized service as motivation to remain comes from the Gallup Organization's (1987) recent survey. Similar arguments were made by Phillips, based on his sample of

Fresh Air Fund volunteer hosts to deprived New York children; those hosts whose own motivation was "egoistic" as well as "altruistic" were more likely to want to serve as volunteer hosts in the future. He suggested:

> While the initial motivation to volunteer may be altruistic (to help some-
> one else), that motivation may also be reassessed in terms of its return.
> Similarly, the decision to continue as a volunteer will be evaluated in
> terms of its costs and rewards.
>
> (Phillips 1982, p. 119)

Thus, volunteer-staffed organizations which depend primarily on service-based recruitment appeals need to consider that this initial burst of enthusiasm, alone, is probably not sufficient to maintain organizational commitment.

Prosocial motives also seemed to play a critical role in maintenance of internal coordination in the sampled organizations. In the studied volunteer-staffed organizations, the perceived self-sacrifice of members of the core served as an important source of status and influence. Certainly those volunteer officeholders and paid employees who were *not* seen as prosocial contributors to their volunteer-run organizations experienced the most severe problems with insubordinate volunteer workers. This complex process is analyzed in detail in Chapter 6.

VOLUNTEERING AS A SOCIAL ACT

This review indicates that the kind of social contact provided by volunteering appears to be consistently important across divergent tasks and types of volunteers. This social contact can take many forms: enjoyment of co-workers' company (Pearce 1983b), conviviality (Sharp 1978), the sharing of common experiences (Minnis 1952), or social contacts to advance one's business or social prestige (Sills 1957).

Further support is suggested by the unique role voluntary associations serve for those in important transitions, which can probably be traced to the opportunities these groups provide for social contact with others. For example, Meillassoux (1968) suggested that voluntary associations served the members of an African community through creating new "social networks" that helped to solve problems created by rapid modernization of their society. Trendly (1949) argued that the Greek ethnic associations of Boston helped immigrants by providing forums for practicing "American" behavior and helped provide a social consensus for members' actions.

Volunteer work provides a particular type of social setting. In Chapter 2 it was noted that volunteers often are subject to confusion about their "associational" and "organizational" ties. This uncertainty, despite its interference with task accomplishment, provides a certain kind of social freedom. Organizational volunteers often enjoy the "associational" dimensions of shared purposes, informal social relations, and the shaping of structures around people. This is in contrast to the greater emotional intensity of the family and the greater economic importance and often depersonalized character of paid workplace interactions. Volunteer settings are among the few social settings in which there is a genuine freedom to construct social relationships without the constraints of tradition or economic pressures. This freedom may serve as one of the most attractive features of volunteering. Volunteers are not limited by their previous training to hold specific jobs, but can, through their own efforts, assume a wide variety of roles. They can become policy makers or service providers; they can become central to the organization's activities or find a vehicle that allows them to help others without a large commitment. The very confusion that can damage task performance can also be a major attraction of the setting to many participants. This suggests that many practitioner attempts to make the organizations more "businesslike" (e.g. Wilson 1976) need to be accomplished with care.

This intensely personal social character of volunteer-staffed organizations helps illuminate the "shyness" of many recruits who seem to want to wait for a personal invitation. It clarifies why only the most determined volunteers join without knowing others in the organization. Most seem to feel uncomfortable volunteering unless they "know someone," a reaction more characteristic of cocktail parties than of workplaces, and the feature Young (1987) called "volunteers' clubbiness." In contrast to the assumed impersonality of the employee-staffed workplace, to outsiders volunteer-staffed organizations may appear to be more exclusive and forbidding.

Thus, the various disparate findings listed above form a consistent pattern. Those who are more sociable are more likely to value the social contact volunteering provides. Those experiencing important transitions, for whom the traditional social ties to kin may no longer be available or satisfying, are more likely to join organizations of similarly placed peers. Those of higher socioeconomic status are more likely to find the voluntary social setting an attractive vehicle for display and social advancement. Further, since personal contact is the dominant recruiting method, a cycle develops in which more middle- and upper-class people volunteer, and they, in turn, recruit their middle- and upper-class friends, and so on. Whether or not a voluntary organization has social contact as its stated purpose, it seems reasonable to conclude that this particular type of social interaction becomes one of the most rewarding aspects of participation for many organizational volunteers.

Social or solidary incentives need closer theoretical attention to determine their importance to volunteer motivation once they are members. Close social ties would be expected to have an important influence on organizational behavior. Yet, this cohesion would seem to be belied by the well-documented tendency of voluntary organizations and associations to splinter (Smelser 1962). In fact, as is detailed in subsequent chapters, social influence appears to be the most important feature of "control" in the sampled organizations.

VOLUNTEERING TO FURTHER THE ORGANIZATION'S GOALS

Finally, many volunteers are attracted to a particular organization because they want to help achieve its objectives. Certainly there are numerous organizations which offer opportunities to serve and which provide social contact, but most volunteers give their time and effort to a cause having some personal meaning, whether it is saving the bay, alleviating poverty, or supporting the arts. This would appear to include Sills' Polio Veterans, who were the only ones likely to volunteer on their own initiative, as well as the members of most expressive associations. It is interesting to note, however, that, like general service incentives, these attractions may not be strong factors in maintaining membership.

Attention to the attractiveness of the purposes of particular organizations also helps to theoretically integrate several research findings regarding the person who volunteers. Voluntary organizations have purposes; even purely expressive associations may undertake service projects, communication, or lobbying efforts directed at those outside the organization. If individuals are going to spend their "free" time organizing, participating in, or working toward a goal, they must feel that these efforts will be effective. Individuals must believe in the efficacy of their actions before they will undertake or persist in volunteer work. This proposition incorporates the findings that volunteers are more self-confident than nonvolunteers. Similarly, those who know other volunteers and have discussed the organization with them are more likely and able to understand that voluntary activities can be effective. Finally, those who feel strongly about an issue – those strongly motivated to achieve a particular goal – are more likely to seek out and organize voluntary organizations dedicated to their goals and to find ways to make them effective.

Finally, evidence from the sampled organizations suggests that the particular missions or tasks of these organizations played an important role in defining the kinds of incentives (or, more accurately, "appeals") used to direct and sustain motivation. Those organizations completing work governed by "professional standards" (newspaper, family planning clinic, orchestra, fire department) would commonly refer to those standards in directing and coordinating the actions of their volunteers. Similarly, the "caring" organizations (day care, poverty relief agency, and the family planning clinic), with their mixed "professional" and "cause" character, were dominated by different appeals and more frequent praise and expressions of gratitude. Volunteers and employees in these caring organizations continuously praised one another for their dedication. In contrast, praise in the professional organizations centered on skills, knowledge, or credentials. Only the volunteer-staffed gift shop, with neither professional standards nor community service appeal, relied *solely* on direct interpersonal ties to motivate. Here volunteers were sustained by their obligations to one another and the parent association. This was the only studied volunteer-staffed organization dominated by a sense of grim duty.

IMPLICATIONS FOR VOLUNTEER ORGANIZATIONAL BEHAVIOR

This chapter contains most of the available research touching on the organizational psychology of volunteers. It has briefly reviewed the extensive literature on the reasons volunteers give for their organizational work, adding the available reports from the sampled volunteers, and integrated it with the even more voluminous literature on the economic, social, demographic, and personality characteristics of volunteers. The conclusions about what attracts volunteers to these organizations have been integrated into a framework of volunteers' motives to join. Yet, in spite of decades of speculation and assessment of volunteers' motives, we know surprisingly little about the experience of volunteers once they are within organizations. What is particularly unfortunate is that this motivational literature provides little evidence about whether those recruited in different ways behave differently once they are members of the organization.

Motivating volunteers to join

This review has suggested that, despite the plethora of individual motives, there are three dominant categories of reasons to volunteer for organizational work: generalized service or prosocial motives, the attraction of the particular social connections that are formed among volunteers, and the particular goals of the organization joined.

Based on Sills' (1957) work, it has been suggested that volunteers with different motives are likely to join the organization through different paths. Those with generalized prosocial motives are likely to join through personal contacts in other volunteer organizations or through volunteer bureaus or action centers that serve to place prospective volunteers in appropriate organizations. Large established community services, what Sills called "matter-of-fact bureaucracies," probably recruit many of their volunteers this way. Alternatively, those volunteering for social contact will most likely be brought in by friends or relatives, with the probable result that organizations relying on this method of recruitment will find that their volunteer workforce is relatively homogeneous. All volunteer-staffed organizations probably rely on this method to some extent (recall that this is the dominant method of recruitment). However, smaller, more specialized, or value-rational organizations are more likely to be singularly dependent on this method. Finally, volunteers who are attracted to the particular mission of the organization are most likely to initiate the contact themselves, either in response to an advertisement, word of mouth or a newspaper article about the organization, or after receiving services as a client.

It is important to restate that volunteers' motives are often complex and even confused. Volunteering is fundamentally unlike employment in an important respect: undertaking volunteer work is usually a modest "initial commitment," unlike accepting a job. Volunteers may leave after a couple of hours' work (and many do) with no disruption of their lives or reputations. Further implications of the low initial commitment needed to begin volunteer work are analyzed in detail in the next chapter.

Motivating volunteers to remain

Wanous (1980), who provided the most extensive discussion of employees' organizational choice, has completed an extensive program of research on how the expectations of entrants influence subsequent organizational behavior. He found that the organizational practices designed to "recruit" (i.e. to sell the job to) employees can result in unrealistically high expectations and, subsequently, in high turnover. Wanous's empirical research demonstrated that "realistic recruitment" led to equal rates of job acceptance but to lower subsequent turnover.

How might these well-established ideas apply to volunteers? It seems that the temptation to use unrealistic recruiting appeals may be even more severe for recruiters of volunteers. Prospective employees must eventually accept some job (and most realize that all jobs have unattractive features). Prospective volunteers are usually not selecting among volunteer jobs, but among the volunteer job and other ways of spending their leisure time.

The best form of realistic job preview for volunteers may be having a friend or associate already working for the organization. Friends and family members are unlikely to mislead (although they may suffer from enthusiasm). The fact that personal contact is the dominant form of recruiting may be an artifact of the lower turnover of recruited friends, family members, and associates. Since dissatisfied volunteers would be expected to leave immediately, with no need to secure alternative employment, volunteers recruited through friends and family may be the only ones not to leave and so are to be found in most organizations at any point in time.

In addition, the retention of volunteers may be affected by the particular reasons why they joined. It was suggested that, following Olson (1965) and Knoke and Prensky (1982), purely normative (general service) motives may prove to be very fragile. There are simply too many other settings that offer these rewards. Thus, the organization must proffer something *particular* for its own members. Most often, this seems to be rewarding social contact, but particular rewards need not be confined to workplace social interaction.

Further, the attraction of the organization's particular goals in retaining volunteers is limited in its ability to foster commitment. These goals are more specific to the organization than are generalized service motives. Yet, in the absence of commitment to the other individuals in the organization (the social rewards the organization offers), goal-attracted individuals are susceptible to schismatic acts, taking themselves and perhaps a subgroup off to form an alternative organization pursuing the same goals but with other methods or colleagues they find preferable. The power of volunteers' social environment to bind them to the organization has not been given the attention it deserves in the maintenance of volunteer-staffed organizations.

Motivating task performance

The motivation of volunteers to perform their work has been neglected by theorists and practitioners alike. Only one study measuring volunteer performance could be located (Puffer and Meindl 1987). In it, paid staff members were assigned to support various committee members. These staff assessments of volunteer performance were correlated with the staff members' other ratings of the volunteers: $r = .29$ ($p < .01$), with the judgment that the volunteer was altruistically motivated; $r = .27$ ($p < .01$) with their level of involvement. Unfortunately, staff assessments of volunteers' performance were unassociated with volunteers' own reports of their motives. Thus, we cannot know whether or not the positive correlations among staff assessments were simply the result of common-method variance or halo error, because we have no independent validation of these measures. This study was methodologically limited, but it does suggest that volunteers' self-reported motives may be *unrelated* to others' judgments of their performance within their organizations. Apparently those studying employee organizational choice have also confined themselves to the effects choices have on turnover rather than on employee effort or performance, and so there is also little to learn from this source.

Young (1987) has commented indirectly on volunteers' task motivation. In his description of nonprofit organizational management, he devoted a section to the impact of volunteer workers on the overall performance of the unit. He suggested that the impact of volunteers is decidedly negative for several reasons: (1) their presence emphasizes the importance of service motives and makes the use of performance-contingent incentives for employee staff members more difficult; (2) they promote the "patronage awarding" of paid positions among themselves rather than hiring based on merit; (3) they undermine their supervisors by going directly to board members with their complaints; and (4) they generally promote "an atmosphere of clubbiness" that detracts from service to clients.

Complaints about the work performance of volunteers are frequent enough that the matter deserves serious attention. There is much from the previous chapters suggesting that organizations do not press their volunteers to maintain work standards. These settings were characterized as chronically understaffed, with the implication that performance standards were lowered to encourage more recruits. Perrow's (1970) proposal that volunteers must receive sufficient symbolic rewards suggests that they must be "catered to" in a way that is inconsistent with stern attention to performance. In addition, reliance on positive social interactions as the dominant incentive implies that it may be difficult for supervisors to hold volunteers accountable while simultaneously seeking to ingratiate themselves to them (Young's "clubbiness"). The question of volunteer performance motivation is the central focus of the remainder of this book.

Chapter 5

Volunteers' attitudes

An exploration of their commitment

Research and theory on employees' attitudes enjoy a long history, enlivened by recent debates concerning the effects of personality and the work environment on these attitudes. As noted in the previous chapter, volunteers' feelings, thoughts, and actions once they have become members have not received commensurate attention. Yet thoughtful analysis of volunteers' attitudes can aid our understanding of the psychological experience of working, as well as reflect on the employee-attitude debates. Throughout this work, it has been noted that volunteers do not work in settings with the same "coercive" power to influence behavior that employees do. The very normative uncertainty of their settings implies that their own psychological states should have greater power to influence their actions than would be the case for the majority of employees. This chapter focuses on an understanding of volunteers' attitudes, both for what they may tell us about their actions as a practical matter, and for how they may reflect on the larger theoretical questions of organizational attitudes in uncertain settings with weak coercive power.

Before proceeding, the term "attitude" as it will be used here needs to be clarified. Katz (1960, p. 168) developed the most widely used definition: "the predisposition of the individual to evaluate some symbol or object or aspect of his world in a favorable or unfavorable manner."

In organizational behavior, the generic category of attitudes has come to include a wide variety of feelings (Staw and Ross 1985). Since the workplace provides many objects about which workers can have positive or negative feelings, there are a vast number of workplace attitudes. For those unfamiliar with the field, the most widely studied workplace attitude has been called "job satisfaction," an overall evaluation of the job. Other widely studied workplace "satisfactions" include pay, co-workers, the job itself, and supervisor satisfaction.

There are a handful of empirical studies of volunteers' attitudes and limited employee–volunteer quantitative comparative data from the study which will be examined here. However, as will be detailed below, the theoretically interesting aspects of volunteers' attitudes cannot be addressed directly by these constrained and rudimentary studies, and so this chapter builds primarily on the study's qualitative data.

The chapter begins with a brief introduction to the better developed employee attitudinal research, touching on the attitude–behavior relationship as well as the current debates about the etiology of employees' attitudes. This is followed by a review of the research on the attitudes of volunteers. Next, a detailed analysis of the particular attitude of "organizational commitment" is presented. Because of its centrality to those concerned with volunteers, its susceptibility to the problems of indeterminate causality, and the extensive attention it has received in employee-focused organizational behavior, organizational commitment is a useful vehicle to explore the role of attitudes in weak behavioral settings. The chapter concludes with a discussion of volunteers' attitudes and the implications of the foregoing discussion for understanding their organizational behavior.

ATTITUDES IN ORGANIZATIONAL BEHAVIOR RESEARCH

Interest in employee attitudes dates back to those earliest studies of organizational psychology, the Hawthorne Studies (Roethlisberger and Dickson 1939). Traditionally, such interest has focused on attitudes as predictors of work behaviors, such as job performance, absenteeism, and turnover. However, the actual predictive utility of attitudes is less than was originally assumed. Vroom (1964) concluded, after a comprehensive review of the literature on the attitude of job satisfaction and job behaviors, that there was a consistent negative relationship between satisfaction and resignation and mixed results concerning absenteeism, but:

> There is no simple relationship between job satisfaction and job performance. Correlations between these variables vary within an extremely large range and the median correlation of .14 has little theoretical or practical importance.
>
> (Vroom 1964, p. 186)

Recent meta-analyses have reported higher but still modest correlations (Petty *et al*. 1984, r = .31; Iaffaldano and Muchinsky 1985, r = .17).

There is wide agreement that employees' attitudes have only a limited direct effect on the most prominent behavior of interest to managers: performance. The effects of attitudes on absenteeism and turnover are consistently positive, if weak. The accepted explanation for the limited ability to predict behaviors from attitudes is that the actual behavioral expression of attitudes is constrained by environmental forces (Porter and Lawler 1968). For example, Mowday *et al*. (1982) suggested that the moderate relationship between job satisfaction and turnover is influenced by such factors as the ability of the employee to find another job and that even if the employee acts quickly on his or her dissatisfaction a job search can take several months and longer. Thus, the theoretical role of attitudes as leading to organizational behaviors of interest to managers is retained, while reconciling the weak empirical relationships by suggesting powerful situational moderators.

Theorists also have made a case for an interest in attitudes either for their own sake or for their role in more spontaneous cooperative behaviors. Hackman and Suttle (1977) have argued that employees' quality of working life is important in its own right. Although employees trapped in disliked positions may be constrained from reducing their productivity by organizational control systems, dissatisfied workers are more likely to suffer from stress, and a humane society would want to ameliorate these problems whenever possible.

More recently, it has been suggested that attitudes influence organizational behaviors directly, albeit those "voluntary behaviors" that are outside of formal control systems. For example, Organ (1988) has analyzed what he calls "organizational citizenship behaviors," arguing that activities such as helping co-workers, because they are voluntary, cannot be mandated by management and so depend to a greater extent on the intentions and attitudes of employees.

The etiology of work attitudes is currently an area subject to debate. There are roughly three perspectives: the traditional one that worker attitudes are affected by objective conditions of the work itself, such as job design and pay; the critique of this perspective insisting that social processes and other contextual cues are more salient than the concrete features of the work environment; and the recent critique of both of these "situational theories" of attitude determination suggesting that attitudes are strongly influenced by individual dispositional tendencies.

As noted, early research on employee attitudes assumed they had important effects on workplace actions, and attention was directed to those features of the organizational environment (particularly those under management control) that led to positive or negative attitudes. Thus, different kinds of leadership styles (Likert 1961), pay delivery systems (Pearce and Perry 1983), and job design (Hackman and Oldham 1980) were examined for their effects on the attitude of job satisfaction. Significant, if modest, relationships were found (Locke 1976). However, the assumption behind this large body of work – that attitudes are a direct function of "objective" features of the work environment – has been questioned.

Salancik and Pfeffer (1978) argued that attitudes arise as much from the social context, the shared definition of the situation developed among employees, as from tangible features of the environment itself. Those working in "objectively dull and alienating jobs" can and do report high levels of job satisfaction. They suggested that it is not that objective environmental features are irrelevant but that they are filtered through an interpretative process, one strongly influenced by others' judgments.

Organizational volunteers provide an interesting opportunity to rethink the assumption underlying these interpretations: that attitudes would influence organizational behaviors, if only they weren't constrained by the power of the strong situations that organizational employees face. There are other equally plausible reasons why attitudes may not affect behavior, including, for example, that attitudes may themselves be highly unstable, transitory impressions (Mischel 1983). Organizational volunteers are less dependent on organizational rewards, and their behavioral settings are weaker. Under these circumstances, if attitudes are relatively stable, we might expect the attitude–behavior linkage to be clearer for organizational volunteers than it has been for employees. Since organizational volunteers face fewer constraints, their feelings and thoughts would be expected to be more clearly expressed in their actions.

Volunteers are a particularly interesting group for a study of these situational arguments, because volunteers' situational constraints are so different from those of employees. In addition to the lack of concrete benefits from (or constraints upon leaving) their volunteer work, volunteering has less clearly defined expectations. As noted above, volunteers enter their workplaces with significant uncertainties in social understandings regarding the role of the worker, the importance of job performance, and even the social importance of the act of volunteering.

To summarize, there are consistently weak relationships between attitudes and employee behavior, with the most evidence supporting the argument that negative attitudes lead to turnover and no evidence supporting the argument that those with more positive attitudes have higher job performance. However, it is possible that the weaker situational constraints faced by organizational volunteers may lead the heretofore "masked" influence of attitudes on behavior to be stronger in these settings. Furthermore, volunteers provide an opportunity to examine attitudes in weak behavioral settings in which the volunteers' dependence on the organization is less and social expectations for their actions are more open-ended than is the case for employees. Thus, the study of the effects of volunteers' workplace attitudes provides an opportunity to learn more about job attitude–behavior connections in the absence of the confounding effects of strong situational constraints.

VOLUNTEERS' ATTITUDES

Empirical research on volunteers' attitudes has been concerned primarily with attitudinal differences between those who volunteer in a community and those who do not – following the same line of research detailed in the previous chapter. Thus, researchers have been interested in attitudes as predictors of the act of volunteering. There has been less interest in the possibility of volunteers' attitudes as predictors of their actions at work, in line with the general neglect of their experience once they have joined the organization. In addition, there has been less interest in the "quality of working life" for its own sake, since volunteers could rarely be seen as coerced into membership, and due, no doubt, to the traditional assumption that volunteer work is a peripheral activity (Chapter 2) and not as important to mental health as paid work.

Mulford, Klonglan, Beal, and Bohlen (1968) argued that both positive self-reported attitudes toward "volunteering in general" and favorable attitudes toward a specific organization increase the likelihood that an individual will volunteer for that organization. Data consistent with this assumption are available from several cross-sectional studies. (See Smith *et al.* 1972 for a comprehensive review.) Smith (1966) found that both generally positive attitudes (e.g. "general obligation to participate" and "general instrumental value of formal voluntary organizations") and positive feelings about a specific organization significantly discriminated between residents with many and few voluntary organization memberships in Chile. In addition, Beal (1956) found that those who affiliated with US Farmers' Cooperatives were more satisfied with the cooperative than those who were not affiliated. Two classic studies reported that the belief that a particular organization is needed is more likely to characterize volunteers than nonvolunteers: Downing (1957) studied social clubs for the elderly, and Scott (1953) studied Civil Defense volunteers in 20 metropolitan areas.

This body of research has been interpreted to suggest that those individuals with more positive attitudes toward volunteering or a particular organization are led by those feelings to volunteer (Smith *et al.* 1972). Unfortunately, no available attitudinal studies provide evidence that positive attitudes toward volunteering or toward a particular organization actually *precede* the act of volunteering. In none of these cross-sectional studies can we confidently infer that these favorable attitudes antedate and, therefore, were a causal factor in the individual's decision to volunteer. We can be reasonably confident that current volunteers are more positive about volunteering in general and about their particular organizations than are nonvolunteers, but the usefulness of this inference in making causal predictions is unclear.

These simple cross-sectional correlations are subject to multiple interpretations. For what reasons do volunteers have more positive attitudes than nonvolunteers? Is it (1) that the organization is attractive and this leads them to volunteer? Or, (2) that, since it is easy for dissatisfied volunteers to leave, only the most satisfied remain (differential retention)? Or, (3) that the insufficient justification for volunteering leads volunteers to enhance their attitudes toward organization (attitudes follow behaviors)? Or, (4) some combination of these? Each of these possible interpretations is analyzed in detail.

Positive attitudes lead to volunteering

There is intuitive appeal to the idea that positive attitudes precede volunteering, consistent with the societal conception of volunteering as an act of "free will." Since volunteers aren't compelled to join these organizations, common sense (and the attributional processes described by Jones *et al.* 1972) suggests that they must want to join them.

However, the evidence of the role of social networks in the actual recruitment of volunteers presented in the previous chapter suggests that volunteering may not depend as much on individual rational calculation as these assumptions imply. It is less the case that volunteers are recruited equally from admirers and detractors of the organization, than that the prospective volunteer may not know enough about the organization or volunteering to have developed any feelings toward it one way or another. In the following section on the attitude of organizational commitment, this process of post-joining attitude formation is analyzed in detail.

Only satisfied volunteers remain

There is a strong intuitive argument in favor of the selective retention of volunteers with positive attitudes. Whatever may have been their feelings about the organization before they joined, volunteers undoubtedly do come to have feelings about various features of their workplace once they have spent some time working. However, in contrast to employees who may find that they must remain working in disliked circumstances until they can make alternative arrangements, volunteers have significantly less dependence on their organizations. All employees earn incomes by their work, and most are quite dependent on this money. Further importance derives from, as Sills (1968) noted, the prominence of "job" in societal and self-definition in our society. Volunteers clearly have no direct financial dependence on their work, but in addition much volunteer work is peripheral to self and societal roles. Friends and relatives will know what one does for a living, but they may be completely unaware of one's changing volunteer activities. Therefore, dissatisfied volunteers can be expected to leave their organizations virtually the moment they become unhappy. Note that this argument assumes that attitudes do cause behavior and that the low coercive power of volunteer settings allows behavior to follow attitude virtually simultaneously. Therefore, job attitudes may be a less useful "variable" in the prediction of volunteers' organizational behavior, since the range of attitudes is restricted.

If attitudes were more variable in employment settings than among comparable volunteers, we would expect to find greater variance in reported attitudes. Table 5.1 contains the self-reported job satisfaction in all 14 organizations. With the exception of the day care centers, the standard deviations of the volunteers' reported attitudes are smaller than those of comparable employees. The exceptional day care center may reflect the fact that it was a cooperative so many parent-teachers' assistants may not have particularly enjoyed their working "hours" for the center. It is noteworthy that the widest volunteer standard deviations appear in the newspaper and the gift shop. As detailed throughout this volume, these two volunteer-staffed organizations did experience significantly greater dissension than did the other five. Therefore, this summary of job satisfaction self-reports does seem to be consistent with the selective retention hypothesis – that the greater needs of employees to find alternative jobs will blunt the effects of dissatisfaction on turnover.

Table 5.1 Volunteers' and employees' mean job satisfaction and standard deviations

Organization	Volunteer		Employee	
	$\bar{X}$	s.d.	$\bar{X}$	s.d.
Day care center	5.79	.89	5.95	.83
Newspaper	6.11	1.19	4.37	1.42
Poverty relief agency	5.60	.72	4.88	1.10
Orchestra	6.48	.74	5.89	1.19
Family planning clinic	6.00	.74	5.94	.99
Gift shop	5.19	1.31	5.00	1.67
Fire department	6.33	.61	5.64	1.29
Grand $\bar{X}$	6.06		5.42**	

** $p \leq .01$

Despite the relative restriction in range of volunteers' self-reported job satisfaction, the measure did reflect the interview and observational identification of those organizations with greater volunteer dissatisfaction. However, as a practical tool in volunteer-staffed organizations, this kind of self-report instrument is less useful simply because dissatisfied volunteers were quick to voice their concerns to anyone who would listen (including their officers). That is, they did not hide their feelings to the same extent as did the studied employees. With no fear of reprisal, volunteers gladly complained to officeholders, and so the opportunity to provide their views anonymously to a researcher did not really lead to any new information in these organizations.

Remaining as a volunteer leads to positive attitudes

From the present study, there is evidence for the third hypothesis, that volunteers may experience insufficient justification for their work, leading them to develop favorable attitudes to justify their actions. Staw (1976), building on the work of Festinger (1961), Charms (1968), and Deci (1975), argued that individuals experience "over-justification" for their work when both extrinsic rewards (those tangible rewards, such as pay, that are provided as an inducement to complete a task) and rewards that are intrinsic to the task itself, such as challenge, are abundant. Individuals experiencing over-justification are hypothesized to reduce dissonance by devaluing the less tangible intrinsic rewards of the task. Thus, a social worker who is paid a salary to perform the personally fulfilling tasks of helping the poor may experience over-sufficient justification and, according to Staw (1976), would be expected to devalue the fulfillment experienced from the work. Similarly, Staw suggested that individuals performing work for which rewards are few will experience "insufficient justification" which leads them to enhance the importance of intrinsic rewards. Thus, volunteer poverty relief workers, because the tangible extrinsic rewards are few, will find even greater personal fulfillment in their relief of the suffering of others.

If Staw is correct, this experienced insufficient justification effect has important implications for understanding volunteers' attitudes. It suggests that the absence of pay itself causes positive attitudes among workers. Therefore, attempts to find ways to reimburse or reward organizational volunteers through tangible benefits or awards will simply substitute one kind of reward for another and will result in an overall reduction in positive feelings about the workplace.

Therefore, it is of practical and theoretical interest that in earlier published work drawing on this study, Pearce (1983a) found results consistent with a sufficiency of justification effect. Volunteers doing the same work as employees reported that they were significantly more likely to work for the rewards of social interaction and service to others, that their work was more praiseworthy, and that they were more satisfied and less likely to leave their organizations (see Tables 2.1 and 5.1). Thus, despite the equivalent primary tasks of their organizations and opportunities for service and interaction, volunteers were significantly more likely to be motivated by service and social rewards and to have more positive attitudes toward their jobs. We cannot tell from these data whether the volunteers were increasing their justification (insufficiency effects) or the employees were reducing their justifications for working (over-sufficiency effects), yet the attitudinal patterns differ in ways consistent with the sufficiency of justification hypothesis.

Combination of effects

Thus, the causes and consequences of volunteers' organizational attitudes are more complex than the early studies indicated. We can be reasonably confident that volunteers' attitudes are, in general, more positive than comparable employees' attitudes, but why this is so and its implications for volunteer organizational behavior need further analysis and empirical research. In the next section, one attitude is selected – the organizational commitment of volunteers – for a detailed theoretical analysis. Because of its centrality to those concerned with volunteers, its susceptibility to the problems of indeterminate causality, and the extensive attention it has received in the employee organizational behavior literature, it is a useful vehicle for exploring the role of attitudes in these weak organizational settings.

ORGANIZATIONAL COMMITMENT

Organizational commitment is the attachment individuals feel toward their organizations, and volunteers' commitment to their organizations is a reflection of the complexity of their organizational experiences. Volunteers usually are assumed to be very committed, since they are not compelled to work by financial need as are most employees. That is, in the absence of compelling external explanations, society, as well as volunteers, attributes high levels of commitment to organizational volunteers. As noted by Jones *et al.* (1972) and other attribution theorists, the apparently insufficient justification for another's actions is frequently justified by assuming strong intention.

In the present case of organizational volunteers, this "intention" is often assumed to be directed toward the organization's tasks or missions. Recall how in Barker's (1968) argument understaffed settings, like volunteer-staffed organizations, tended to be composed of members strongly committed to the outcomes of the setting. Thus, volunteers must be more committed to their organizations' outcomes or objectives.

Yet commitment *to the organization* cannot be assumed to be high for all members. Recall that Knoke and Prensky (1982) argued that volunteers may be strongly committed to the goals of their organizations but have weak ties to the particular institution, hence the frequency of schisms (Smelser 1962) or simple abandonment that are real threats to volunteer-staffed organizations. For example, volunteers who worked for the poverty relief agency because of their commitment to assisting the poor could find many alternative ways to make this contribution. Thus, the building of *organizational* commitment is of serious practical import to those concerned with volunteer organizational behavior.

There is limited research or theory on the organizational commitment of volunteers. This review begins with the one theorist who has addressed volunteers' commitment to their organizations: Etzioni (1975). However, the commitment of both "utopian community members" to their communities and of employees to their organizations has received significant research attention. Therefore, the present initial attempt to understand the development of volunteers' commitment to their organizations and its implications for both volunteers and their organizations builds from these three literatures. It begins with a review of the body of related literature concerned with commitment of employees to their organizations. Next, Kanter's (1968, 1972) research on the processes by which members of utopian communities become committed is examined. Neither of these literatures is directly concerned with organizational volunteers; the first addresses organizations, but only their employed members, and the second is concerned with volunteers who commit themselves to segregated, all-encompassing communes. Yet, both perspectives on commitment help us to build a more complete understanding of volunteers' attachment to their organizations by addressing both kinds of organizational settings of volunteer work – its matter-of-fact institutional settings and its value-rational settings. Subsequently, building on these three related theories of organizational commitment, a characterization of the organizational commitment process for volunteers is developed.

Organizational involvement

The discussion of volunteers' commitment begins with the work of the one organizational theorist who has directly addressed the organizational commitment of volunteers. Although Etzioni (1975) was interested in the different mechanisms by which organizations exert control over their members, his wide-ranging theory includes the suggestion that different forms of control are associated with different kinds of member involvement with the organization: alienative, calculative, and moral (defined in Chapter 2). Recall that moral involvement is assumed to characterize most volunteers. He argued that, in this case, the members are intensely involved with their organization (emotionally committed), internalizing the organization's goals and values. Etzioni suggested that these forms may be mixed in practice and that it seems likely that volunteers' relationships with their organizations can range between the extreme associational norms of moral involvement to the disinterested calculative involvement of someone working "required volunteer hours."

It is noteworthy that Etzioni would characterize volunteers as more intensely (or emotionally) involved than calculatively involved employees. This places him in conflict with Knoke and Prensky (1982), who suggested that volunteers had weaker commitment and were less bound to their organizations than employees. Like Barker, Etzioni assumes that moral involvement, by virtue of its absence of external compulsions, must result from a strong internal commitment. But commitment to what? He seems to equate commitment to some facet of the workplace, whether that be the enterprises' mission, fellow co-workers, or the work itself, with emotional commitment to the organization itself. This is probably not a viable assumption. For a better understanding of volunteer organizational commitment, we turn to those who have focused directly on this area.

The organizational commitment of employees

Since the early 1970s, attention to employees' commitment to their organizations has increased. Unfortunately, the various researchers have often used the concept of commitment in widely varying ways. One of the most important differences in their definitions is whether organizational commitment should be seen as the result of relatively rational calculation of the benefits of organizational membership or as an emotional, rather self-sacrificial, attachment. As an example of the former meaning, Hrebiniak and Alutto use the following definition: "A structural phenomenon which occurs as a result of individual–organizational transactions and alterations in side bets or investments over time" (1972, p. 556). Alternatively, Buchanan expressly excludes "calculated" involvement from his definition of organizational commitment: "A partisan, affective attachment to the goals and values of an organization, to one's role in relation to goals and values, and to the organization for its own sake, apart from its purely instrumental worth" (1974, p. 533).

This distinction is an important one, because these two kinds of organizational commitment imply differing processes of commitment formation and have different implications for both employees (and volunteers) and their organizations. Unfortunately, employee organizational commitment researchers and theorists have not resolved this conflict; instead, they have developed broad definitions of organizational commitment that include both calculative and affective commitment. This decision to define organizational commitment as both calculative and affective appears to be adequate for the study of employees, but it will pose difficulties when applied to volunteers. This is because the benefits of volunteering are usually less concrete, and self-sacrifice plays an important role in the studied volunteers' control systems, as will be detailed in Chapters 6 and 7. These definitional ambiguities are reflected in the two distinct theoretical and research approaches to employee organizational commitment. Since each approach can contribute to our understanding of volunteers' organizational commitment, both are briefly introduced below.

Behavioral commitment

Salancik termed his conception of organizational commitment "behavioral commitment": "A state of being in which an individual becomes bound by his actions and through these actions to beliefs that sustain the activities and his own involvement" (1977, p. 62). This theoretical focus is on how past behaviors or actions bind the individual to future courses of action. Not all actions are binding on future actions, and his discussion of the necessary features of committing actions is particularly useful for understanding the commitment of volunteers. Drawing on Kiesler's (1971) social-

psychological model of commitment, Salancik (1977) posited four characteristics of actions that make them binding and, therefore, determine the
degree of commitment. First, a committing act must be *explicit* – that is,
unequivocal. Second, binding actions must be *irrevocable*. As he suggested,
some actions are like trials, allowing us to change our minds if we don't
like the outcome. The third characteristic is the individual's *volition*; that
is, did the individual commit the act of his or her own free will? Salancik
did note the difficulty, both for the individual and society, of determining
whether or not an action was intentional, constrained, or influenced by
uncontrollable events. The final feature of committing actions is the *public*
character of the act. If the people whose opinions are valued know of
explicit, irrevocable, and intentional actions, the actor is more likely to be
committed to the future actions these imply.

In applying this general definition of committing actions to employees'
commitment to their organizations, Salancik examined one of these four
components, volition, in detail. This attention derives from the fact that
taking a paid job is virtually always explicit and public, and so these
committing features can be assumed. Finally, the reversibility of the act of
taking a particular job will vary for different individuals, and Salancik
described certain general features that will influence the reversibility of a
particular employment relationship. For example, he suggested that the
substantial body of research demonstrating that those with longer tenure
in organizations are more organizationally committed can, in part, be traced
to the fact that the longer employees have been with an organization, the
more difficult leaving becomes. Over time, the decision to continue with
the organization becomes less easily revoked, because employees may lose
substantial pension benefits and their organization-specific expertise may
be much less valuable in other organizations. Salancik also suggested that
other binding factors, such as greater self-confidence in their ability to do
their jobs, could contribute to the tenure–commitment link.

The easy revocability of the decision to join an organization is particularly
problematic for volunteers. Taking a volunteer job is probably as close to
a trial action as any organizational membership can be. Certainly, leaving
the organization entails no financial hardship. Furthermore, the decision to
volunteer can be less public than the decision to take a paid position. The
decision to work as an employee is considered an important one by friends
and family, and they would expect to be promptly informed, making the
action more public, hence more behaviorally committing. Doing volunteer
work is not usually as important to others (see Chapter 2), so it would be
quite appropriate for volunteers to wait until they have worked long enough
to find out whether or not the volunteer job is attractive before making
their actions public. Therefore, the easy reversibility and less public nature
of the decision to take a volunteer job would tend to dampen the behavioral
commitment of volunteers to their organizations. This feature will be

explored at length in the final section on commitment of organizational volunteers.

The final two components of Salancik's (1977) conception of committing actions are the explicitness of the act and the volition or intent of the actor. Volunteering is usually an explicit act, but in Chapter 3 it was suggested that there are many cases of friends and family helping volunteers, reducing the explicitness of some "acts of volunteering." Determining an individual's intent – the degree to which the actor is relatively constrained or is acting "on purpose" – is a complex problem for both employees and volunteers, but for different reasons. For employees, the problem is one of building organizational commitment in the face of unambiguous economic pressures to take a job. That is, it is easy for employees and observers to feel that since employees were required by necessity to take their jobs, they need not infer that employees want to work for their organizations. Employees need to earn the best possible salary, given their skills and prevailing labor market conditions. As Salancik suggested: "Members are hired rather than invited into the organization. Commitment under such circumstances will obviously be more difficult" (1977, p. 12).

For volunteers, the problem of volition is in some ways exactly reversed. As noted above, individuals volunteer for numerous reasons – reasons that can include the externally compelled, such as pressure from a close friend or a family member, or the need to make social contacts to expand the number of customers for one's business. Yet these reasons are usually not socially acceptable (Smith 1981). Therefore, volunteering is usually assumed to be based almost exclusively on the volunteer's own volition. To again quote the volunteer from Chapter 1, "If you are paid, you probably don't question it, you assume you are doing it for a living. Volunteers don't know why they are working; they don't know the answer. I guess they assume they do it because they want to do good." If Salancik is correct, this inference of volunteer intentionality should lead to greater organizational commitment. That is, since they see no clear external force compelling them to work there, volunteers will decide that they must like working for their organization. Yet, as detailed later in this chapter, when combined with the easy revocability of volunteering, the volunteers' commitment is more complex than this simple assertion would imply.

Behavioral effects of organizational commitment

Mowday *et al.* (1982), in their work on the psychology of employee organizational commitment, provided a comprehensive review and integration of the second stream of research on employee commitment that is relevant to volunteer organizational commitment. They integrated their review of research and their own empirical work into a model of organizational commitment giving special attention to the causes and consequences of employee organizational commitment. For example, they argued that age and tenure lead to employee commitment but that formal education has a reverse effect; that a member's organizational commitment is affected positively by job scope and negatively by role conflict; that worker ownership leads to greater commitment, but hierarchical level does not; and that feelings of personal importance to the organization, perceived equity, and greater social involvement lead to increased organizational commitment.

Finally, in a longitudinal study, Porter, Steers, Mowday and Boulian (1974) found that organizational commitment increased for those who stayed with the organization and declined for those who left, suggesting that commitment to an organization develops over time. In another longitudinal study of commitment and turnover, Porter, Crampon, and Smith (1976) discovered that stayers maintained a relatively constant commitment during the 15-month study period but leavers started with a lower commitment which declined steadily as they got closer to the point of quitting.

The effects of each of these antecedents of organizational commitment for employees are supported by empirical research, and several generalizations to volunteers seem plausible. Particularly relevant are Mowday *et al.*'s "work experiences" antecedents: it might be expected that (1) greater feelings of personal importance to the organization and (2) greater social involvement with other organizational members would lead to higher volunteer organizational commitment.

Further support for the importance of "personal importance to the organization" comes from Lathram and Lichtman's (1984) study of the commitment of a Protestant church's members and from the present study of volunteers. Lathram and Lichtman studied the effects of various kinds of "social linkages" on behavioral indicators of commitment (church attendance, organizational satisfaction, and percentage of income contributed to the church). Although general social interaction variables were positively correlated with the commitment indicators, by far the greatest percentage of commitment variance was explained by the report, "I feel wanted and needed in my church."

The importance of this feeling of personal importance in the building of organizational commitment is reflected in the problems of retaining volunteers experienced by the student newspaper described in Chapter 3. In Table 5.2, it can be seen that the exceptionally high turnover in the student newspaper is accompanied by membership organizational commitment that is significantly lower than that of the other six organizations. The newspaper reporters did not feel needed (as is reflected in the introductory quotation). One contributing factor may have been the volunteer-run newspaper's practice of assigning new volunteers to "stand around and wait" for an assignment (that might or might not be made) by a harried core volunteer. Several volunteer reporters suggested that they were likely to "not show up" if they didn't feel they were really needed.

Table 5.2 Mean tenure and extent to which incumbents reevaluate their participation in volunteer-staffed organizations

Organization	Percent turnover (in last year)	Organizational commitment
Day care center	13	2.27
Newspaper	67	1.37
Poverty relief agency	14	2.06
Orchestra	8	3.02
Family planning clinic	0	2.10
Gift shop	4	2.49
Fire department	3	2.68

The importance of social involvement with other members of the organization has also been noted. This work has repeatedly emphasized the importance of solidary or social incentives in the maintenance of voluntary association membership, which is consistent with the reported research findings of Buchanan (1974) on federal managers. Co-workers are "particular" to an organization and can come to represent the organization itself. The web of informal obligations that evolve when people work together, help each other, and grow to like one another would be expected to be as powerful in building the organizational commitment of volunteers as it is in the case of employees.

In addition to antecedents, Mowday *et al.* (1982) also posited several behavioral effects of organizational commitment. They suggested that organizational commitment should have a positive effect on employee attendance and retention. This is because employees who feel positively about their organization would be expected to want to continue their association. In addition, consistent with the job satisfaction research, they expected only a weak relationship between an employee's organizational commitment and job performance. They countered this finding by arguing that commitment probably leads to greater job *effort*, but that other factors also affect performance – factors such as ability and role clarity – and so a strong positive relationship between effort and performance could not be expected.

What, then, about these organizational behavior effects for volunteers? First, it seems reasonable to assume that greater organizational commitment will lead to reduced turnover, as has been demonstrated for employees (Mowday *et al.* 1982; Arnold and Feldman 1982). Yet, employee-based results may have only limited implications for volunteer retention. First, Mowday *et al.*'s (1982) definition of commitment included "calculative" as well as "emotional" commitment, and volunteers generally have more limited calculative benefit. If environmental pressures change (one needs to take a full-time paid job or to move home with parents during the summer), emotional commitment probably cannot sustain a volunteer's membership. Further, Mowday *et al.* suggested that significant drops in employee organizational commitment can be used to anticipate and perhaps to counteract employee turnover. However, it is reasonable to expect that employees would take more time between their decision to quit (low commitment) and the actual act of quitting than volunteers would. This is because employees would normally be expected to search for alternative employment before voluntarily quitting. Volunteers probably have little need to remain in organizations to which they are no longer emotionally committed. However, a calculatively committed volunteer, such as a student obtaining attractive work experience, would probably act much like a calculatively committed employee.

Volunteers' organizational commitment

There are two empirical studies of volunteer organizational commitment and retention. Jenner (1981) found that the organizational commitment of Junior League members could be used to predict number of volunteer hours contributed two years later (r = .46, p < .01). Seltzer, Miller, and Powell (1988) suggested that the organizational commitment–turnover relationship may be mediated by situational factors for volunteers, as well as for employees. Volunteers may quit because of personal changes, such as moving or returning to work or school. Since volunteering is often viewed as a peripheral activity, it may be influenced more heavily by outside events than employment is. Thus, the effects of organizational commitment on volunteer turnover would be moderated by situational factors. Seltzer *et al.* (1988) tested their hypothesis by administering questionnaires to hospital volunteers, using Mowday *et al.*'s (1982) nine-item short form to measure organizational commitment, and then returning six months later to assess actual volunteer turnover. They found that organizational commitment (1) indirectly affected turnover through intentions to quit, and (2) had weak direct effects on turnover. Thus, volunteers' organizational commitment, like that of employees, is associated with subsequent turnover, but the relationship is situationally constrained. Yet, whereas employees are likely to be constrained by their dependence on income from employment, volunteers are often constrained by their greater commitment to other activities.

The effect of a volunteer's commitment on absenteeism is less certain. Certainly, volunteers who don't care about the organization may not honor commitments. But, here again, volunteers are usually less financially committed and so can quit if they are dissatisfied (so the "safety valve of absenteeism" may be unnecessary for volunteers). Nevertheless, whatever their self-reported commitment, absenteeism among volunteers is rife, and this important practical problem is analyzed in detail in the following chapters.

Finally, there is the question of whether volunteer organizational commitment leads to greater effort on the job. It is important to note that the commitment-to-effort hypothesis has not been tested for employees and is, at present, a theoretical extension of theories of commitment. So, although it is intuitively plausible that higher levels of employee organizational commitment would lead to higher levels of effort, we have no concrete evidence to support this view.

Among volunteers, the Jenner (1981) study supported this commitment-to-effort argument, since the correlation between organizational commitment and subsequent number of hours worked was significant. There are no more direct tests of the argument that a volunteer's organizational commitment will lead to greater effort or any other feature of job performance.

Since the concept of "effort" itself presumes a job structure that may infrequently apply to volunteers, additional difficulties are introduced. Effort suggests energy that is directed toward some known outcome. That is, workers know *what* to do and need only decide how hard to try. Yet, recall the mention in Chapter 3 of how many sampled volunteers' jobs could better be characterized as "non-jobs" in which the incumbents stood around and waited for an assignment. Effort in its traditional meaning simply wouldn't apply. "Persistence" would be relevant, but it is different from the exertion implied by the term effort.

In fact, employees' jobs may also be more complex than is implied by these attitude–performance hypotheses. Theoretically, performance may have been too narrowly defined as solely quantitative production or effort on a constrained, repetitive job. The absence of significant relationships between attitudes such as organizational commitment and job performance may have resulted from tests using only the most constrained (and easily measured) samples of job performance. These narrow and nonrepresentative measures of job performance do not capture the more complex and "voluntary" facets of performance that may, in fact, be affected by commitment.

To summarize the employee–organization commitment literature, the limited empirical evidence indicates that the antecedents of organizational commitment most relevant to volunteers are feelings of personal importance to the organization and greater social involvement with organization members. Greater organizational commitment was modestly associated with lower subsequent turnover, with some evidence that this attitude–behavior relationship is also situationally constrained for volunteers. In addition, the established consequences of absenteeism for committed employees was suggested to have limited and complex relevance to organizational volunteers. Finally, research with volunteers supports the causal relationship between organizational commitment and the number of hours worked in a subsequent two-year period. This suggests support for a commitment-to-effort causal link and implies that previous tests of employee performance-attitude relationships may have been dependent on overly narrow measures of job performance.

Commitment and community

Kanter (1968, 1972) has studied the processes by which individuals become committed to utopian communities. Such commitments are much more extensive than most employment relationships, since communitarians commit all aspects of their lives to community governance. Although such communities require more intense commitments than working for voluntary organizations, there are two reasons why the "voluntary" commitments they develop may reflect facets of volunteer commitment that cannot be seen in studies relying exclusively on employment relationships. First, utopian communities take us away from the strong utilitarian and rational bureaucratic norms of many work organizations. Many organizational volunteers work in value-rational settings that may have more in common with utopian communities than with the organizations studied by those concerned with employee organizational commitment. In addition, Kanter focuses more on the antecedents of commitment to the community, whereas most employee commitment researchers have concentrated on its behavioral consequences.

Kanter (1968) suggested that different types of community commitment result from the different kinds of requirements imposed on members. She distinguished three forms of commitment. *Continuance* commitment is a commitment to the survival of the organization. Her second form is *cohesion* commitment, which is a commitment to the social ties developed in the organization. The third form, *control* commitment, is defined as belief by a member that the system's norms and values are the appropriate guides for action. Kanter (1968) argued that these three forms of commitment are related and can reinforce one another, and each of the utopian communities in her study used more than one of these strategies to develop the intense community commitment required of its members.

Applying this typology to organizational volunteers suggests that the strongest form of volunteer commitment in less intense volunteer-staffed organizations may be cohesion commitment. In Chapter 4, it was noted that the vast majority of volunteers in the studied organizations were recruited through personal contacts and reported that personal relationships increased in importance after they began working. In Chapters 6 and 7, data from the studied organizations are presented which suggest that influence and control patterns depend on these social ties. It seems that commitment to co-workers and social interactions of the voluntary organization was the dominating form of commitment for the studied volunteers.

Kanter (1972) suggested that cohesion commitment is built, in part, through a public renunciation of previous social relationships. Such extreme ceremonies would clearly not be possible for part-time organizational volunteers, yet these organizations could invest in "milder" ceremonies, such as public investiture or welcoming ceremonies. These would communicate to the volunteer and others that he or she is now a part of the social community of the organization. All too often, new volunteers are treated as outside the organizational social community, since nothing marks their entrance or membership. Similarly, Kanter's other basis for strong cohesion commitment, group ceremonies and symbols, is not used as often as possible. Without events to highlight volunteers' entrance and membership, these organizations miss opportunities to enhance their volunteers' commitment.

Continuance commitment would seem to be relatively weaker for organizational volunteers. Volunteers do not make the organizational investments, nor are they as financially dependent as are either employees or communitarians on the organization's prosperity as an institution. Yet, as noted throughout, continuance commitment is critical if these organizations are going to avoid schisms and retain their volunteers.

Kanter (1972) suggested that continuance commitment is developed when personal sacrifices are made upon joining. A modest form of this is available, yet remains virtually untapped. Organizational volunteering is itself a "personal sacrifice" of leisure time. Yet in the studied organizations, this sacrifice was rarely described or understood as a common sacrifice that could bind members together. It was seen as the result of "individual decisions," which reflected on individual merit, rather than as a contribution to the collective effort. In Kanter's utopian communities, sacrifices were viewed as contributions that all members and only members of the group made. As will be detailed below, personal sacrifice is important to the organizational psychology of these volunteer workplaces, yet, again, it was not often recognized as such.

For example, the volunteer-staffed organization with the highest turnover and lowest self-reported organizational commitment, the newspaper, had the built-in impediment to continuance commitment of membership roles restricting positions to certain groups ("students"). Clearly, such policies limited the potential organizational commitment of the organization's members and, thereby, contributed to its more severe problems with turnover and to other manifestations of "unreliability," such as absenteeism and indifferent performance. This is discussed in detail in the next two chapters.

Finally, Kanter's (1972) control commitment would seem to be weakest for part-time organizational volunteers. They do not spend the time with their organizations that either employees or communitarians do and so have fewer opportunities to pattern as many of their actions after fellow organizational members. Furthermore, the freedom implied by the voluntary associational norms discussed in Chapter 2 would most likely lead to more personal freedom in organizational actions than is usually thought to be characteristic of either employment settings or utopian communities.

BUILDING VOLUNTEERS' ORGANIZATIONAL COMMITMENT

There are two themes drawn from the preceding review that bear directly on our understanding of the development of volunteers' commitment to their organizations. The first theme is the greater revocability of the volunteer's decision to work for a voluntary organization and the subsequent inferred volition of the act of volunteering. This suggests that commitment may be more important to volunteers than to employees, implying greater felt commitment. The second is the hypothesized importance of cohesion commitment to the establishment of volunteers' organizational commitment.

Revocability and volition

As noted above, Salancik emphasized the importance of the irrevocability of committing acts. That is, decisions that are perceived to be tests-of-the-waters are not as likely to bind the individual to implied future actions. Salancik (1977) has argued that the act of taking employment with an organization, under many circumstances, is not easily revoked. In this chapter, it has been suggested that volunteering for an organization is substantially more revocable – more of a decision to see if the organization suits the worker – than a paid job would be. Therefore, we might expect volunteers to be, on the whole, less behaviorally committed to their organizations than employees would be.

Yet this inference apparently contradicts Etzioni, Barker, and the common sense assumption that volunteers are more committed than "alienated wage earners." Further, it contradicts another component of Salancik's (1977) definition of committing actions: that the act was intentional, not clearly compelled by external circumstances. Volunteers are usually not compelled to work and so are assumed to be donating their time and energy because they are personally committed. The very fact that volunteers are not as behaviorally committed to their organizations to the extent that employees are would seem to imply that they are more genuinely dedicated.

This apparent paradox – that volunteers are less and more organizationally committed than employees – can be resolved by recalling the dichotomous definition of commitment. The concept of commitment has been used in two very different ways by organizational behavior researchers. Some have emphasized the instrumental ties to the organization, suggesting that individuals become more behaviorally committed to their organizations because the benefits of membership outweigh the costs. Others have used the term commitment to mean an affective or emotional dedication that goes beyond instrumental calculation. This discussion of volunteer commitment illuminates this dichotomy and illustrates the confusions that can arise when these different meanings are attached to the same term.

Organizational volunteers may be considered to be members who are usually not as behaviorally committed to their organizations as are employees and, therefore, may be assumed to be affectively committed to organizations. This is a societal assumption about volunteers, an assumption that may not be accurate in all instances. Volunteers can reap many benefits from their work, yet it is probably true that these benefits do not have the coercive potential that employment can have for employees. Employee behavioral commitment without affective attachment can result in the alienated involvement described by Etzioni (1975) and others (e.g. Erikson 1986; Walker and Guest 1952). Therefore, we might expect that volunteers, on the whole, will be affectively and emotionally committed to some feature of their work (or, at least, that they judge themselves to be so committed) – be it to fellow workers, the organization, or its mission.

Note that, as with other aspects of the organizational behavior of volunteer work, absolute statements about commitment are not possible. Some employees may be more emotionally committed than some volunteers. It is more a relative absence of behavioral or instrumental commitment that distinguishes volunteers from employees. The instrumental benefits gained from volunteering are rarely as great as a yearly income, and very few volunteers are compelled to remain in their organizations.

This observation finds some support in Weiner's (1982) theoretical model of commitment. He conceptualized commitment as solely the affective attachment, characterizing commitment as personal sacrifice for the organization that does not depend primarily on environmental controls such as reinforcements and punishments. He argued that commitment and rewards can substitute for one another. Yet when they are in opposition to one another, as would often be the case for volunteers (who must give up valued free time), Weiner speculated that instrumental calculation will "usually" predominate.

Thus, we would not expect the strong association between the affective dimension of commitment and the dependent variables of attendance and retention found among employees. As noted above, Mowday *et al.*'s (1982) measure of organizational commitment explicitly includes a self-report of the instrumental benefits of membership. Volunteers who are emotionally committed to their organizations will not necessarily calculate that continued volunteer work is in their interest, and so they would not necessarily come to work or remain in the organization, as would a behaviorally committed employee. For example, volunteers can continue to believe in the importance of helping others and in the value of their organization's accomplishments, and, at the same time, find that they have become too busy to keep up their volunteer work. Hence, high affective commitment among volunteers should not necessarily lead to less absenteeism or turnover.

Reflection on the commitment of volunteers also suggests that a representation of commitment as solely (or even predominantly) the result of "committing acts" is itself limited. Evidence of the causal effects of the affective attachment of volunteers on the hours they contribute suggests that the affective dimension of commitment may be the more important one in predicting on-the-job actions. Organ (1988) suggested that citizenship acts are more likely from employees with positive attitudes. Certainly an alienated worker "trapped" in a detested job would not be expected to contribute beyond the minimum job requirements. Further, millions of individuals work as volunteers every day with only the most limited behavioral commitment compelling their services.

Cohesion commitment and volunteers

Kanter's (1972) cohesion commitment appears to be particularly important to the development of volunteers' organizational commitment. That is, volunteers' commitments to their co-workers and to their organizations as social settings appear to be important components of their commitment to their particular voluntary organizations.

This balance of commitments – high commitment to co-workers (and often to the goals or values of the organization), but low behavioral or instrumental commitment to the institution – would be expected to lead to organizational behavior quite different from that of either communitarians or employees. For example, volunteers have more positive job attitudes than do employees, since the dissatisfied volunteer leaves at relatively little cost. Volunteers rarely refrain from speaking their minds, since they are not dependent on the goodwill of the institution. Further, since they care about the organization's mission, volunteers have more about which they want to speak. Yet commitment to co-workers binds members to one another, and this can have implications for their behavior. It may account for the "clubbiness" and "patronage" charges against volunteer organizational members leveled by Young (1987). Certainly individual performance-contingent rewards would be discouraged because they are divisive. Further, close co-workers may not always identify with all facets of the organization's mission, thus providing a "support group" for counter-organization actions.

CONCLUSIONS

This chapter has focused on understanding how volunteers' workplace attitudes may reflect on the larger theoretical questions of organizational attitudes in uncertain settings with weak coercive power. Volunteers have relatively more positive attitudes than employees but their self-reports and recruitment patterns suggest these positive attitudes may reflect the insufficient justification phenomenon and selective retention; the suggestion that

positive attitudes cause individuals to volunteer is only one plausible interpretation. Drawing on studies of communitarian and employee organizational commitment, it has been suggested that post-joining experiences,
particularly the perception that one is needed and the value of social bonds
formed with other organizational members, dominate the establishment of
volunteers' organizational commitment.

Yet, what can be said about the relationships between volunteers' attitudes and "on-the-job" behaviors – their effort, persistence, willingness to
solve problems, to take direction from or to provide direction to others?
Limited evidence suggests that positive attitudes do influence important
work behaviors among volunteers. Yet, Jenner's (1981) finding concerning
the number of hours worked still provides a rather barren picture of volunteers' workplace behaviors. Despite the extensive research on volunteers,
we still know next to nothing about the organizational behavior of
volunteers. Initial attempts to provide a rich description of the actual
organizational behavior of volunteers and to present an integrated theoretical understanding of their work lives appear in the next two chapters, with a
focus on the problematic behaviors as reported by practitioners – volunteer
unreliability.

Part III

Member reliability and independence

Unreliability is the serious organizational behavior problem facing organizations staffed by volunteers. Despite the best efforts of many, it certainly is true that many volunteers cannot be relied upon to perform or attend consistently. They simply do not integrate as completely "into the system of organizational behavior" (Simon 1957) as employees do. This fact of life concerning volunteers is taken for granted by all who work with them in organizational settings. (See e.g. Young 1987.)

This question is addressed in the following two chapters. In Chapter 6, "The organizational control of volunteers," the question of volunteer unreliability is reviewed. Relevant theory and research, as well as evidence from the studied organizations, form the basis for a proposed theoretical explanation of the organizational control of volunteers. One of the central features of this form of volunteer control – active interpersonal influence – was found to be the primary form of control in the studied volunteer-staffed organizations. For this reason (and the fact that it is the least explored facet of volunteer control), it is examined in depth in Chapter 7, "The management of interpersonal influence."

Chapter 6

The organizational control of volunteers

It is widely assumed by those who work with volunteers that they, as a whole, cannot be relied upon to perform or to attend as consistently as employees. Certainly no evidence from the studied organizations contradicted this truism. For example, in the voluntary food distribution agency, the board of directors decided that it was appropriate to provide longer-term support to their clients who called for free food. Therefore, in addition to obtaining sufficient information to get the food to the caller, volunteers were also instructed to inquire whether the caller qualified for or received support from a social service agency. The volunteers were given descriptions of the various agencies and were expected to provide this information to appropriate callers. However, the new information was rarely provided. Apparently many volunteers felt uncomfortable making these kinds of inquiries; other volunteers did not like the local "welfare office" for some reason and did not want to refer callers to it. Thus, the agency could not rely on clients receiving information because some volunteers complied and some did not.

Other illustrations of how free volunteers felt to do their work (or not), however they pleased, are indicated in the following interview passages:

> One interviewee summarized these beliefs about volunteers and employees by saying that volunteers are either much better or much worse than employees. When asked to elaborate, she said that by better, she means they are enthusiastic and do the extra things that need to be done. By worse, she means they cannot be relied upon to come to work or to perform at a minimum level. By implication, employees can be expected to come to work and perform at an acceptable level, but they are unlikely to approach the job with zeal.
>
> (Field notes, post-interview conversation with a gift shop volunteer)

> They referred to the hassle they had had with the State Office in reopening their clinic. Since there was a hospital-run clinic in the area they had to prove there was a need in order to get State funds. [The Chapter Chairwoman] laughed as she reported that the State people had said "Oh

you people! You know if you were paid we'd come down a lot harder on you." I asked them if they really thought that was true. They said, "Oh yes, they require us to do things but we say we just don't have the time." [The Volunteer Chairwoman] then told me about an incident in which the State Office Head of Services had suggestions . . . . "She wanted us to be more professional." I took her idea about the smocks to my volunteers and they weren't interested. So I just told the State Office we didn't want to wear smocks.

(Field notes 6/21, conversation with volunteers in the family planning clinic)

Apparently, this difference in the reliability of volunteers and employees is seen by interviewees as one of the central distinguishing features of the two groups. As shown in Table 3.1, the one characterization of volunteer–employee differences broadly shared by volunteers and employees is that "employing organizations have the power to insure performance." As noted above, it is also an important source of the sneering antipathy sometimes expressed toward organizational volunteers. Some of the reasons why this freedom develops among volunteers have been introduced earlier:

1 Uncertainty about roles (as worker, associational member, and client) reinforces the notion that the volunteer knows what is needed. Young (1987) complained that volunteers often had "policy agendas" of their own and could carry their disagreements with their salaried supervisors to friendly trustees, thereby undermining hierarchical control (Chapters 2 and 3).
2 Volunteers have less powerful incentives than employees to remain with the organization, with the implication that employees can be coerced into reliability. Further, the need to draw on volunteer labor usually indicates that the workplace is understaffed, suggesting a greater dependence on workers with a concomitant "lowering" of performance standards (Chapters 4 and 5).

These factors contribute to a powerful degree of freedom of action for volunteer organizational workers. Yet, what is seen as freedom to the worker is inevitably viewed as unreliability by those seeking task accomplishment and continued environmental support. Ways in which these free workers can be brought into the system of organizational behavior are analyzed in this and the next chapter. In this chapter, the relevant theoretical and empirical work addressing this problem, including the data from the comparative study of the matched volunteer and employing organizations, is reviewed and summarized as three features of control systems used to manage organizational volunteers.

The literature review begins with a review of those theories which have directly addressed the problem of "control" in voluntary associations or

collectivities. Few of these theorists focused directly on volunteers performing organizational work roles, yet their analyses of association and church
member control are a useful adjunct to what we know about employees.

This perspective is necessary because interest in the control of employees
has developed in a way that has limited usefulness for understanding the
control of volunteers. Most importantly, theorists concerned with
employee-staffed organizations have taken for granted the need for more-
or-less compelled behavior. The design of control systems is seen as a
straightforward technical problem in which the difficulty is to design a
comprehensive measurement or surveillance system, with the assumption
that the organization should find no difficulty motivating the required
behavior once it is identified (e.g. Lawler and Rhode 1976).

This is not to suggest that there has been no interest in eliciting preferred
behaviors from employees. The interest is usually labelled "motivation"
and centers on the fact that most employees have substantial choice in their
organizational behavior beyond the minimum levels established by control
systems. Thompson (1967) distinguished "perfunctory effort" (doing that
which the control system requires) from "consummate effort" (proactively
trying to do one's best). Galbraith (1977) elaborates by noting that formal
control systems, by their very nature, cannot anticipate change, nor can
they cope completely with large complex problems requiring extensive
interdependence among individuals or groups. There are many prominent
examples in a large body of writing which emphasize that measurement
and authoritative command cannot possibly cover all of the necessary organizational behaviors without throttling the organization (for a recent discussion see Shapiro 1987).

This is consistent with the observation of the above-quoted gift shop
volunteer who suggested that employees tend to conform with the control
system requirements but often are not willing to contribute beyond those
requirements. Yet, rudimentary control of the most basic and visible actions
are *assumed* in the study of employee organizational behavior, with attention directed to understanding why employees might contribute beyond
these minimal requirements. In contrast, volunteers' neglect of even the
most basic and easily measurable acts, such as attendance, are legendary.
Instilling enthusiasm is not the problem; it is attracting the potential
workers' attention and focusing their efforts on necessary, if routine, tasks
that is the great difficulty.

Although the problems of employee and volunteer organizational control
are different, clearly there is some overlap. As noted earlier, Organ (1988)
has characterized the nonmonitored, spontaneous, and cooperative
employee behaviors as "volunteered," since they are contributions beyond
the minimal required level. Therefore, attempts by organizational behavior
theorists to understand the circumstances under which employees will "volunteer" their efforts can provide useful insights. This is particularly so

because there is virtually no theory of volunteer control systems at the individual level – it remains the province of social theorists rather than of organizational behavior theorists. Therefore, the relevant employee organizational behavior theory and research are reflected throughout this and the next chapter's discussion of the approaches to control used with organizational volunteers.

However, the present description of the ways in which volunteers' efforts are directed and integrated relies primarily on the sociological literature concerning control of the membership in voluntary associations. This is a rich tradition in sociology and provides a framework for the discussion of the individual and interpersonal processes analyzed in these chapters. These social theorists share an emphasis on the role of ideals or values in the control of volunteers. However, here it will be argued that values have only a limited usefulness in understanding the concrete processes by which some volunteer-staffed organizations obtain virtually faultless volunteer reliability while others, like the student newspaper among the sampled organizations, face such severe unreliability problems that they ultimately fail.

Earlier the importance of interpersonal influence was emphasized. However, although sociologists have noted in passing that social or interpersonal control may be present in associations, they do not explore this process in any detail. Until the present work, only one available empirical study had addressed interpersonal influence in volunteer-staffed organizations – Smith and Tannenbaum's (1963) classic comparative analysis of the relative hierarchical influence in a business firm and a voluntary association. This work has been extended and completed in the present study of 14 organizations. Both of these studies are analyzed in detail in this chapter. Therefore, this chapter contains a review of available theory and research on the organizational control of volunteers and concludes with the suggestion that effective management of volunteer unreliability seems to depend most on strong interpersonal influence processes, including, for example, stable group membership, crystallized normative expectations, peer conformity pressures, and charismatic leadership. The role of interpersonal influence is introduced in this chapter, with key features of these processes examined in depth in the next chapter.

THEORIES OF ASSOCIATIONS' CONTROL OF THEIR MEMBERS

An analysis of control systems for volunteers touches on the long-standing scholarly study of the necessity for coercive methods or controls in voluntary associations. As noted in Chapter 2, one of the reasons for social theorists' earliest and continuing interest in these social settings was for their symbolic value as non-coercive, "free" social entities, and one of these theorists' primary foci has been the manner in which these entities exert control over individual members. Further, the study of control in voluntary associations has been central to the establishment of several key sociological principles. For example, Greer's (1955) study of voting patterns in labor unions helped to demonstrate that formal associational actions (such as whether or not to go out on strike) could *not* be predicted from a simple average of members' individual preferences. His work suggested that even the least coercive of institutions can compel their members to act in ways that are not the result of their own personal inclinations. Certainly, many volunteers are brought into the "system of organizational behavior" of their organizations, and an understanding of how this is done has been of long-standing interest to organizational sociologists.

Control through shared values

Weber (1968) was concerned with the bases on which leaders claim legitimacy – on the types of authority they exercise. As noted earlier, in addition to the better known authorities, traditional, charismatic, and bureaucratic, he proposed a type of authority called "value-rational faith." This form is a belief in the importance of the value itself and that whatever contributes to the value is good. However, Weber never developed an authority based on this type of faith, leaving that to Rothschild-Whitt (1979). She proposed that this form of authority rests, not on the person as in charismatic authority, but on faith in the value of a rationalized set of norms, with obedience to methods that are useful in achieving the ends or desired values. Hence, in Rothschild-Whitt's collectives, in support of the value of participatory democracy, endless discussions are held over relatively trivial administrative matters. As noted in Chapter 2, volunteer-staffed organizations may be expected to range from extremely value-rational to bureaucratic legal-rational, but we can probably assume that all volunteers work in settings in which appeals to values can be made. They all work for organizations dedicated to service or to societal improvements, that is, for organizations dedicated to furthering a particular value. Although it has been noted that individual motives cannot be inferred from organizational goals, appeals based on the values of the organization would certainly be legitimate, even if not always completely effective. This form of control is elaborated below.

Control of volunteers through esteem

Etzioni (1975) argued that normative (a values-based) control consists of two components, "pure normative" and "social esteem." These observations concerning the mechanisms by which normative power is achieved are particularly relevant:

> There are two kinds of normative power. One is based on the manipulation of esteem, prestige, and ritualistic symbols (such as a flag or

benediction); the other, on allocation and manipulation of acceptance and positive response. Lacking better terms, we refer to the first kind as *pure normative power*, and to the second as *social power*. Social power could be treated as a distinct kind of power. But since powers are here classed according to the means of control employed, and since both social and pure normative power rest on the same set of means – manipulation of symbolic rewards – we treat these two powers as belonging to the same category.

(Etzioni 1975, p. 6)

These two forms of normative power are undoubtedly related, but unfortunately Etzioni did not provide an extended discussion of social power. He suggested that pure normative power is more useful from the viewpoint of the organization, since the hierarchy can control its exercise. In contrast, social power becomes organizational power only when the organization can influence the group's powers, as when a teacher uses the class climate to control a deviant child or when a union steward agitates the members to use their informal power to bring a deviant into line.

In his discussion of normative power, Etzioni did not devote extensive attention to voluntary associations or organizations but concentrated on the stronger normative settings, such as religious orders. One reason seems to be the weakness of "vertical relations" in volunteer-staffed organizations. However, he mentioned that he felt voluntary associations relied primarily on social power, with additional varying degrees of pure normative power.

Unfortunately, Etzioni did not discuss how this kind of power would be exercised. However, he did proffer the specific structures which facilitate the wielding of pure normative influence, and these ideas are useful for understanding the more value-rational kinds of volunteer-staffed organizations. He suggested that effective pure normative influence relies on (1) intensive socialization, (2) high selectivity of all members, or (3) both. These ensure that symbolic rewards used by the organization are valued by the members.

Yet these requirements seemed too stringent for many of the studied volunteer-staffed organizations, which were understaffed settings, and so accepted recruits with few barriers. There was no selectivity at all in these organizations, and no formal attention to socialization (although brief training was required by the relief agency, and skill training was provided at intervals for family planning volunteers and all volunteer firefighters). If these volunteer-staffed organizations achieved any consensus on values, it certainly was not achieved through selectivity or socialization.

Similarly, Etzioni further proposed that normative organizations will require greater consensus on normative expectations than will utilitarian or coercive organizations, with the degree of consensus dependent on the centrality of the activities to a particular organization.

This emphasis on the variability in the centrality of different values is worth elaborating with examples from the studied organizations. In none of these were volunteers unreliable when their actions directly affected the central mission of their organizations: relief volunteers got food to those who called; firefighters put out fires; family planning clinic volunteers were scrupulous in their medical procedures and education; day care center volunteers wouldn't dream of neglecting the children in their care; and volunteers in the orchestra may have skipped rehearsals, but never a concert. In each case, the potential damage of dereliction in these core areas was starkly visible to the volunteers. Unreliability was centered in the more abstract, peripheral areas, around those tasks for which the volunteer did not feel, for whatever reason, personally responsible. When volunteers could see the importance of their actions, they were reliable. (In the few cases where unreliability did occur on a core task, such as a missed concert, the volunteer was dismissed.)

The studied volunteers were selectively, not unthinkingly, unreliable. This selectivity has important implications, for it suggests that there is a control system operating but that it covers a narrower range of actions than controls in employee-staffed organizations. It also implies that "problematic unreliability" may result from differences in the definitions of "core tasks." This issue is explored below.

Finally, Etzioni (1975) suggested that persuasion is the actual mechanism by which values-based influence is exercised (see also Mason 1984). However, neither Etzioni nor any other theorist has described how this form of influence operates in organizations in practice, other than to note that charisma or personal influence is an important requirement for members of all ranks of the hierarchy in normative organizations. The charismatic power of key individuals did seem to play an important role in the sampled organizations and will be analyzed in detail in the next chapter.

Control of volunteers through self-selection

Gamson's (1968) work contributes to the present discussion through his insight into how voluntary associations, which must appeal to shared values to maintain control, do so without the careful selection and socialization procedures characteristic of stronger normative institutions. Like Etzioni, he also suggested that voluntary associations need to rely on selective recruitment to insure reliable behaviors: "Societies, like other forms of social organization, try to simplify their subsequent control problems by refusing entry to those elements most likely to aggravate such problems" (Gamson 1968, p. 117). He argued that self-selection dominates in the case of voluntary associations. Volunteers would not donate their time to organizations representing values they did not hold, a fact which may help to explain the volunteer reliability on core organizational tasks. This is also consistent with the evidence that these organizations tend to attract demographically homogeneous volunteers.

However, these general values provide only weak guidance for concrete control of workers' actions. The core values of many of these organizations, particularly the large established institutions, are usually quite broad and vague, leaving vast opportunity for disagreement about tactics and procedures. Further, many volunteers do not seem to exercise much selectivity in their decision to volunteer. For example, some are routed to specific organizations through general recruitment mechanisms (such as neighborhood voluntary action centers or community social service organizations). In addition, many large established organizations, such as museums and hospitals, attract volunteers who want to be of service but have only a general commitment to the broad values these institutions represent. Following from the discussion in Chapter 5, it could be that self-selection plays a role for these volunteers through selective retention rather than through initial self-selection.

Yet, although Gamson's insight probably holds true less often for the large matter-of-fact volunteer-staffed institutions, the more an organization is ideological or value-rational, the more likely it is that shared values through self-selection play a dominant role in control.

Control of values by leaders

The final social theorist to address values in organizational control is Wood (1981). His research examined the bases for beliefs in the legitimacy of leaders. He was concerned with the phenomenon of how American Protestant church leaders directed their churches to greater social activism on behalf of civil rights in the 1950s and 1960s and later on behalf of the poor, despite opposition to those public policies by a majority of church members. His analysis of why leaders were able to influence members to support organizational actions contrary to their own beliefs provides insight into how leaders of volunteers exert influence.

Wood argued that organizations of the type he calls "value-fostering organizations" are based on fundamental values that can provide the legitimacy for organizational actions. In the case of the religious organizations studied by Wood, leaders framed policies on social action to reflect the fundamental values of the church and then used those values as a basis for claiming legitimacy for controversial policies by bringing to consciousness the members' beliefs in those general values; that is, they encouraged members to apply the church's general values to specific policies (Wood 1981, p. 85).

Thus, Wood's study revealed church leaders who were actively changing and modifying members' beliefs, even when these actions risked the institutions themselves. These leaders did not respond to membership majority rule and did not see their roles as passively reflecting the memberships' views. Wood did not see the influence of values-based voluntary organizations over their members as necessarily weaker than that of other kinds of organizations.

Theorists of employee organizational behavior have noted the increased power that leaders can obtain by drawing on the goals, values, or mission of the organization. Selznick (1957) suggested that one of the primary functions of leaders is the articulation and embodiment of the organization's values. In addition, Barnard (1938) emphasized the importance of organizational goals in leaders' influence on subordinates' behavior, suggesting that collective goals are a basis for appeals for transcendence of individual objectives. Recently, Peters and Waterman (1982) have suggested that if they had to select "One truth that we were able to distill from the excellent companies research. . . . We might be tempted to reply, 'Figure out your value system' " (p. 279).

Each of these four social theorists emphasized the importance of values in the control of organizational volunteers. Certainly appeals to shared values can provide an important source of influence for organizational volunteers; however, these arguments do not completely capture the nature of influence in many kinds of volunteer-staffed organizations.

First, these theorists ignore the fact that volunteers frequently feel free to interpret the implementation of the organization's values in their own way. Even though volunteers may support the values the organization is seeking to promote, they are under no obligation to support the means chosen by others. Thus, the volunteers in the family planning clinic believed the values of the organization could be achieved without wearing smocks, and the telephone volunteers could help poor people receive food without asking questions about recipients' personal lives. Appeals to values must be credible, and many volunteers will not abdicate their judgment about these matters to someone else. In contrast to religious groups in which members of the clergy are usually assumed by the laity to have more insight into the implementation of core values, many organizational volunteers do not assume that their leadership has any particular insight that they lack.

Secondly, these organizations usually would not be expected to have a monopoly on the expression of values. Alternative vehicles (schisms) can be formed easily. Most of these organizations not only must influence through shared values but must do so in an environment in which the organization and its workers cannot claim any special monopoly.

Finally, these theorists provide little insight into how these procedures are operationalized at the individual level. What does it mean to "control through values"? For this, we must turn to the available evidence from organizational behavior.

INTERPERSONAL INFLUENCE

In contrast to the sociologists' general concern with maintaining collectivities, there has been comparatively negligible interest in understanding direct interpersonal influence. Even Etzioni (1975), who provided the most comprehensive discussion of control in voluntary associations, devoted his attention to the one mechanism – pure normative power – that could be analyzed at the institutional level, simply mentioning the more interpersonal social and charismatic power in passing. However, there are two available sources of information about actual organizational volunteer interpersonal influence. The first, Smith and Tannenbaum (1963), provided a comparison of relative hierarchical influence in a voluntary association and a business firm. The other information source is the present study.

Comparative interpersonal influence

Smith and Tannenbaum (1963) compared the relative influence of different hierarchical ranks in the League of Women Voters with the relative influence of groups in a national delivery company. Influence was measured by questionnaire items in which members of all ranks assessed the "actual" and the "ideal" influence exercised by the different ranks in their organization. They found that "rank-and-file" members of the League were reported to have significantly more actual and ideal influence than their counterparts in the delivery company. The researchers suggested this difference rested on the greater actual "reward and coercive power in the business firm," as well as on the fact that all members of the firm accepted and expected the hierarchical system of authority associated with business organizations. These results are consistent with common sense notions of the differences between these two kinds of organizations as reflected in Table 3.1 and provide an account for the observed greater unreliability of volunteers.

Yet this study was limited by its comparison of two very different kinds of organizations. The League of Women Voters has a primarily educational mission, and it is reasonable to suppose that educational organizations, whether staffed by employees or volunteers, extend relatively more influence to lower ranking members, such as professors and teachers, than do delivery companies who employ semiskilled drivers to complete very routinized and predictable work (under what can be assumed to be severe pressures for efficiency).

Replication and extension

Smith and Tannenbaum's original scales, as well as questions concerning organizational reward and sanction power, were given to volunteers and employees in the task-matched studied organizations to provide a test of their findings that controlled for task. Surprisingly, when controlling for organizational tasks, the hierarchical patterns of influence differed in important ways from those found by Smith and Tannenbaum (see Table 6.1). Consistent with their findings, the employees reported that their organizations' reward and sanction power over members was significantly greater than the reward and sanction power reported by the volunteers. Yet, surprisingly, this greater organizational power was not reflected in relatively greater influence for the officeholders and supervisors who represented the organization to the workers. Volunteers reported that their officeholders wielded significantly greater influence than did their employee counterparts. Thus, non-office-holding volunteers were judged to have more influence than employees doing comparable work, but so, too, did their officeholders. In volunteer-staffed organizations there did not seem to be any kind of trade-off in the relative influence of those at different hierarchical levels, with all participants reporting more influence than matched employee samples.

Table 6.1 Means and intercorrelations among power and influence variables

Variables	Volunteer $\bar{X}$	Employee $\bar{X}$	1	2	3	4
1. Organizational reward and sanction power	2.34	3.33**	–			
2. Officeholders' influence	3.82	2.04**	−01	–		
3. Non-officeholders' influence	4.08	1.96**	−20*	77**	–	
4. Personal influence	3.14	3.02	−03	07	11	–
5. Ideal personal influence	2.13	2.48**	26**	−17*	−37**	−49**

n = 216
* p ≤ .05
** p ≤ .01

Observational data also suggested a mismatch occurred in volunteer-staffed organizations between the reward and sanction of power and the influence of officeholders. This discrepancy in volunteer and employee influence appeared to result from two sources. First, all of the sampled employee-staffed organizations (except the gift shop and community newspaper) received governmental funding, either directly or indirectly, and with this funding came the civil service procedures and policies that tended to restrict the influence of supervisors. In addition, the employees of the poverty relief agency, orchestra, and fire department were unionized, which set additional limits on the influence of supervisors. Further, the employee-staffed organizations spent more and were more visible in their communities than were most of the sampled volunteer-staffed organizations. Leadership in these volunteer-run organizations had substantially more autonomy from external scrutiny, perhaps due to their small size and their "private character," than did the leadership of employee-staffed organizations doing the same work.

These volunteer-staffed organizations often found themselves in relationships with their environments that differed significantly from employee-staffed organizations, which in turn seemed to have important effects on internal influence and control. Volunteers donated their time and services to worthwhile services or ideas. When society had decided that these tasks deserved greater support through funding for employees, this support carried a cost. With societal support necessarily came scrutiny – income must be reported, employment regulations observed, and so forth. These volunteer-staffed organizations were simply more "peripheral" to the larger society's attention, and this feature provided a great deal of freedom for all organizational members.

The second reason for the comparatively high levels of volunteer officer influence appears to be that officer influence was expertise-based rather than position-based. Apparently these officeholders gained influence in their volunteer-staffed organizations because of their willingness to assume time-consuming responsibilities, not because of any authority inherent in their office. Since they spent more time on organizational matters than fellow part-time members did, they acquired greater expertise and knowledge. Rothschild-Whitt (1979) described how her ideologically egalitarian cooperatives implemented procedures to try to counteract this natural power imbalance that occurs when doing organizational work. Yet, since all of these organizations had as their primary purpose the delivery of some service to nonmembers, members did not seem to be particularly worried about these counter-egalitarian processes. In fact, for the most part, only the officeholders worried about their own "excessive" power. Table 6.1 indicates that these volunteers expressed a preference for significantly *less* influence than they presently held (a mean ideal personal influence of 2.13 compared to a reported actual influence of 3.14).

Cohesive groups and social power

Thus, formal office-holding did not have the same implications for influence in volunteer-staffed organizations as it did in employee-staffed ones. A better description of the patterns of influence in these settings is reflected in the distinction between core and peripheral members. Certainly it would seem plausible that core members would be expected to exert more social influence on one another than would peripheral members on either members of the core or on other peripheral members. That is, the groups of core volunteers could be viewed as what social psychologists have called "cohesive groups." The relative cohesiveness of a group has been defined as the relative attractiveness of the group to its members. A group with members who highly value their membership is a cohesive one. Social psychologists have presented evidence that the more cohesive the group is, the greater the conformity to fellow member influence (Shaw 1976); thus a cohesive work group operates a potentially powerful control system.

As noted earlier, for the studied core volunteers the social interaction taking place as part of organizational membership was a more important part of their lives than it was for peripherals, and thus they would be expected to be more likely to conform to social pressure exerted by other core volunteers. Similarly, this form of influence would be expected to be less powerful for peripheral members. Volunteers who were indifferent to the opinions of their co-workers would be much more likely to follow their own personal work standards, whether those standards were high, low, or simply inappropriate to the work situation, than would members of a cohesive work group (Nadler *et al.* 1979).

Further, the power of social conformity pressures would be expected to be greater for those volunteer-staffed organizations that played a more important role in volunteers' lives, even when they were not core group members. This may be because "the group" is the only available expression for certain values of volunteers. For example, Milofsky and Elion's (1987) rural alternative school embodied the counter-culture values of its members, and there were very limited alternatives in that setting. Similarly, recruitment based on personal contact would reinforce the social influence of other members, since expulsion or failure in the organization would be known by friends and family members. Thus, organizations having volunteers who value membership in good standing are more likely to be able to exert influence over one another, that is, to obtain more reliable behavior.

Table 6.2 Mean self-reports for core and peripheral volunteers

Variables	Core	Peripheral
Officeholders' influence	5.74	5.55
Non-officeholder's influence	3.00	2.88
Ideal officeholder's influence	5.84	5.62
Ideal non-officeholder's influence	3.26	3.22
Material rewards/instrumental gain	5.06	5.50
Material rewards/intrinsic interest	5.26	5.26
Symbolic rewards/service	5.90	5.46*
Symbolic rewards/social	5.67	5.37†
n	35	116

*p ≤ .05
†p ≤ .10

In fact, Table 6.2 indicates that core volunteers were more likely to report that they worked for the symbolic social and service rewards. The relatively greater importance that core volunteers placed on the social rewards of their jobs supports the argument that they, at least, are relatively more likely to submit to the interpersonal influence of fellow core group members. Further, the relatively more "altruistic pattern" of self-reported rewards by core group members indicates greater commitment to the organization's mission and hence more susceptibility to values-based normative influences. This pattern is consistent with the "martyred" role that Milofsky and Elion (1987) suggested activists in volunteer-staffed organizations needed to maintain their influence. This martyred leadership role is analyzed more thoroughly in the next chapter.

In summary, although appeals to shared values would be expected to play an important role in the coordination of volunteers' efforts (especially for value-rational organizations), they played a more limited role in the studied organizations. They seemed most salient only for those tasks that unambiguously expressed the organization's core mission, but they seemed less effective for "maintenance" types of activities. Rather, in these organizations, interpersonal influence was a more important force. Evidence from the studied organizations suggested that volunteers varied in the extent to which they would submit to one another's influence. The theoretical implications are explored below.

IMPLICATIONS

Observations of the studied organizations imply the existence of the following processes: the effects of interrupted group formation, the practice of selective unreliability, and the effects of the limited formal control of social influence.

Interrupted group formation

Volunteer-staffed organizations with practices that interfered with the formation of cohesive groups would be expected to forego an important source of control. This is reinforced by Mason's (1984) observation that "continuity of leadership" was one of the most important requirements for the effective management of volunteer-staffed organizations. Therefore, it is surprising how often volunteer-staffed organizations seem actively to discourage the formation of cohesive core groups of volunteers. Many volunteers join these organizations through personal contacts and report that the social contact of volunteering is a salient reward, and so they would seem ready to value a cohesive work group. Yet those making staffing decisions often do not take the social setting of volunteers into account when placing them. The way new volunteers in the family planning clinic and student newspaper were simply "slotted into" an available task if they came to work was noted in Chapter 3. Large institutions also use volunteers to "fill in." Thus, the volunteers work with different co-workers at different times, and this, compounded by their part-time status, can make the formation of stable social relationships all but impossible. Staffing practices like these actively destroy one of the most powerful incentives available to volunteer-staffed organizations.

Similar control problems are created in those organizations that are staffed, either through policy or necessity, by volunteers with a known finite tenure in the organization. Students who volunteer are a prominent example. They volunteer for training or as a contribution while they are in school, and the organization knows it can have, at best, only a few years of their time (often only a few months). Thus, these volunteers have no strong investment in the social approval of their co-workers, and in many cases they know that they are not likely to ever see those fellow workers again after a few months. This, rather than any particular character flaws in young adults, is probably the more parsimonious explanation for the notorious unreliability of student volunteers.

Most remarkably, some volunteer-staffed organizations adopt formal policies that disrupt the formation of cohesive work groups in their organizations. Requirements for the rotation of offices, justified as fostering wider participation or providing "training," are examples. When offices are rotated frequently, incumbents know they will soon step out of that role. The relationships they form in completing that work are short-lived (they may continue to interact with the same people, but not as their treasurer, for example). Therefore, these temporary incumbents have little incentive to ensure that difficult or controversial decisions are made. The best example is the continual battles between the gift shop's chairwoman and the manager described in the following chapter. All of these gift shop officeholders were always "new," others always forgave their errors because of the incumbents' newness, and all were continually frustrated and (publicly) silent. This pattern seems to be broken only under circumstances of relatively permanent – and often charismatic – leadership. The influence of such leaders is analyzed in more detail in the next chapter.

The importance of cohesive groups in volunteer-staffed organizations is also illustrated by an example of volunteers' responses to events staged for them in the absence of strong social ties. Nadler et al. (1979) have argued that cohesive organizational work groups are most likely to be built around the "real work" of participants. This may be particularly powerful for volunteers who were attracted by the organization's mission. Separated social events may work well as "group builders" for full-time employees, who have had ample time to get to know one another, but for peripheral volunteers most fellow workers are strangers and, therefore, such a gathering would be a different sort of experience for them than for core volunteers or employee planners.

For example, one of the most disturbing events reported by core members of the poverty relief agency concerned the potluck dinner they organized to "thank" the organization's volunteers. They were humiliated when only a handful of the volunteers even bothered to show up for this event. In this organization, many volunteers worked short shifts once a month, and most volunteers really knew only the coordinators and a few other prominent core volunteers. Even when working, they spent their time in their own homes on the phone or driving deliveries of food to clients. They hadn't attended the banquet in their honor because they didn't expect to see friends, and they were happy to continue to work a few hours a month to help the poor in their community. Unfortunately, the members who had worked hard to stage the event were hurt and angry, and more than one blamed "apathetic volunteers." It would seem the importance of strong social relationships, which develop among full-time employees whether or not they are wanted, was not well understood by those working with volunteers.

Selective unreliability and crystallized norms

Above it was noted that volunteers were not indiscriminatingly unreliable but selective in their insubordination. One way of trying to understand this selectivity is by drawing on the work of social psychologists who have studied the relative clarity of norms or normative expectations in groups. This research suggests that group members are not always clear or in agreement about what constitute the "important behaviors" (Shaw 1976).

There was, indeed, a great deal of uncertainty among volunteers concerning what was expected in these organizations. Many volunteer-run organizations seem to be continually in the process of clarifying their expectations about appropriate tasks. For some volunteers, this process of definition may itself be an important aspect of membership. For example, members of a particular public interest or "rights" organization may enjoy the debate and articulation of their group's missions at least as much as the actions they undertake for their goals. Of course, distinguishing when such activities are simply expressive and when they are signs of dysfunctional uncertainty is difficult, even for many of the participants.

Norms, like more formal rules, become crystallized when the membership has decided that particular behaviors are important enough to the group that reliable action is necessary. It is often the case that a group member who differs with the rest of the group about appropriate behavior (social psychologists call them "deviants") can help a group to crystallize and articulate important behaviors (Dentler and Erikson 1959). Yet again, the freedom and independence volunteers enjoy may lead them to quit rather than to suffer the social pressure resulting from their different views. Hence, volunteer groups may have poorly crystallized norms simply because dissenters leave too quickly, that is, before forcing members to clarify and articulate their expectations.

Interestingly, there is some evidence from the studied organizations that expectations were knowingly kept vague due to a mistaken assumption that volunteers will not tolerate structured work relationships. Volunteer officeholders were consistently pressed by the researcher to explain why unreliability was tolerated. Respondents would often suggest their lack of power or the pressures of understaffing described above. However, the studied organizations with the least tolerance for unreliability had less turnover than the tolerant organizations. For example, the day care center, the family planning clinic, and the fire department were quick to describe the actions that would lead to a volunteer's being fired, and they could recount their most recent experience in terminating a volunteer. It seemed as if many officeholders in the other organizations simply assumed their volunteers would not work under stringent, clear work expectations and, therefore, none were provided. Some organizations survived this debilitating laissez-faire climate by substituting a dedicated core group with high levels of commitment who completed virtually all of the organization's work.

It is also worth noting that the matter-of-fact institutions that cannot rely on social network recruiting and cohesive work groups often provide a very structured, even "bureaucratic," environment for their volunteers. When volunteers work for large established nonprofit organizations that are dominated by employees, they work at relatively low-skilled jobs and are subject to formal organizational controls. In these cases, new volunteers usually receive training and manuals and are treated in many other respects like the employees working within formal control systems. Thus, it seems that volunteer-staffed organizations maintain control through either strong social influence or clear formal procedures, or a combination of the two.

The use of either a cohesive core group or a formal organizational structure in the studied organizations seemed to be influenced by organizational size. When volunteer-staffed organizations grow in size, they face potentially insurmountable problems in the use of cohesive groups for control (and simply scheduling all of the volunteers becomes overwhelming). Organizations often manage this by decentralizing into autonomous local chapters – as was the case for Sills' (1957) National Foundation for Infantile Paralysis, the sampled family planning clinic, and the sampled volunteer poverty relief agency (both the clinic and the agency were affiliated with similar ones throughout the United States). In fact, the largest of these small organizations (poverty relief agency and gift shop) reported substantial difficulties in managing their scheduling tasks, had the greatest proportion of peripheral members, and relied more on formal structuring of work than did the smaller organizations. Note, also, that the tasks in these two largest organizations required significantly less skill than was needed for the others (day care center, newspaper, orchestra, family planning clinic, and fire department), and so surveillance could be more distant and formalized.

Limited organizational control of interpersonal influence

Since cohesive groups seem to have such potential for reducing the unreliability problems of organizational volunteers, it is noteworthy that Etzioni (1975) argued against this form of control. He suggested that group influence isn't always exercised in the interests of the organization. Informal interpersonal influence can encourage favorable actions, such as working hard and maintaining high quality standards, or can encourage restricted production and the withholding of information – actions that do not contribute to overall effectiveness. Therefore, a group with powerful interpersonal influence over its members is not necessarily beneficial to the larger organization. There is ample evidence that employees in cohesive groups respond readily to the influence of fellow group members, even when it contradicts the organization's reward system and results in a loss of income (Nadler *et al.* 1979; Whyte 1955; Roethlisberger and Dickson 1939). It is for this reason that Etzioni (1975) argued for the hierarchical manipulation of esteem and prestige, since these are more easily controlled by the organization.

Yet, however controllable purely normative incentives are, they cannot be effective unless they are valued by the membership. And the value placed on these symbolic rewards is determined socially – through consensus. Even more widespread than the stories of volunteer unreliability are the withering observations of failed attempts to manipulate prestige symbols. Jokes about the indiscriminate granting of impressive titles (with pointed reference to the absence of salary) are routine in volunteer-staffed organizations. Certificates, awards, and the right to wear certain articles can be either ludicrous or profoundly moving depending on whether or not they represent the good opinion of valued others. Particularly for the sampled volunteer-staffed organizations, which were not dominant social institutions in their communities, officeholders simply could not assume that their own declaration of the symbolic value of something would necessarily be accepted by the rest of the membership. The poverty relief volunteers' indifference to the laudatory banquet held in their honor is but one example of how prestige symbols can flop. Volunteer-staffed organizations of the kind described here do not have strong vertical structures of either prestige or power. These organizations cannot avoid their dependence on the interpersonal influence of their members.

CONCLUSIONS

Volunteers are not as dependent on their organizations as are employees, and their independence, combined with societal assumptions about the relative tractability of volunteers and employees, leads to less volunteer subordination to the system of organizational behavior. Subsequent variability, as attractive as it may seem to the volunteers, can create serious difficulties for organizations seeking to provide a reliable service to outsiders or to achieve goals that require smoothly integrated activities. Yet volunteer-staffed organizations continue to provide numerous services, many doing so with only limited problems of volunteer unreliability. In this chapter it has been suggested that the control of potentially unreliable volunteers is achieved primarily through interpersonal influence, appeals to shared values, and selection of task and domain. The first two have been introduced and will be examined in depth in the next two chapters, so the concluding comments will focus on the third mechanism.

The selection of particular tasks or domains provides the basis by which shared values and interpersonal influence can be exercised. As noted earlier in this work, appeals to values are a fragile form of social control. They are not weak when they can be mustered (see Wood 1981), but they are effective only under certain conditions. Organizational volunteers must share the values, see that their efforts directly contribute to those values, and believe that the individuals to whom they submit share those values. Such conditions imply that these organizations must necessarily be restricted to those values, ideas, or services that can appeal to a sufficient number of volunteers. For most organizations, the appeal lies in helping the less fortunate or contributing to a better community. Sometimes organizations that do glamorous or interesting work can attract volunteers (such as the orchestra and the fire department studied here). Volunteer-staffed organizations find that their missions go in and out of fashion, which directly impacts their ability to attract and retain volunteers. Thus, the use of appeals to shared values suggests a fundamental restriction of volunteer-staffed organizations to certain service domains and attractive tasks.

Similarly, it has been noted that work that clearly contributed to the organization's mission was reliably done. In fact, it was the managerial, maintenance, and support tasks which experienced the most reliability problems. This paradox – the shirking by volunteers of those managerial or "leadership" roles which hold such attraction to comparable employees – is examined in the following chapter.

Finally, as noted above, volunteer-staffed organizations can maintain better control through interpersonal influence when they remain small enough to maintain face-to-face relationships. Thus, volunteer-staffed organizations restrict themselves to limited (and, perhaps, to more concrete and attractive) tasks. The sampled volunteer-staffed organizations simply did less – the day care did not provide lunches, the orchestra played fewer and less demanding concerts, the fire department did not undertake fire prevention education, and the poverty relief agency did not attempt longer-term solutions to their clients' poverty. In other words, an important way in which control was maintained was by restricting what the organization did to the less demanding, as well as the more attractive, domains.

Although the observation of the restriction of volunteer-staffed task and domain would seem obvious, in practice many of the failures of volunteer-staffed organizations seem to stem from an inadequate analysis of what would attract volunteers to join the organization and motivate them to conform to organizational requirements. The practical steps for those concerned with designing tasks for volunteers are offered in Chapter 9. The following chapter completes the analysis of volunteer unreliability with detailed attention to the role of leadership and to the effects of the presence of employees.

Chapter 7

The management of interpersonal influence

In the previous chapter, the role of interpersonal influence in the integration of volunteers' actions into the system of organizational behavior was introduced. Here several features of the management of these processes in the volunteer-staffed organizations are selected for detailed attention. The features that seemed to distinguish the studied volunteer-staffed organizations with problematic unreliability from more effective ones were lack of charismatic leadership, the problem of attracting members to assume the additional burdens of holding office, and the poor relationships between paid staff and volunteers.

CHARISMATIC LEADERSHIP

Charismatic or personal leadership provided an important source of stability and direction in these organizations, and when it was missing, severe problems arose. Charismatic leadership is the power a leader has over a follower based on the personal qualities of the leader:

> The term "charisma" will be applied to a certain quality of an individual personality by virtue of which he is set apart from ordinary men and treated as endowed with supernatural, superhuman, or at least specifically exceptional powers or qualities. These are such as are not accessible to the ordinary person, but are regarded as divine in origin or as exemplary, and on the basis of them the individual concerned is treated as a leader.
> (Weber 1968, pp. 358–9)

As this quotation indicates, charismatic authority centers on the devotion of followers to powerful religious or political leaders, and at first glance it may seem inapplicable to the workaday organizational world. Yet charismatic leadership in organizations is gaining attention (Conger and Kanungo 1987; Trice and Beyer 1986; Bass 1985; House and Baetz 1979). Conger and Kanungo (1987) reviewed the empirical research on charismatic leadership in organizations and stated that certain personal attributes of charismatic leaders have been consistently identified: vision or ideological goals, behavior that instills confidence, ability to inspire, self-confidence, dominance, and rhetorical ability. In addition, they proposed several characteristics of the relationships between followers and their charismatic leaders: followers' trust, willing obedience, affection, feelings that they are able to contribute to the leader's mission, and shared beliefs. This kind of devotion appeared to be present in those volunteer-staffed organizations with the most effective coordination and fewest unreliability problems.

The indifference volunteers felt toward formal office has already been described. As indicated by the family clinic volunteers' refusal to wear smocks and the poverty relief volunteers' neglect of organizational procedures, to a greater extent than employees, these volunteers felt free of formal hierarchical commands. Rather, in these volunteer-staffed organizations, as in many employee-staffed ones, members allowed themselves to be guided by others because of the personal qualities of those others. This form of authority may or may not have had the emotional and spiritual intensity of the stereotypical charismatic religious leader. For example, in the studied organizations, it was more often based on a rather dispassionate respect for the individuals' expertise. However strong the intensity of the relationship, it was fundamentally a personal rather than a bureaucratic form of authority.

This personal charismatic authority is vested not necessarily in one particular individual, but sometimes in a small cadre that Milofsky and Elion (1987) have characterized as "activists," who were usually called "the leadership." The studied organizations all had a core leadership group, as has been indicated, yet these particular organizations also were dominated by single individuals. This individual dominance may have derived from the paucity of paid staff members, or perhaps from other reasons related to their technologies (e.g. orchestras are rarely egalitarian, but are dominated by the artistic vision of their musical directors). Therefore, an understanding of the management of interpersonal influence in these organizations begins with a description of the effects of charismatic individuals on them.

It probably isn't surprising that forms of influence based on individual personality should play such a large role in these small organizations. The studied volunteer-staffed day care center, poverty relief agency, orchestra, and family planning clinic each had a "beloved founder" who seemed to assume almost mythical dimensions. These founders were all still "involved," if not currently holding formal offices. The one organization with a charismatic leader who was not a founder was the fire department, which had recently celebrated its 125th year. The leading individual – the fire chief – had been a firefighter for 40 years and followed his father before him in the single paid position of town fire marshal and elected (volunteer) fire chief. His son was the youngest captain ever to be elected. Since this fire department had existed for over a century, the chief was not actually a founder, but he was certainly the dominant figure, and it was inconceivable that he would lose reelection, since no one would dream of opposing him.

The heroic stature of the founders was reinforced through stories of the difficulties they had to overcome in founding the day care center, the poverty relief agency, the orchestra, and the family planning clinic. The stories of the establishment of these organizations contained similar patterns of "opposition" or difficulties which the founders overcame. The volunteer-staffed day care center was founded by a woman who discovered that the divinity school where she and her husband were both beginning graduate study had no child care for their infant. She struggled valiantly against the opposition of the divinity school dean, who was reported to "be opposed to the day care center because it would encourage divinity students to have children instead of waiting until their studies were completed." Similarly, the founder of the poverty relief agency continued to work tirelessly in recruiting volunteers, overcoming the complacency of suburbanites who assumed that there were no hungry people in their community. Everyone contacted, even the most peripheral volunteer, knew and revered her. The musical director of the volunteer-staffed orchestra grappled with financial austerity to continue to receive the meager funding from his employer necessary to provide free symphony concerts. Finally, the chapter chair-woman of the volunteer family planning clinic had founded the chapter when she moved to that town several decades ago. Her state had had very restrictive laws governing the dispensing of birth control at that time, and she loved recounting the caravans she would organize one night a week to drive over the bridge to the less restrictive neighboring state. She was very proud of her own involvement in the court case in which the Supreme Court declared that it was an invasion of privacy for the states to restrict women's access to birth control.

In each of these organizations there was a leader who not only embodied the values of the organization but who worked tirelessly for it. The sheer number of hours given by these individuals to their voluntary positions was staggering, with the highest being the nearly 40 hours a week reported for the family planning clinic's chapter chairwoman.

The impact of these individuals was as strong as that of any other success-ful entrepreneur. Their views of their organization's mission predominated. For example, the founder of the poverty relief agency believed that the suburbanization of society allowed residents to "hide from" the poverty of their fellow citizens. For this reason the organization decided against the practice of similar organizations – the establishment of "centers" in the poorer neighborhoods where residents could walk over and pick up their food. Rather they retained the "inefficient" system of volunteers to staff telephones and deliver the food to the clients' homes. She felt that it was as important to get the middle class into those neighborhoods and talking to their residents as it was to get food and transportation to the indigent. Similarly, the chapter chairwoman's vision of the distinct contribution of a voluntary family planning clinic was instrumental in obtaining state support for their clinic:

> When talking about why they had restarted their clinic even though the local hospital now ran one, the chapter chairwoman said "Well, you know we have the missionary zeal. The hospital has so many serious problems, people are dying and that's what they are geared for. If someone forgets to take her pill, they yell at her. You can't do that."
>
> (Field notes, 6/9)

These founding champions attracted adherents who shared their personal visions. In addition, their energetic work for their organizations also meant that they had the knowledge about organizational affairs – Wilensky's (1967) organizational intelligence – that a lengthy and full-time involvement brings. Thus, these successful leaders shared two characteristics: a personal vision of the organization's contribution to the community, and excellent technical knowledge about the mechanics of revenue, licenses, and organization, as well as professional expertise when appropriate (family planning and firefighting).

However, this combination of personal vision and technical expertise does not sufficiently convey the degree of emotional attachment these individuals inspired. The potential for schisms in voluntary associations has been described, and these five organizations had been able to avoid these splits through what Milofsky and Elion (1987) described as the "activists' images as self-sacrificing martyrs" for their organizations.

In each of these organizations, the mention of the leader's name would evoke anecdotes about their contributions to the organization – their time commitment or some action that exemplified the values the organization was promoting. Some indication of the relatively more altruistic contributions of these individuals is suggested by the core–periphery comparisons in Tables 3.2 and 6.2, which indicate that core members worked significantly more hours, reported greater job demands, and had motives that were relatively more service- and social-oriented compared to the more instrumental peripheral volunteers.

These leaders not only held technical expertise and rallied members to their vision of its mission, but the members also "owed" the leaders. That is, the peripherally involved felt an obligation to these contributors. However much nonleaders contributed, their leaders contributed more.

The importance of this potent combination of vision, technical expertise, and martyrdom can best be seen in the two organizations that did not have it. Both the student-run newspaper and the volunteer-staffed gift shop had bylaws requiring the rotation of offices on a yearly basis. Further, these two organizations also restricted potential volunteers to a finite time period (college students for the newspaper, and a required "graduation" out of the gift shop's parent association in early adulthood). These bylaws stemmed from the fact that both organizations identified themselves as providers of "training" for their members. This is a common pattern for many volunteer-staffed organizations, and its serious limitations for both commitment-building and the use of social influence have been described.

There is no question that one of the reasons for the collapse of the student newspaper was that the editor-in-chief did not command the personal influence of comparable leaders in the other studied organizations. He was acknowledged to be technically expert, holding the skills and standards of professional journalism, but he had not been successful either in recruiting those who shared his standards or in fostering them among his editors. He specifically attributed his difficulties to the fact that there was no journalism major at that college – implying that he could not obtain volunteer editors and reporters with sufficient training or professionalism. Yet, he saw himself and was seen by others as forwarding his own journalism career, and he laid, therefore, no special claim to a vision for the newspaper or to martyrdom. In his very understaffed setting, he became editor-in-chief for his journalistic skills, not because of his interpersonal or leadership skills. He did not personally have a commitment to this particular student newspaper (only to decent professional standards) and, therefore, could neither attract nor obligate other committed participants.

The absence of charismatic leadership in the volunteer gift shop stemmed from different sources. The shop was owned by the parent voluntary association primarily as a fundraising enterprise. It was run by an elected shop committee, with the chairship of the committee rotating every year. The shop committee was responsible for the gift shop, and members joined the committee full of enthusiasm for the kinds of gifts and displays they would like to see. However, the shop also had a full-time paid shop manager who had worked in retailing for several decades, and clashes between the manager and committee chair occurred every year:

> Another problem stems from the temporary leadership of the shop. The chairwomen have difficulty asserting authority over the long-term manager, what's more [the volunteer] reported that the manager tries to suppress problems, because she sees each one as a temporary personality problem that will be solved in a few months. [A different volunteer] suggested that another problem is that the manager's "bosses" also work for her as sales clerks. . . . there are constant clashes over display, marketing and purchase of merchandise.
>
> (Field notes, 7/30)

It seems that stocking and displaying merchandise in a gift shop was a matter of personal taste that provided many opportunities for disagreements. Volunteers became shop committee chairs because they wanted to make shop improvements according to their own tastes. Neither the shop manager nor the committee members accepted the legitimacy of the other's dominance in this area, with continual strife and bad feelings as a result. That this organization did not fail completely, as did the student-run newspaper, was due in part, perhaps, to committee members who had important relationships with other members of the parent association and did not want to harm them by abandoning this important fundraising entity. However, the continual animosity was well known and had led to frequent reconsideration of whether or not the shop was "worth it."

In summary, those organizations that had individual leaders who had strong personal visions for the missions of their organizations and technical and interpersonal expertise, as well as a martyr image, were able to keep their organizations from disintegration. Through example and persuasion, they were able to attract other volunteers and to keep them working reliably enough to maintain the organizations. The two studied organizations that did not have individual leaders with all three of these characteristics experienced dissension severe enough to destroy the one and to threaten the survival of the other.

Yet, as effective as the charismatic-leader solution was for the immediate problems of control, it left these organizations very dependent on a single individual. In fact, House (1977) suggested that charismatic leadership in (employee-staffed) organizations may be dysfunctional for the long-term health of the organization, whatever its short-term benefits in high employee commitment. Organizations dependent on single individuals are vulnerable, since that individual can leave, or his or her interests can change. This dependence highlights the limitations of a sole reliance on interpersonal influence for organizational control. It is unstable (Smelser 1962) and highly dependent on the skill and dedication of one or a few individuals. Thus it isn't surprising that the management of interpersonal influence also involves practices that seek to build stability and reduce dependence. In fact, each of the studied organizations had tried to compensate by both the active recruitment of other core members and hiring employees. However, the first solution proved difficult for these organizations and the latter changes the social dynamics underlying the use of charismatic leadership. The management of these approaches is analysed below.

RECRUITMENT TO THE CORE

Of course some volunteers moved from the periphery to the core because of their personal interest in the organization's mission or in these kinds of roles. Yet, in each of the studied organizations, the supply of naturally inclined individuals was not sufficient to complete the organization's work, and members of the core were continually recruiting among the peripheral volunteers. The primary vehicle through which they tried to obtain "greater involvement" of fellow volunteers was through the recruitment of volunteers to formal offices. These officeholders held the formal authority in these organizations; examples include captains in the fire department (who directed firefighters at the scene of a fire), treasurers (who were responsible for allocating and monitoring the finances), board or committee members (who collectively were responsible for the organizations). The allocation of responsibility and authority is as necessary to volunteer-staffed organizations as it is to other formal organizations seeking to achieve objectives. Yet all of the volunteer-staffed organizations had difficulty recruiting members to these positions, which was in striking contrast to the strong interest many employees had in comparable positions.

The relative permanence of officeholders in volunteer-staffed organizations has been widely noted by students of voluntary associations (Michels 1959; Rose 1954; Sills 1957). They have uniformly characterized the problem as resulting from the indifference or "apathy" of the majority of volunteers. These theorists have gone on to analyze several of the structural features of these associations that contribute to greater amounts of membership apathy; these include large organizational size, specialized tasks, and the development of a leadership with a vested interest in perpetuating its position.

However, observations in the studied volunteer- and employee-staffed organizations suggested that apathy was not an accurate or useful characterization of the causes of members' office avoidance. The term apathy implies a lack of emotion, a listlessness or disinterest. Rather, it appeared that avoidance of formal offices in these organizations could be better explained as a calculated intention to avoid the burdens of holding office. To be fair to these previous nonpsychologists, the actual exploration of members' cognitions and affect was not their intention. They used the term "apathy" to refer to a structural phenomenon without considering the individuals' actual dispositions. Unfortunately, this affect attribution has been accepted unthinkingly.

There can be no doubt that these volunteers and employees had opposing views on assuming authority. In the volunteer-staffed organizations responsibility could be obtained simply by seeking it (by pursuing an office) or by acquiescing to it (by relenting in the face of entreaties). However, as noted above, offices were not widely sought, and, in fact, often were actively avoided by these volunteers. Never in the histories of the day care center, poverty relief agency, and family planning clinic had there been enough volunteers interested in board positions to actually hold contested elections. In contrast, formal positions of authority in the employee-staffed organizations (supervisory jobs) were aggressively sought after and difficult to obtain. In practice, they involved "promotions" – and the pyramidal nature of these organizations meant that many could never assume these coveted positions, no matter how well qualified they were.

These differences were reflected in members' responses reported in Table 6.1. Although there were no differences between volunteers and employees in actual personal influence, the employees wanted significantly more influence than did the volunteers; further, many volunteers reported a preference for less organizational influence than they currently held (a 2 indicates "about the same influence I have now") while no employees – neither supervisors nor rank-and-file workers – expressed that desire.

An examination of what employees and volunteers actually said about positions of responsibility in their organizations provided further indication of the polarity of their views. The following employed firefighter's response to the question of "Would you like another job in this organization?" was typical:

> Sure, everyone wants to move up, but there's nowhere for me to go really. There are 36 firefighters and only four battalion chief jobs. I would have to wait for one of them to retire or be promoted, and when is that going to be? Five years or more.
>
> (Firefighter, employee-staffed fire department)

The employee-staffed family planning clinic is another example. Job level was dependent on educational credentials as well as merit. The highest ranking administrative officer held a master's degree in administration and the highest ranking clinical officer was a nurse-practitioner. Their subordinates could not be promoted to these positions without additional education.

The following reports by volunteers stand in contrast: the first, from a non-office-holding volunteer, and the second, from an officeholder, were typical of the responses of volunteers to the interview question, "How much say would you say you personally had in the way things are done around here?"

> Just a vote. Really, I'm happy with what I have. I've got no time for more responsibility.
>
> (A parent who was a teacher's assistant, volunteer-staffed day care center)

> Quite a bit, if I want to use it. My judgment is respected in the center. Maybe I have too much; I would like to see other people more involved.
>
> (Treasurer, volunteer-staffed day care center)

These themes – that responsibility requires time and that leadership is exercised through personal qualities ("respect") rather than position power – were common among volunteers. The "time" requirements of leadership positions seemed to be a paramount consideration (see Table 3.2). The requirement that volunteer officeholders contribute more of their "free-time" appeared to be the major barrier to peripheral volunteer interest in pursuing core roles.

It appears that the primary reason why these volunteers avoided offices while employees actively pursued comparable positions was that formal authority positions in these two types of organizations offered very different amenities. Higher positions in employee-staffed organizations brought perquisites in addition to the ability to influence policy. The supervision of employees is usually characterized by higher salary, more autonomy, less tedious work, more clerical assistance, and more status symbols, such as a private office. In the studied volunteer-staffed organizations, those holding formal authority positions received none of these perquisites. In fact, their tasks were more tedious – more meetings and proportionately less time in direct contact with clients. Most importantly, holding office was more time-consuming – officeholders were responsible for certain tasks and had to do these tasks themselves if no one else could be found to help. For example, the treasurer might have to type the annual financial report or the president might spend a day in the office answering the phone if no other volunteer could be found to do this work. The very term "activist" implies an individual who takes on tasks, and holding office is simply a mechanism for insuring that an individual has a "contract" to take responsibility for certain types of tasks. In short, in volunteer-staffed organizations, holding office entails the promise to commit more labor, provides no more real autonomy than any other volunteer has, and results in virtually none of the reward power available to many employee supervisors.

There is little need to refer to such psychological constructs as "membership apathy." When volunteers have little to gain and much to lose by assuming offices in their organizations, it is clearly in their self-interest to maintain their peripheral status. It is only necessary to posit that the benefits for those who do assume offices – such as greater impact on the organization's direction, instrumental personal contacts, a sense that one is contributing in a vital way to the community, and the like – outweigh the substantial costs. With evidence of salient punishments for officeholders, there seems little need to posit vague affective states as explanations for other members' indifference to them. Even researchers such as Barber (1950) and Sills (1957), who also developed structural explanations for volunteer avoidance of office-holding, retain the term "apathy" in their discussions. Among the studied volunteers, there was no evidence that inactivity derived from a lack of feeling or interest. Holding office was merely too costly.

Before the construct of apathy can be dismissed completely, it is important to note that the previous research on member apathy was conducted in large organizations, while the studied volunteer-staffed organizations were small (see Appendix, Table A.2). There are three reasons why apathy may be less likely in smaller organizations. First, psychologists argue that tension – or emotion – is more evident in smaller groups (Bales 1950), and so the small size of the sampled organizations could act to counteract that affectless state. Second, in larger organizations the routes to leadership positions are probably longer and more difficult. Volunteers in larger organizations may be more likely to shrink in the face of this more forbidding effort. Finally, larger organizations are probably able to marshal more economic resources than small ones (they can tap more potential contributors and are more visible in their communities). This could result in more of a "vested interest" for the activist core to protect (e.g. the larger volunteer-run organizations are more likely to pay salaries). Therefore, it is quite plausible that the studied organizations were simply too small for apathy to develop and for an entrenched oligarchy to have attractive positions to protect.

However, they were not too small for the majority of members to avoid active participation. It may be that an emotional state, such as apathy, is present in larger organizations but it may not be the sole reason why the majority of volunteers avoid activism. It seems plausible that membership apathy is epiphenomenal to broad membership inactivity, not a cause of it.

Finally, one interesting result of this difference in the relative benefits received by officeholders in the studied volunteer-staffed and employee-staffed organizations is that members tended to attribute different motives to their officeholders. Volunteers, although they may have disagreed with some members of the core or not cared for them personally, were always quick to praise core members' selflessness and commitment to the organiz-ation. Core volunteers were respected because they were seen as "giving" a great deal to the organization and its mission. This is, perhaps, another demonstration of Staw's (1976) contention that attributions of personal causality are made in the absence of apparent extrinsic inducements for the activity. It also coincides with Milofsky and Elion's (1987) analysis of the martyred role required of the activists in their rural alternative school.

In contrast, employees did not attribute altruism to their supervisors. These employees often respected their leaders' knowledge, liked them per-sonally, and feared or resented them, but they did not praise their selfless dedication. Core volunteers were viewed as giving more than they received, whereas ranking employees were seen as receiving, if not more than they gave, at least enough to reward them amply for their work.

In practical terms, this avoidance of volunteer offices would be expected to affect the organizations negatively. First, as noted above, it left these organizations dependent on one or a very few individuals who were willing to work at genuinely self-sacrificial levels to keep the organization going. In fact, because of the paucity of individuals to do many tasks, these organizations were often prey to one of the most damaging cycles in volunteer-staffed organizations: the few dedicated and reliable volunteers are heaped with more and more work until they become exhausted and find that the only way they can break the cycle is by leaving the organization completely (commonly called "burn out"). Thus many volunteer-staffed organizations punish, rather than reward, their best workers.

Six of the studied volunteer-staffed organizations avoided the pitfall of punishing the meritorious through reasonably precise job descriptions and clear hours of obligation. Only one had a debilitating vicious circle – the student-run newspaper. Editors did not rely on their reporters (sometimes sending two on a story or going along themselves). The reporters did not feel necessary and so wouldn't turn in a story; then the editor had to write it him- or herself. Thus the editors found they were spending even more thankless hours "covering for unreliable volunteers."

In addition, with offices being the most severely understaffed settings within these understaffed organizations we might expect that job performance criteria would be substantially lower than within the comparably overstaffed positions of the employee-staffed organizations. That is, the overall quality of the management of volunteer-staffed organizations could not be expected to be very high. Certainly it was true that newly appointed (or more accurately, strong-armed) treasurers may never have examined a budget before being thrust into the job. This is one of the reasons these organizations depended so completely on their experienced founders and a small group of long-term core members. Alternatively, the time requirements of these positions can provide a face-saving option for those who have not performed their functions well. They may relinquish their positions for rank-and-file membership roles, claiming other demands on their time, whereas employee-staffed organizations may retain poor supervisors because demotion may be seen as too extreme or as blows to their status.

In summary, volunteers were much less likely than employees to pursue formal positions of responsibility. It was argued that this could be understood better when viewed as the result of the differences in the benefits and costs of holding these positions in these two types of organizations rather than as an affective state like apathy. While employees' supervisors receive many perquisites in addition to the ability to influence organizational policy, volunteers receive few or none of these and must normally expend even greater amounts of their free time in the organization's service. This phenomenon contributes to vicious circles of membership irresponsibility and officeholder burn out, as well as to organizational inefficiency. Interestingly, the most popular method by which these organizations are made more adroit is through the retention of employees. The introduction of employees into volunteer-staffed organizations presents a new and complex set of interpersonal pressures, and they are now examined.

VOLUNTEER–EMPLOYEE RELATIONS

Most organizational volunteers work with employees, and employees are almost always members of the organization's core. As noted in the introductory chapters, whether or not organizational workers are paid for their work has powerful effects on the workers' own and others' expectations of their behavior. When volunteer-staffed organizations introduce employees into their organizations to work alongside and over volunteers, this has profound implications for the interpersonal relationships in the organization.

Tensions seem to result from the fact that employees combine high status (based on the organizational intelligence developed through more continuous work in the organization as well as on the value ascribed to "professionalism" in many occupational settings) with the implicit rejection of the importance of self-sacrifice that results from their "taking" of salaries. That is, employees have both more legitimacy (expertise) and less legitimacy (they are not as dedicated) than their volunteer co-workers, and this contradiction creates tensions that require skillful management.

Before discussing this tension, it is important to note that the following discussion is based on volunteer–employee relations in a particular kind of setting – one in which the volunteers unambiguously dominate and run the organization. As can be seen in a summary of the roles played by employees in the seven volunteer-staffed organizations studied (Table 7.1), there were very few employees in these organizations. Recall that these particular volunteer-staffed organizations were selected as representative of ones that do work similar to that done by employees and that they were controlled by the volunteers. However, many volunteers work as adjuncts to employees in organizations controlled by employees – usually in the larger matter-of-fact institutions, such as hospitals or schools – and in those settings, volunteers "help" the employees, are directed by them, and usually are governed by clear formal procedures, such as job descriptions.

Table 7.1 Employees in volunteer-staffed organizations

Day care center	Four part-time teachers.
Newspaper	Editor-in-chief received a partial scholarship; ad salespeople earned commissions; production work by outside contracts.
Poverty relief agency	Two part-time coordinators.
Orchestra	Musical director received additional summer salary to produce concerts.
Family planning clinic	Full-time secretary; physicians paid for clinic work; state and national offices for this chapter had large professional staff.
Gift shop	Full-time shop manager; part-time bookkeeper.
Fire department	No employees.

Although some of the following discussion may apply to these larger institutional settings, the tensions that are to be described here have usually been resolved; the professionals and their norms dominate, and, therefore, the volunteers expect to follow formal procedures as if they were themselves employees. The volunteers are still volunteers, and no doubt many of them feel freer than employees to voice their views and to improvise in their jobs, and employees may resent indulgences granted to these volunteers. However, this license occurs within a known and confined boundary, and volunteers are removed if they cannot remain within bounds. The only exception might be a volunteer who either individually or through social connections represents an important source of revenue to the organization. In this case, however, the individual is rather more a "prima donna" who happens to be a volunteer and, like all prima donnas whether they are paid six-figure salaries or not, must be suffered by co-workers.

Professional status

An important effect on the relations between volunteers and employees resulted from the higher professional status employees have. This status is greater than that of volunteers in direct proportion to the degree of special skill and training required of members of the occupation. In all seven of the volunteer-staffed organizations, "professionals" completing the same work were regarded as more skilled and as having higher status. One illustration:

> I can't help but notice that of all the volunteer–employee comparisons there is the least amount of mutual animosity between these firefighters. However, the paid workers still have more status. An example is [volunteer] telling me that in neighboring [town] they have a volunteer company with paid drivers. He was amazed, though, and wanted to point out to me that the volunteer officers gave the orders. Clearly that seemed counterintuitive to him.
>
> (Volunteer-staffed fire department field notes, 7/31)

In the volunteer-staffed day care center and the poverty relief agency, volunteers pointed with pride to the professional credentials of their paid members. In the newspaper, orchestra, family planning clinic, and fire department, volunteers would boast of the professional credentials of fellow volunteers. In these occupations professional credentials were an important sign of quality, lack of which left the volunteer-staffed organizations subject to charges of providing inferior service.

In the one organization with the serious rift between an employee and the volunteers, the gift shop, the dispute appeared to be over definitions of areas of professional expertise. The volunteers were quick to praise the shop manager's "knowledge of the business," particularly the mechanics of ordering and managing inventory. The volunteer shop committee and paid manager disagreement concerned whether or not the manager's professional expertise extended to the choice of merchandise. The shop manager clearly felt she "knew what sold." The members of the shop committee wanted a store stocked with merchandise they could feel proud of (the shop manager was several decades older than the shop committee members and they felt her choice of merchandise was dated). Since the volunteers were unwilling to concede that the manager's expertise extended to merchandise selection and the manager was unwilling to see purchasing as within the policy-making domain of the committee, the tensions continued to smolder.

In the other organizations, the balance between the professional employees' expertise and the maintenance of volunteer dominance was managed through both an integration of credentialled status with volunteer office-holding and a careful deference on the part of paid members. Examples of credentialled core volunteers included the family planning clinic, which was dominated by its nurse-founder and which recruited many of its volunteers from the health care community. In the fire department, volunteers took care in electing the most skilled firefighters to the command offices, since their lives could depend on these commanders' judgments (e.g. ordering firefighters into a building that was about to collapse). The ways in which paid members in the other six organizations "gave status" and took care to not overstep their technical roles is described in the section on managing relationships.

Profiting from charity

However great the status of the employees in these organizations, in four of them there was a counter pressure that worked against their legitimate dominance – the fact that these employees reaped financial gain from the organization. As long as volunteers remain in clearly voluntary roles (such as fundraising for worthwhile causes) and employees are found working for profit-making enterprises, no one questions the legitimacy of their actions. Yet in the sampled organizations volunteers and employees frequently found themselves in direct competition with one another.

In the poverty relief agency and family planning clinic, the introduction of employees had posed serious threats to the character of the organizations. Once employees were present, they introduced a different set of personal goals – for example, long-term employment security rather than experimentation. Further, employees had an interest in bolstering the organization's professional credibility (it was the paid coordinator credentialled as a social worker who suggested that the telephone volunteers refer callers to the local welfare office).

Finally, although most of the direct employee–volunteer relationships in these volunteer-staffed organizations worked well, the extremely negative views of volunteers held by many of the employees of the employee-staffed organizations need to be mentioned. These usually took the form of employees claiming they could not make any comparison between what they and volunteers did – that what volunteers did was so completely different and inferior that no comment was possible. Often this hostility resulted from a direct competition with the volunteers that threatened the employees' livelihood. Professional musicians could not make enough to support themselves if volunteers performed without pay. If the welfare office's paid social workers could not really lift their clients out of poverty, there was less justification for their cost. One indication of the very power-ful threat this direct competition posed was the unsolicited insistence of volunteer officeholders in the orchestra and in the poverty relief agency that they really did not compete with, but supplemented, the work of the professionals.

The exceptions were the day care and fire department employees who tended to have a more matter-of-fact view of volunteers. The employee firefighters frankly praised the role of volunteer firefighters in supporting their recent strike for higher wages. They saw them as – it goes without saying – less skilled than professionals but as an efficient use of resources in rural areas with less demanding fires. Volunteer and employee firefighters and day care teachers did not directly compete with one another; less affluent community members could share this kind of work among themselves, but whenever possible they would have these tasks done professionally.

Thus, in the studied organizations, those employees who were most hostile to volunteers were the ones most threatened by them. Sometimes employers exacerbate the insecurity of employees by advocating the expanded use of volunteers as a cost-saving measure, putting employees in the position of justifying themselves (and, incidentally, of discovering that well-trained and responsible volunteers are now a threat).

Therefore, when volunteers and employees work together, they tend to provide a form of silent criticism of one another. The volunteer suggests to society that it is "paying too much" for the work of the employee. The employee threatens the self-sacrificial character of the volunteer's social setting and shames the dilettantes with their competence. Yet, despite this threat to the legitimacy of one another, the volunteer–employee relations were excellent in five out of the six studied organizations that retained employees. This seemed to be the result of careful management by core volunteers and employees alike.

Delicate management

The potential for damaging disruption appeared to be managed in the studied organizations in two ways. First, through continuous rotation between core volunteer roles and employee positions the distinctions between these roles were blurred. A good example of this occurred during data collection in the poverty relief agency when the coordinator retired to volunteer status. Similarly, when one of the teachers in the day care center said she would have to leave when her baby was born, the volunteers suggested that she stay and place her baby in the infant center (despite the fact that she had no divinity school connection), and she did. She worked her hours as a paid teacher in the toddler room and as a volunteer teachers' assistant in the infant room. Rather than seeing such situations as potential jurisdictional crises, they were seen as affirmations of the organizations' missions.

Milofsky and Elion (1987) described how even the paid staffs needed to maintain their martyr roles in order to retain their influence:

> When participatory organizations have paid staffs, this means the staff members receive an income that is dramatically lower than people doing equivalent work elsewhere. This happens not just because the organizations are cash poor. One of our free schools had under-payment as a self-conscious policy. New parents who themselves were well-paid regularly objected to taking advantage of the teachers. In a meeting where these concerns were voiced, however, the president explained that the under-payment helped make the parents feel obliged to invest more volunteer time in the school and to give more generous monetary or in kind donations. In fact, there were several occasions where the teachers had refused raises, insisting that the money budgeted for their salaries be spent on new equipment or other material necessities.
>
> (Milofsky and Elion 1987, p. 13)

Although none of the studied organizations presented such an extreme case, the teachers in the day care center, the musical director of the orchestra, and the poverty relief agency coordinators were clearly considered underpaid "for what they contributed." These employees considered themselves – and were considered by the volunteers – to be as self-sacrificial as the majority of volunteers (if not quite as much as founding volunteers). In no case could any of these employees be characterized as using the organization for economic gain or advancement, and none saw work as "just a job".

Second, the volunteers and employees in most of these organizations treated one another with great care and deference. Employees placed volunteers (especially founders) on pedestals and praised their self-sacrifice (and often were more than a little protective and paternalistic). The employed secretary at the family planning clinic was the individual who sang the praises of the founding chapter chairwoman most insistently. These employees were also careful (in contrast to the gift shop manager) not to take undue authority for themselves. For example, at the first meeting with a paid coordinator of the poverty relief agency, the researcher was sternly rebuked for calling her the "director." The volunteers directed the organization, and she simply perceived herself as helping to coordinate its work.

Thus, these successful employees were careful to maintain the self-sacrificial values of the organization and to keep to their proper technical place.

Similarly, the volunteers praised the selfless dedication of their underpaid employees. They would brag about the technical credentials of their employees and heap as much praise on them as the employees did on volunteers. No one even thought of regarding the employees' contributions as less worthy because they took money from the organization. They were seen as committed to the cause, just like other members of the core. One indicator of this was the fact that many peripheral volunteers in the newspaper, poverty relief agency, and family planning clinic were not aware that some members of the core were paid.

CONCLUSIONS

Control in these organizations was based on a careful management of interpersonal influence and the dependencies that this approach created. The studied volunteer-staffed organizations were dependent on key individuals who provided vision, technical and interpersonal competence, and acted as role models of self-sacrificial dedication to the organization. Through their willingness to take on the organization's work and their ability to inspire others, they kept their organizations functioning. This charismatic authority did not completely substitute for formal rules and job descriptions, but it did seem to substitute for "hierarchical command." However, these organizations found that the additional burdens of holding office led to an avoidance of these positions, which left them dangerously dependent on a few core members. When this understaffing was addressed through retaining employees for key roles, it was suggested that the threat employee and volunteer co-workers pose to each other's legitimacy was effectively managed through a blurring of volunteer and paid roles (which included underpayment to employees) and a careful deference to one another.

Part IV

Toward inclusive organizational studies

This examination of organizational volunteers has provided an opportunity to reflect on several general aspects of organizational behavior, as well as on volunteer organizational behavior more specifically. In the following two chapters the information presented in the foregoing chapters is summarized and discussed. The material has been divided into two chapters directed at the two distinct readerships of this work: those interested in a wider understanding of organizational behavior as applied to all kinds of work organizations and those interested in the more effective management of volunteer-staffed organizations themselves. In Chapter 8 the implications of the material for the wider field of organizational behavior – specifically focusing on how the material reflects on unexamined assumptions about employee-staffed organizational behavior – is presented. Chapter 9 provides a discussion of the research and practical management implications of these ideas for those specifically interested in the management of volunteer-staffed organizations. To aid in guiding future research, the generalizations developed in this work are summarized in propositional form. As is indicated in both chapters, this work is quite preliminary and exploratory; it is hoped that the following attempt to apply the conclusions from the previous chapters to specific organizational behavior topics and managerial policies will help to spur additional debate and research.

Chapter 8

Implications for theories of organizational behavior

The organizational behavior of volunteers has been neglected by the field of organizational behavior. Perhaps this is because, as Sills (1968) noted, volunteer activities are seen as peripheral to the important institutions of society and to topical problems such as international competitiveness. Although this comparative neglect has been a particular disservice to those who must manage organizations staffed by volunteers, another serious effect has been the narrowing of our understanding of organizational behavior. When studies are restricted to employees and the focus is narrowed even further to only the largest organizations, our understanding of organizational behavior is diminished. With nothing to offer contrast, many of the most important features of employees' environments and expectations simply are not seen, because they are "constants" in those settings. For example, it was only when American researchers became familiar with the distinctive management practices in Japanese firms that their understanding of the effects of cultural assumptions in American management practices blossomed. In this chapter, some of the implications of this study of the organizational behavior of volunteers for our general theories are offered.

UNCERTAINTY IN FORMAL ORGANIZATIONAL ROLES

In the foregoing chapters, it was suggested that volunteers experience significant uncertainty stemming from the fact that they frequently find themselves holding contradictory formal positions in relation to the organization. (See Table 8.1 for a summary of these ideas in propositional form.) As association members, they are "owners" of the organizations; as "direct service volunteers," they are workers obligated to perform in accordance with directives and subject to performance surveillance. Finally, volunteers are also a kind of client of the organization, sometimes in the literal sense, most visibly in self-help organizations, but also in a more indirect sense, since the participation itself must serve volunteers' intrinsic or intangible needs (Perrow 1970). Each of these distinct formal organizational roles comes with its own set of behavioral expectations. For example, owners determine the direction of an organization, and this implies that they participate in determining the organization's strategy and policies. In contrast, they are also workers carrying out others' decisions. Thus volunteers and those who work with them are free to choose to emphasize one role or another or to combine them in an idiosyncratic way. Hence their widely decried "insubordination" is simply an emphasis on their ownership role. Of course, this role conflict is only a potential difficulty – many organizations do successfully reconcile this confusion into clearly defined setting-specific expectations on which the participants agree.

Table 8.1 Contradictory roles propositions

P_1 Volunteers will hold contradictory formal and contradictory implicit organizational roles.

P_2 Individuals who hold contradictory organizational roles will experience uncertainty in behavioral expectations.

P_3 Individuals who hold contradictory roles will tend to give priority to meeting the expectations associated with the higher status and more attractive roles.

P_4 Work associates of an individual who holds contradictory roles will tend to pressure the individual to fulfil the role which makes each associate's own work easier or more attractive.

P_5 Individuals with greater interpersonal sensitivity will adjust more effectively to the shifting roles of associates who hold contradictory roles.

P_6 Public articulation of the presence of contradictory roles will decrease the incidence of behavior being perceived as role-inappropriate, thus will lessen frustration and anger.

However, it is clear that much of the condemnation of volunteer workers' effectiveness described above comes from individuals who wish volunteers would stay securely in the role of (lower status) workers, while the volunteers persist in claiming the (higher status) prerogatives of owners. Since it is reasonable to expect participants to prefer that volunteers assume those roles that best suit their own interests, this role-related stress is probably the inevitable outcome in those organizations that do not effectively manage this potential conflict.

This kind of problem is probably more common among employee-staffed organizations than has been widely acknowledged. Employees, particularly managers and professionals, commonly carry more than one formally recognized role in their organizations. A manager may hold the post of Vice President of Marketing, and in that role be expected to vigorously fight for the interests of the Marketing Department, and simultaneously be a member of the firm's Executive Committee and in that capacity perhaps be expected to avoid "parochialism" and to act in the organization's overall interests. Certainly, university professors wear many different "hats": they serve on many departmental, school, university, and accreditation policy-making committees in which they oversee themselves as classroom teachers and students' advisors. Such role multiplicity is extended to other nonmanagerial workers through quality circles, employee stock-ownership, co-determination, and other such programs. Although these programs may provide many benefits to both employees and their employers, they do introduce additional formal roles that need active management. Despite the proliferation of formal organizational roles with differing expectations, organization theory is virtually silent concerning the effects of this phenomenon. Likert (1961) did characterize supervisors and middle managers as "linking pins," emphasizing their dual formal roles. However, he did not explore in any detail the implications of holding multiple roles.

Following the experiences of volunteers, we might expect that participants would adopt the role that best serves their own interests and needs and that members of participants' task environment would want them to adopt the role that best serves their (different) interests. Thus secretaries see themselves as administrative assistants, while the lawyers they serve may see them as typists carrying out their commands. Further, individuals may attempt to pursue their interests by evoking the demands and expectations of the favored role, in effect cloaking political behavior in the language of obligations that the others freely contracted. When the participants did identify and articulate these differing expectations (as occurred in the day care center, poverty relief agency, family planning clinic, orchestra, and fire department) these pressures were manageable. Yet, when these differences remained unarticulated, they seemed to escalate rapidly into the personal animosities that crippled the student newspaper and gift shop. There is some recognition that employees are quite sensitive to status differences, as reflected in popular writers' emphasis on equalizing such differences (Peters and Waterman 1982; Ouchi 1981). Yet the political effects of formal role conflicts and how they have been managed have not been analyzed in any detail.

Further, we might expect that even individuals who do not seek to benefit from this confusion, but who seek to carry out their responsibilities straightforwardly, might find their interpersonal perceptiveness and skill excessively taxed by having to learn to recognize and deal with subtle shifts in role-appropriateness. Unfortunately, much of the interpersonal theory and training we give our students assumes that formal relationships among individuals are relatively simple (boss–subordinate, for example). Further, it assumes that the only complexities in relationships are in the personalities and emotional states of the individuals. Our teaching and theory would benefit from dropping the presumption that formal, as well as informal, relationships among members of organizations are simple and one-dimensional. This study of volunteer-staffed organizational behavior suggests that the complexity of formal role demands was at least as important a strain on interpersonal relationships as the participants' personalities.

UNCERTAIN BOUNDARIES

The study of volunteers forces the researcher to recognize that precise organizational membership cannot always be clearly determined. Since volunteers are not paid, their organizations face no pressures to clearly differentiate "members" from "clients" or other outsiders. In practice, only the one organization that was not chronically understaffed, the fire department, had an accurate membership list (see propositions in Table 8.2). As noted, in the other organizations, members would drag friends and family in to help whenever they could, often without anyone's "official" knowledge. The uncertainty of membership was exacerbated by these organizations' officers' hestitation to remove those contributing little (or nothing), no doubt because of understaffing. Further, the fact that many of these organizations served as informal gathering places meant that there would often be many nonmembers congregating in the workplaces.

Table 8.2 Uncertain boundaries propositions

P_7 Organizations which markedly underpay their members will attract insufficient members (become understaffed), unless (1) the tasks or social setting are very attractive, (2) the members have no alternative organization through which they can meet their objectives, or (3) both.

P_8 In understaffed organizations, poor performers will not be removed unless they cause undisputably severe damage to the organization.

P_9 Members of understaffed organizations will actively recruit new members, using any means they can command, including their personal ties to others.

P_{10} Understaffed organizations will bifurcate into an activist core and a periphery of partially-involved members.

P_{11} Peripheral members in understaffed organizations will tend to become acquainted with only a few other members.

P_{12} Peripheral members will tend to become dependent on guidance from core members, which will then further isolate peripheral members, diminish their importance, and increase the time demands on and responsibilities of core members.

P_{13a} Peripheral members who become isolated and less significantly involved will tend to feel excluded and devalued.

P_{13b} Core members who experience escalating time demands and responsibilities will tend to feel exploited.

P_{14} Clear, closed-ended job descriptions for peripheral and core members will counter the development of contradictory roles, encourage complementary relationships, and limit bifurcation of the organization.

P_{15} As the size of the understaffed organization increases, the greater will be the discrepancy between core and peripheral members in their knowledge of co-workers.

These uncertain boundaries had significant implications for the ongoing organizational behavior of these organizations. With the volunteer work-force bifurcated into a tightly knitted core group with peripheral members only partially involved, an important problem thus resulted. Peripheral members did not always "know" their co-workers. They could not know whether they should ask these co-workers for assistance, or what their skills, knowledge, and job assignment might involve. Individuals did get to know who the core members were. Therefore, the tendency to rely heavily on core members and insufficiently on others led to the vicious circle described earlier in which core members became increasingly exploited while peripheral members felt useless and so quit.

Although uncertain membership is particularly acute and visible in many volunteer-staffed organizations, there are many employee-staffed settings in which boundaries are not as distinct as is assumed. The most obvious example is in the increasing use of temporary or contract workers (Pfeffer and Baron 1988). Although these temporary workers have a clear status and duties, there are many activities in which it is unclear whether or not they should be included: for example, staff meetings, after-hours social events, training programs. Further, their supervisors may find that they cannot require as much from them, in either overtime or willingness to help others. These workers are neither completely in nor out. We might expect temporary workers to suffer from some of the same feelings of exclusion that troubled many new volunteers.

Another current trend in business organizations is "dis-integration," in which firms do not vertically integrate as they grow but rely more on long-term contract relationships (Ouchi and Bolton 1988). These networks-of-organizations also foster uncertain boundaries. Individuals working in different divisions of a single organization acknowledge that they should be working toward the same objective, and this assumption (and the fact of a shared boss somewhere) should assist in dispute resolution (Williamson 1975). Participants in these new, dis-integrated organizational networks are, by contrast, in a market-type relationship. There is no shared boss, but there may, perhaps, be some loyalty to the long-term success of the relationship itself. Experience with volunteer networks suggests some questions about this phenomenon. Do network participants find that they must spend substantial time in clarifying their relationships with one another? Do "core members" of the network arise to take on a disproportionate share of the coordination of activities? Do these networks depend on the personal influence (charismatic and martyred) of one or a few leaders to maintain integrated action? Volunteer-staffed organizations provide one model of the management practices that arise in the absence of a clear vertical hierarchy. It will be interesting to see if these new dis-integrated organizational networks also evolve similar coordination and conflict-resolution practices.

THE ATTRACTIVENESS OF DECISION-MAKING

One of the most fruitful contrasts between these employee-staffed and volunteer-staffed organizations concerned the attractiveness of "managerial work" when it had to be accomplished without large pay and status rewards (propositions appear in Table 8.3). Much of organizational behavior has simply assumed, rather than examined, the effects of large pay and perquisite differentials between jobs. It had been observed that many employees value organizational upward mobility ("a promotion"), and so many students of organizational behavior simply assumed that most employees share the same perception of these tasks as attractive, in and of themselves (e.g. Alderfer 1972; Vroom and Yetton 1973). Yet, the studied volunteers avoided these responsibilities if at all possible. Only a few attended meetings, and the majority avoided office-holding leadership positions.

Table 8.3 Decision-making propositions

P_{16} Managerial tasks will be unattractive to the majority of organizational members.
P_{17} Organizational members will want to influence decisions that affect them in important ways. Participation without discernible personal influence on decision outcomes will not be attractive to participants.

Researchers seem to have ignored the very real extrinsic rewards that leadership/management activities have in many employee-staffed settings. Managers make more money than their subordinates; employees want to influence (not "participate in") decisions affecting the real allocation of resources that may benefit or harm them. The behavior of the volunteers suggested that many may find the actual managerial activities themselves loathsome. This aversion is probably not limited to volunteers. How many people really enjoy sitting through a meeting in which every single co-worker has the opportunity to fully air his or her opinions? Managerial jobs, particularly at lower levels, are genuinely frustrating and exhausting. Some of the failures of employee participation programs and managerial appointments may stem from this apparently false assumption about what people value in their work, as distinct from the outcomes of that work. Participative management practices, whether in volunteer-staffed or employee-staffed organizations, could benefit from more precision regarding what participants really will obtain from them. The study of volunteers' reactions to assuming managerial work helps to differentiate the (often frustrating and difficult) work itself from the perquisites and pay inevitably associated with it in large employee-staffed organizations.

PART-TIME WORKFORCE

The studied volunteer-staffed organizations had to rely on the intermittent, part-time, contributions of their workers. This forced fractionating of jobs into part-time pieces highlighted the significant amount of coordination that takes place naturally when all members of the workforce are at work at the same time (propositions in Table 8.4). Organizations staffed by part-time volunteers had coordination problems that simply did not exist for their counterparts with full-time employees. Problems that will take three days of exchanged phone messages to solve can be done in ten minutes if the parties work in close proximity. What superficially looks like unproductive hallway chatting among full-time employees may be building relationships that can be called upon when cross-functional problems arise. Co-workers who continuously work together get to know each other's strengths and weaknesses and so know on whom they can rely. Furthermore, performance expectations are clarified; Whyte (1955) provides evidence that employee co-workers develop normative expectations about levels of productivity that can be a source of reassurance to workers (as well as reducing the variance in individual productivity).

Table 8.4 Part-time workforce propositions

P_{18} Organizations employing part-time workers will need to create formal mechanisms to coordinate the work that is informally coordinated by full-time co-workers.

P_{19} Full-time workers will spend more time engaged in nontask social interaction with co-workers than will part-time workers. These greater levels of nontask social interaction will build familiarity and will facilitate solutions to unexpected and novel organizational problems.

P_{20} Full-time workers will be more likely to develop shared expectations and perspectives about workplace requirements (such as levels of productivity) and events (such as the meaning of a new managerial policy) than will part-time workers.

All of this suggests that there are significant costs to organizations that disperse their workers temporally or spatially. Part-time and "telecommuting" employees will result in the need for increased formal coordination to substitute for previously "natural" informal coordination. Similar effects might be expected when plants or other operations are located in distant countries, perhaps nine time zones away. In the studied volunteer-staffed organizations, this integration was usually completed by a formal coordinator position, but in employee-staffed organizations these duties may just be added to a supervisor's or full-time senior worker's responsibilities. For example, an accountant in California now has to call the German facility's managing director at midnight, from home, to ask about a relatively minor problem in the recent monthly financial report. Further, even with a successful coordination of dispersed job tasks, the experience of part-time volunteers suggests that the more subtle processes of building confidence in one another and collaboration on nonroutine problems can be slowed and disrupted by dispersion. Given the increasing internationalization of the workforce and the use of computer-aided telecommuting, these problems may become increasingly important in employee-staffed organizations.

ROLE OF COMPENSATION DIFFERENTIALS IN WORK DESIGN

The present study uncovered striking differences in the way in which tasks were allocated to individual jobs between employee-staffed and volunteer-staffed organizations doing essentially the same work (propositions in Table 8.5). Volunteer-staffed organizations were less likely to group tasks by type, and volunteers shared equally in the interesting client-contact work, policy setting, and routine clerical functions. In contrast, employee-staffed organizations were more likely to group tasks by homogeneous skill or responsibility. Different forms of compensation seemed to be one reason for this difference. Volunteers were "paid" with the experience of the work itself (and the knowledge of its importance), and so they needed to share the more interesting as well as the more tedious tasks. In contrast, employees were paid in money, resulting in pressures to keep the (expensive) skilled workers focused on tasks that required their skills and to group less-skilled support activities into jobs for lesser paid employees. Thus, employees' interactions were influenced by finer divisions of labor, which may have resulted in greater skill development, but also may have led to a less egalitarian workplace and, often, to less task efficiency (since whole jobs are fragmented to take advantage of wage differentials across occupations).

Table 8.5 Effects of compensation on work design propositions

P$_{21}$ In practice, attention to the attractiveness of tasks and configurations to workers will be as important in the design of organizations as efficient information processing.

P$_{22}$ In understaffed organizations, attractive tasks will be shared as widely as possible among workers, which will result in less occupational specialization.

P$_{23}$ When understaffed organizations add sufficiently compensated jobs, these jobs will tend to include the least attractive organizational tasks.

P$_{24}$ The greater the wage differentials among different organizational occupations, the greater will be the task specialization.

P$_{25}$ The minimization of overall labor costs will be more important in the design of organizations than efficiency through facilitation of information processing.

These observations are not surprising except for the fact that modern theoretical discussions of organizational design virtually ignore the effects of wage differentials (Galbraith 1977; Mintzberg 1979; Perrow 1979). Detailed analyses of task requirements are provided with no acknowledgement that it may be strictly more efficient for organizations to sacrifice some coordination "costs" when the wage differentials across occupations more than compensate. In industries where the wage differences are quite large – in health care, for example – we can observe an increasing trend toward finer occupational specialization that seems to be cost- rather than task-driven. Thus the study of volunteers suggests that the field's theories of organizational design are missing what appears to be a vital component. They direct our attention to "efficiency in communication," whereas "cost efficiency" is probably the more important consideration. An exploration of the design and behavioral effects of relative labor costs would seem to be a fruitful area for researchers.

RECRUITING: SOCIAL NETWORKS AND NONRATIONAL DECISIONS

The present study reinforced the findings of previous research that volunteers are primarily recruited through friends, co-workers, and family members (propositions in Table 8.6). Volunteers usually joined their organizations because they were introduced through someone they knew. There is some variance – the large, matter-of-fact nonprofit institutions do rely more on impersonal recruiting than smaller, intense value-rational organizations. Thus, it seemed that few volunteers weighed the advantages and disadvantages of volunteering before joining, but rather "tried it out" and decided, after they officially had joined, whether or not to commit themselves. This may be one reason why many volunteer-staffed organizations experience such high turnover among new volunteers, and it suggests that the experiences of new volunteers need special managerial attention.

Social network recruiting apparently also plays a dominant role in the recruiting of American employees (Bureau of Labor Statistics 1975). Despite the practical importance of this method of recruiting, it has not received direct attention from those interested in selection and recruiting. Wanous (1980) did acknowledge its importance by suggesting that the higher retention levels of those recruited by existing employees may result from more realistic job previews given by the current employees. In addition, as in volunteer-staffed organizations, the friend-recruiter may help to integrate the new recruit socially and so ease the transition into the organization.

Unfortunately, however, we know little about the organizational effectiveness of such recruiting. For example, current employees may coach friend-applicants on how to negotiate the selection process successfully and so artificially inflate their scores on tests. Such forms of recruiting may put

Table 8.6 Social network recruiting propositions

P$_{26}$ Only individuals who (1) have a strong personal interest in achieving the organization's goals, or (2) see the organization as the only likely vehicle for that goal attainment, or (3) have a strong sense of self-efficacy, or (4) have some combination of these will be likely to volunteer for organizations without personal intermediaries.

P$_{27}$ The more important interpersonal influence is in the control of a volunteer-staffed organization, the more likely potential volunteers will be to view the organization as an exclusive social setting that requires an invitation from an insider.

P$_{28}$ Many people will regard volunteering for an organization as a "trial act" and will not weigh the costs and benefits of volunteering before joining as thoroughly as they would if they were considering paid employment.

P$_{29}$ Organizations that depend on social network recruiting will have a more homogeneous membership than will organizations that make greater use of impersonal recruiting methods.

P$_{30}$ It is likely that workers recruited through acquaintances will receive more realistic job previews and more assistance in becoming socially integrated into the organization than will impersonally recruited workers.

P$_{31}$ Recruits who receive realistic job previews and assistance in social integration will be less likely to leave their organizations early in their tenure.

women and ethnic minorities at a disadvantage, since they may have fewer such coaches or contacts in jobs traditionally occupied by white males. Alternatively, social network recruiting may help reinforce organizational control, as current employees exhibit exemplary work behaviors in a bid to insure that their friends or relatives are also offered jobs. For example, in the United States, many well-paid blue-collar jobs in government or large, stable businesses receive many more applications than they can possibly accommodate (e.g. firefighters, oil refinery pipefitters). Openings for these jobs can be a valuable source of "patronage," and the high proportion of family members recruited into these occupations suggests that the organizations may be using the positions to extract desired behaviors from current employees. A more complete understanding of organizational selection would seem to depend on a better knowledge of the effects of different forms of recruiting.

NONDEPENDENT WORKERS AND LEADERSHIP

Volunteers depend on their organizations for very little that is truly vital to their lives (propositions in Table 8.7). Many do, of course, develop strong emotional ties to their cause and co-workers, but these develop over time and characterize the minority of working volunteers. Therefore, the leaders of successful volunteer-staffed organizations have had to become adept at motivating without powerful rewards or sanctions. That every community abounds in such successful volunteer-staffed organizations demonstrates that it can be done. Managers of employee-staffed organizations might do well to learn from these successful leaders. Below are discussed three features which seemed to characterize such successful leadership practices.

Table 8.7 Leadership of nondependent workers propositions

P$_{32}$ Leaders of nondependent workers who communicate more about the importance of the organization's accomplishments will be more influential than those who do not communicate about the organization's importance.

P$_{33}$ Leaders of nondependent workers who can foster the workers' perceptions that they are personally important to the organization's accomplishments will be more influential than leaders who do not foster the impression of worker importance.

P$_{34}$ Leaders of nondependent workers who demonstrate to workers that they demand more of themselves than they do of their workers will be more influential than those who are not demanding of themselves.

P$_{35}$ Workers who are subject to open-ended escalating demands will come to feel exploited and will reduce their contribution to the organization in order to maintain what they perceive to be a fair balance of contributions and inducements.

P$_{36}$ Organizational members with stronger social ties to others will be more likely to submit to the influence of others to whom they are socially tied.

The importance of the workers' contribution to the effort

The successful organizations spent inordinate amounts of time talking about the importance of the organization's contribution. They kept copious statistics: number of people fed, clients seen, fires fought. They abounded with glowing testimonials to courageous volunteers, recreated scenes in which deserving clients were helped, and had many warm anecdotes. Further, and most critical, not only was the importance of the effort continuously emphasized but the vital role of each and every volunteer was made clear through the task assignment itself. Those organizations in which volunteers felt they, personally, were not needed (newspaper reporters, family planning intake volunteers) suffered from the "volunteer unreliability" problems analyzed above.

It seems that many employee-staffed organizations miss opportunities to demonstrate to individual employees the important role that they play. It sometimes seems as if ranking executives view low-level employees as "expendable" since replacements are easy to hire (*Wall Street Journal*, 5/10/1989). This attitude is communicated by word and deed, and employees come to feel that what they do isn't vital. If what they do isn't important, they have only enough incentive to produce what it takes to retain their jobs, nothing more. The employee enthusiasm that often is attributed to small companies may come from the fact that it is easier for all employees to see the importance of their own actions in these more intimate settings. Certainly, even very large organizations can develop programs that help to demonstrate the importance of all employees.

Martyred leadership

In the studied organizations, successful volunteer leaders genuinely led by example. If most volunteers put in ten hours a week, their leaders put in twenty. Whatever these leaders asked of other volunteers, the volunteers knew that their leaders had already asked more of themselves. That is, successful leaders, by their own personal dedication to the effort, built moral obligations between individual volunteers and themselves. For example, a volunteer would not skip a shift because he or she knew that the selfless leader would then have to work it. The organization where this worked best (poverty relief agency) also coupled it with clear limits on the obligations each volunteer owed. After a time, open-ended appeals would rightly come to be seen as manipulative and would be resisted.

Despite the widespread popular acknowledgement in normative writings of the principle of leading by example (e.g. Kouzes and Posner 1987), it is surprising how little attention the principle receives in current academic research on leadership. It may be that the audience (managers and future managers) is not receptive to this message, unless forced by extreme need (battle, volunteer motivation). Yet the effectiveness of leading by example would seem to be promising and deserving of rigorous research.

Close friendships at work

Finally, volunteers worked for one another. They reported that their relationships with co-workers became increasingly important over time. Core volunteers developed a particularly close involvement with each other. Such involvement is one way of building more rewards and sanctions into the workplace. No one wants to let friends down. In addition, the greater the contact among volunteers away from work, the greater the chance that irresponsible behavior will become more widely known. As discussed previously, student volunteers seem to be particularly "irresponsible," and the lack of this kind of fairly permanent social linkage among student volunteers was argued to be a major cause of students' poor performance. To these students, there is no long-lasting unpleasant social consequence of their inappropriate behavior.

Many years ago Roethlisberger and Dickson (1939) discussed the powerful influence co-workers had on one another's productivity. They described how peer influence was exercised for either high levels of productivity (Relay Test Assembly Room) or lowered levels of productivity (Bank Wiring Room). Yet, with the exception of Krackhardt and Porter (1985), research interest in peer influence seems to have faded. It certainly does not have the central place its potential workplace influence would suggest it warrants.

DISTINCTION BETWEEN BEHAVIORAL AND NORMATIVE COMMITMENT

An analysis of the organizational commitment of volunteers supports the distinction between normative and behavioral commitment as described by Weiner (1982). Although volunteers would inevitably have weaker behavioral commitment than employees – since volunteering is more revokable, less public, and less likely to be externally compelled – they are popularly believed to be "more committed" than employees (propositions in Table 8.8). That is, they are assumed to be more committed to the goals of the organization, since they have fewer compelling reasons than employees to participate. The present study suggests that the importance of Weiner's clarification should not be underestimated.

Table 8.8 Commitment propositions

P$_{37}$ Volunteers will tend to have weaker behavioral commitment to their organizations than employees.

P$_{38}$ Volunteers will be committed to at least one aspect of their workplace (e.g. the organization, its goals, fellow workers, or attendant social status, etc.).

P$_{39}$ Behaviorally committed organizational members will be less likely to leave the organization.

P$_{40}$ Behavioral commitment will be unrelated to nonmaintenance or extra-role work behaviors (e.g. organizational citizenship).

P$_{41}$ Normatively committed organizational members will be more likely to promote the welfare of the object of their commitment (that is, the organization, if they are organizationally committed; clients, if committed to the service mission, etc.).

Behavioral commitment simply indicates that it is difficult to leave – that the individual is tied to the organization. This says nothing about the individual's affect toward the organization or anyone else working there. Yet much of the practical interest in commitment stems from interest in fostering the enthusiastic identification of members with the organization and its goals. Certainly behavioral commitment would be an excellent predictor of retention, but it is not clear that it would tell us anything about the workplace actions of individuals. In fact, the work of Kiesler (1971) would suggest that the more clearly workers see themselves as behaviorally committed to their organizations the less likely they are to feel the need to justify their actions by assuming they must like working there. Just because an individual is handcuffed to an organization does not necessarily mean that that person will be inclined to adopt its goals or engage in any of the other actions expected of those dedicated to a collective purpose. Thus, this work with volunteers suggests that there may be a negative correlation between behavioral commitment and the kind of enthusiasm and dedication most observers usually mean when they speak of "organizational commitment." The observation that volunteers have more positive job attitudes while being less behaviorally committed than employees supports this argument. So, too, do the theories of Barker (1968) (understaffed vs overstaffed settings) and Staw (1976) (insufficient vs oversufficient justification). Both behavioral and normative commitment may lead to greater retention, since the trapped and dedicated are equally likely to stay. Yet they suggest very different forms of on-the-job behavior. There has not been sufficient attention to the effects of affective or normative commitment on employee organizational actions other than turnover.

WHEN THE VALUE OF THE EFFORT IS QUESTIONED

The field of organizational behavior is surprisingly silent on the subject of the effects of larger societal expectations on the attitudes and actions of individuals in organizations (propositions in Table 8.9). In the present study, it was suggested that the widely publicized critiques of social service volunteering led to a "devaluing" of this organizational work and subsequently to a "defensiveness" among many volunteers. The cross-pressures that volunteers face – being unpaid so their efforts are regarded as worthless, yet sacrificing for their communities – are simply starker versions of the judgments many employees may face. Organizational behavior is treated as if it were subject only to forces completely within the organization – for example, reward systems and supervisory leadership. Yet all organizational participants work in a larger society that makes judgments about the value of their work. For example, working to build better armaments may be seen as noble during overt national hostilities, but as "profiting from death" during periods of disarmament. Van Maanen (1974) has described how the police are often distrusted by outsiders and so over time develop friendships solely with other police insiders. Such societal judgments can affect recruitment, can result in more defensive and brittle relationships with clients, can increase the pressure on new recruits to "become one of us" quickly, and may have numerous other complex effects on the actions of employees at work.

Table 8.9 Devalued effort propositions

P₄₂ The judgments of people who are not members of the organization regarding the value of individual members' work or of the organization will have an impact on members' evaluations of the worth of their own work and of the organization.

P₄₃ Members will try to defend against negative external evaluations by restricting their social interactions to those with positive views.

P₄₄ Organizations with positive external evaluations will find it easier and less expensive to recruit new members than will those with negative external evaluations.

THE SYMBOLIC ROLE OF COMPENSATION

Pay is the defining characteristic of employees and is widely assumed to be the one necessary feature binding them to their organizations. Yet the presence of millions of volunteer organizational workers gives lie to this confident assumption. Certainly it is not that pay is unimportant, quite to the contrary. This study of volunteers helps to illuminate the powerful role of pay in our organizations (propositions in Table 8.10). It is not that no one would work without pay, but that pay – its amount and the ways it is administered – conveys important meanings to members of organizations.

The ways in which organizations compensate their members has come to convey important symbolic messages about the kinds of contributions participants can make to organizational effort. Again, the experiences of organizational volunteers are simply more extreme variations of the experiences of different employees. Because of the symbolic importance of pay in our society, volunteers find themselves placed in inherently unclear positions. They are paid nothing, yet their organizations certainly do not want them to be left with the implicit message that their efforts are worth

Table 8.10 Symbolic role of compensation propositions

P₄₅ The nature of an organization's pay system will convey a powerful message about the members it expects to attract and what kinds of behavior it values.

P₄₆ Since the absence of pay for volunteer organizational work can convey the message that the work is valueless, volunteer-staffed organizations will be more successful in recruitment and retention if they successfully communicate the value of the work.

P₄₇ Egalitarian compensation and reward systems will communicate egalitarian expectations, as reflected in less occupational specialization, less withholding of information, and greater trust among members.

P₄₈ Precise closed-ended compensation systems communicate that members will have a specified closed-ended contract with the organization, with members expecting additional compensation for any additional contribution.

nothing. Working without pay leads to the paradox of volunteer labor: it is both "work" and "leisure," each implying contradictory expectations for volunteers' actions in their organizations. When these expectations were not carefully managed, they led to debilitating conflicts.

The manner in which organizations compensate their members has come to assume powerful symbolic connotations about the value the organization – and, by implication, society – places on their labor. Organizations are widely viewed as arenas for economic exchange in which employees contribute their time and efforts in exchange for money. This popular view of organizational work is reflected in the language of scholars of organizations and organizational behavior. Theorists of the behavior of individuals in organizations borrow concepts from the economic marketplace, as in Simon's (1957) "inducements-contributions contracts" and Schein's (1980) "psychological contracts," to describe the relationships between organizations and their members. Recent theorists may have de-emphasized the rational character of organizations but retained the emphasis on economic transactions (cf. Goodman and Pennings' [1977] characterization of organizations as a "negotiated order"). If anything, the use of marketplace analogies for workplace relationships has increased in recent years (see, e.g., Eisenhardt 1988). Implicit is the assumption that people work for gain and that they "negotiate contracts" in which the terms of the economic exchange are established.

These assumptions about organizational participation in exchange for economic gain are exacerbated by the symbolic importance money has come to assume in our societies. Our incomes have become surrogate indicators of the importance of our labor to the organization and of our social status in the fluid, modern world. Wallace and Fay (1983, p. 14), like many other compensation writers, note that pay has important symbolic connotations for employees. They note that many employees come to view their level of compensation as both a relative and an absolute symbol of their accomplishment and value to their employer.

Yet, few authors have sought to study exactly which features of pay symbolize what messages. Wallace and Fay suggested that its symbolic importance leads to "overreaction" to all features of compensation. Pearce and Perry (1983) provided supporting evidence for this suggestion in their study of federal pay reform. Yet the present work suggests that the actual form and, certainly, the level of pay send important differential messages about what the organization values.

In the volunteer-staffed organizations, all volunteer workers were paid equally, and so it isn't surprising that these organizations were characterized by strong egalitarian norms. Everyone was expected to "pitch in" and share the burdensome tasks; anyone attempting to claim to be "above" certain tasks would have been laughed out of the organization. Certainly, no volunteers were alienated and resentful, and aggressive, secretive political behavior was unknown – a claim few employee-staffed organizations can make. Clearly, there was nothing to hold a dissatisfied volunteer to the organization, and there were few resources to bother fighting over, yet, the symbolic function of working without pay – of "volunteering" – played an unmistakable role in supporting these behaviors.

There are also many ways in which the form of employee compensation influences their organizational behavior. For example, pay secrecy is a widespread organizational practice, one often deplored by academic researchers (Lawler 1971). Such secrecy helps inflate the value of knowing what a co-worker is paid and creates an aura of illicit excitement about any bit of information or rumor concerning pay. Often the exchange of confidences about one's salary can be an important event in the development of office friendships. Further, pay secrecy is a strong symbol of information restriction and can contribute to some social relations which are characteristic of closed, fearful, totalitarian societies.

In addition, the major status categories in most organizations are demarcated by compensation categories. The workforce is stratified into "exempt," "salaried," "hourly," "salary-plus-commission," "temporary," and, of course, "volunteer." The equation of different pay categories with different levels of importance to the organization is reflected in Ouchi's (1981) book describing the implementation of his management theory, "Theory Z." He described the experience of one firm in seeking to develop employee commitment to the organization through the combination of all of the different pay categories into one status for all employees to demonstrate the new egalitarian management approach.

Pearce (1989) found that one organization did not, in fact, distribute pay differently despite having three different compensation programs varying in their emphasis on "merit pay." She concluded that the organization was more interested in symbolically distinguishing the importance of various categories of employees. Policy-makers wished the world to know that the higher ranking employees' pay was more precarious – depending more on their individual performance. Yet they found that actually making large distinctions in raises was more difficult.

It is not only the form of pay administration but the absolute amount that carries strong symbolic content. For example, the assumption that pay should reflect the labor's value to society is apparent in the current debates concerning "comparable worth." Lapham's arguments are typical (*Los Angeles Times*, 7/6/1983):

If people mean what they say about the quality of education, then there's nothing for it except to raise the levels of pay and status for the whole teaching profession. Such a measure might reward waste, fraud and incompetence, but so does every other distribution of public or private funds. It is a question of what society thinks important enough, for what values it stands willing to pay the surcharge that is exacted by its belief in the sanctity of profit. If it comes to pass that society thinks teachers are as useful as doctors and lawyers, then it will have answered its own question.

The debate over "comparable worth" has developed from the assumption that pay should reflect what labor is worth, rather than the historical labor market differences which were based on sexual or racial segregation. Its proponents argue that pay differentials between female-dominated and male-dominated jobs are fundamentally unfair. One need not advocate higher pay for teachers and those working in female-dominated jobs to observe that their arguments about the worth of jobs to society appeal to widespread assumptions about the appropriateness of pay levels.

That these pay debates have only recently been raised, while the inequities they concern have existed for many decades, may reflect the increasing importance of pay as a surrogate for social status. As members of advanced post-industrial societies become more mobile with the consequence that individuals are no longer closely tied to single communities throughout their lives, people begin to rely more on portable attributes – such as income, cars, and clothing – to gauge social status. We all look for cues to tell us about one another; when we cannot use family or neighborhood, we rely on substitutes.

This research suggested that volunteers reacted strongly to their "unpaid" status. They took pride in its symbolism of sacrifice and service and reacted strongly to suggestions that they might be "unprofessional" or that their labor was worth nothing. The increasing fragmentation of stable communities and greater emphasis on money and financial success place volunteers in an increasingly awkward symbolic position. As the symbolic value of money in organizational life grows, the emphasis on volunteerism necessarily shrinks. Further, since employers need to rely on their employees for a myriad of small voluntary acts, this shift to market-focused contracts could hurt them as well. In many ways, volunteer-staffed organizations reflect the least controlled, most uncertain and "voluntary" side of organizational behavior and so may serve as a forewarning of forces confronting employee-dominated organizations.

CONCLUSIONS

The previous discussion reflects the wide-ranging implictions of the study of unpaid workers for organizational behavior. This exploratory work cannot hope to resolve these issues, or even to identify all of the relevant questions for the field of organizational behavior. Rather, it is intended to stimulate reflection and research that will broaden our understanding of organizations.

Chapter 9

Implications for volunteer management and research

The reported research has important implications for volunteers and paid staff members who are interested in managing and learning more about organizations staffed by volunteers. Volunteer organizations have received attention from social theorists because they are important to their societies; these organizations do valuable work. For most of us, the work done as organizational volunteers provides a major opportunity to make a meaningful difference to society, to make life better for others. For the vast majority, in their volunteer jobs, they are not constrained by the decisions and limitations of youth, nor by the bounds of current economic and social roles. No matter who you were or are, volunteer work provides the chance to make a lasting contribution.

Yet thousands of volunteers withdraw from this opportunity out of frustration. They do so because they find they have joined disorganized enterprises in which good people seem, somehow, to exploit and insult one another. The success of the many volunteer-staffed organizations that do not fall into this trap shows that it is not inevitably a feature of volunteer-run organizations. Yet, volunteer-staffed organizations are difficult to run successfully. Good will is no substitute for a clear-eyed understanding of the nature of volunteer organizational behavior. What follows is a discussion of the implications of the foregoing chapters for volunteer-staffed organizations. The implications cover both the practical observations concerning what seemed to work in the successful organizations and possible avenues for further research on volunteer-staffed organizations.

UNCERTAIN ROLES AS OWNER/WORKER/CLIENT

One characteristic of volunteer organizational workers is that they often hold conflicting roles in relation to the organization (propositions in Table 9.1). The resultant uncertainty is exacerbated by the egalitarian cultures of these organizations that emphasize independence and autonomy. Thus, two problems may be created for the management of these organizations. First, it can be confusing for new volunteers. Beginning work as an employee

Table 9.1 Effective management of volunteers propositions

P$_{49}$ Volunteer-staffed organizations with formal training and orientation programs for new recruits will have less turnover among recruits than those without such programs.

P$_{50}$ Volunteers in settings where the technology is not highly developed and where mistakes are not life-threatening will feel more free to make their own judgments about work than will volunteers in environments where mistakes have more serious consequences.

P$_{51}$ Volunteers will follow directives and conform to formal controls when they believe that these acts are necessary to achieve organizational goals.

P$_{52}$ Most volunteer-staffed organizations will consist of an activist core and a less active peripheral membership.

P$_{53}$ Core members will have significantly more knowledge of the organization and its members, will attempt more active interpersonal influence, and will submit more readily to others' interpersonal influence than will peripheral members.

P$_{54}$ The larger the proportion of organizational members in the core, the more smoothly integrated will be members' activities.

P$_{55}$ Peripheral members will assume core roles either because the core activities themselves are attractive or because they are strongly motivated to see the organization succeed.

P$_{56}$ Organizations which make open-ended demands on their volunteers will have more difficulty retaining volunteers than those which make more specific requests.

P$_{57}$ The longer volunteers work for their organizations, the more likely they will be to assume core roles.

P$_{58}$ Volunteer-staffed organizations with finite tenure for membership will have weaker social ties among members and weaker influence over members than those with open-ended tenure.

P$_{59}$ "Martyred leaders" will contribute to the effectiveness of their organizations by (1) working long hours during crisis periods, (2) embodying the organization's values, and (3) developing positive personal relationships with other members.

P$_{60}$ "Martyred leaders" will have greater influence over others than less zealous leaders because their own sacrifices will create feelings of moral obligation in others.

P$_{61}$ Having employees and volunteers do similar tasks will undermine the legitimacy of both inherently.

P$_{62}$ Tension between volunteers and employees in volunteer-dominated organizations will be lower when employees assume more volunteer-like attributes and accept volunteers' priorities.

P$_{63}$ Tension between volunteers and employees in employee-dominated organizations will be lower when volunteers assume more employee-like attributes and accept employees' priorities.

P_{64} Volunteers will tend to perform at lower levels than employees because (1) volunteers are less willing to complete unattractive tasks and (2) they work fewer hours, which reduces their job-relevant knowledge and increases coordination costs.

P_{65} Volunteer-staffed organizations will maintain effective levels of volunteer performance and coordination through either (1) high levels of informal social controls or (2) comprehensive bureaucratic controls, or (3) both.

P_{66} Organizations which emphasize that volunteer jobs are a form of work will foster greater volunteer attention to job performance and organizational goal achievement.

P_{67} Organizations which emphasize that volunteer jobs are a form of leisure will diminish volunteers' feelings of responsibility for their work and will foster employees' resentment of their volunteer co-workers.

P_{68} The actions of volunteers will most likely be coordinated through interpersonal influence, not through the administration of formal rewards and punishments.

P_{69} Organizations in which volunteers' work is recognized as worthwhile and is actively managed will experience less turnover and performance unreliability than will be experienced by organizations which manage volunteer work passively and provide no recognition.

carries with it significantly stronger norms about what the neophyte should be doing. Employees learn that they need to discover who their boss is and what it is he or she expects of them. Employees are usually explicitly directed to their supervisors, and supervisors know that they are expected to "take charge" of the new person initially. Contrast that pattern to the experiences of many volunteers. A neophyte may walk into a setting in which many of the individuals are socializing with their friends and be ignored completely as the friends continue their conversation (as the researcher was when she entered the student newspaper). Often the individual with whom the prospective volunteer spoke initially is not there, and the "volunteer-on-duty" may not even know that a new person was expected. The new volunteer may be seen as an interruption of planned tasks and so is instructed to sit and watch. The same independence and egalitarianism that experienced volunteers value can lead a new volunteer to feel neglected and ignored. Under these circumstances it isn't difficult to see why the majority of new volunteers are brought in by friends or to see that only the most self-confident or goal-dedicated persist in volunteer roles. Most individuals find the uncertainty of any new organization and job to be stressful, and for new volunteers it can be overwhelming.

Therefore, it isn't surprising that the organizations with the most formalized training and orientation programs (poverty relief agency and fire department) also had the least turnover. Such programs not only teach the volunteers the necessary skills (their formal purpose) but also serve to clarify expectations and help to integrate them socially into the organization.

It seems to be particularly difficult for volunteer-run organizations (without large employee workforces) to make these investments in their new volunteers. Recall that these are understaffed settings, and so the volunteers are struggling to complete their core service tasks. Yet the neglect of orientation and training increases their turnover rates and so exacerbates the staff shortage.

A second influence of the multiplicity of volunteer roles is that volunteers and those who work with them often find that they interpret their responsibilities differently from one another. When faced with a choice of expectations, it isn't surprising that many individuals will select the ones that serve their own interest, such as enhancing their status or making their work easier. Thus volunteers' supervisors, particularly employee supervisors, may tend to see a volunteer in the role of "worker" or even "para-professional assistant," while a volunteer would emphasize his or her role as owner or community leader. When the technology is highly developed and mistakes are deadly (e.g. medicine, firefighting) volunteers may willingly subordinate their judgments to experts. In the arts, human services, political action, and other more subjective areas, fewer volunteers seem willing to defer to others.

This conflict is exacerbated by the fact that such understaffed settings are usually quite dependent on their volunteers. Volunteers are not as behaviorally committed as employees and so are in a better "bargaining position" than comparable employees. Thus, many volunteers feel quite free to ignore those directives and policies that, in their own judgments, are unnecessary. Despite these different sources of volunteer insubordination, they are both amenable to the same solution.

It was found that volunteers were never insubordinate in those tasks they believed to be important. Thus, volunteers need to be convinced that particular policies or directives are necessary. The importance of consistent and clear coordination can be emphasized to volunteers with examples of serious damage to clients when workers ignored direction. Organizations can clearly designate certain times and places for different roles (weekly staff meeting, "owners," but during service delivery, "workers"); they can also openly discuss the conflicts inherent in their multiple roles.

There is, however, a more subtle difficulty. Volunteers often can see for themselves when practices are damaging to direct client service, but they may have less understanding of the importance of practices that serve a more symbolic function of reassuring important actors in the institutional environment (Meyer and Rowan 1977). Yet these needs can be explained and debated among volunteers until a consensus develops. This requires that the organization's leadership articulate these needs. For example, a previous anecdote described the volunteer family planning volunteers' refusal to wear smocks. However, the state office, in justifying its directive, responded only that "it looked more professional." The office may have had important reasons for wanting their clinics to look professional, such as maintaining legitimacy with accreditation or funding bodies or building political support in the community for their other projects. However, they did not seek to explain these reasons to the volunteers; they simply dismissed the volunteers as recalcitrant (and possibly silently vowed to seek funding for more paid staff). With some attention to articulation and management, organizations with independent members holding multiple organizational roles can run as smoothly as ones with the opposite characteristics.

MOTIVES AND ATTITUDES

Because volunteer-staffed settings are understaffed and staffed by individuals who have no clear financial motive, surveys of volunteer motives and attitudes continue unabated. The hope seems to be that information on why volunteers volunteer could help in the development of more effective recruitment and retention strategies. However, this work clearly demonstrates how misleading such surveys are. At the most general level the motives of volunteers remain stable across different countries and over time: volunteers work for generalized service or prosocial reasons ("to do good"), for the organization's attractive social interaction or status, and to forward the organization's particular goals. Certainly, specific organizations may attract individuals for particular reasons, such as the parents studied by Milofsky and Elion (1987), who were attracted to their rural alternative school because it reinforced their desired self-identity. But these specifics are usually well known to core organizational members.

Further, the self-reports of volunteers' motives and attitudes were shown to be so seriously confounded by social desirability, selective retention, and insufficient justification effects that substantive interpretation of the results is virtually impossible. Since there is little that such work can tell us about how to attract new volunteers or the behavior of existing volunteers, this line of research should be discouraged.

Yet the feelings and perceptions of volunteers are certainly very important, particularly since they are not as constrained by their need to remain in an organization they dislike as are employees. And it is just this propensity of volunteers to leave so quickly when unhappy that makes broadbrush questionnaire techniques useless. Questionnaires provide dependent employees with the anonymity they need to be frank, yet independent volunteers usually speak their minds quite openly. Similarly, the normative expectations regarding the appropriate "use" of volunteer work operate strongly against the free expression of self-interested views, and questionnaires are more likely than in-depth interviews to elicit only superficial presentational data.

Thus research on the causes and effects of variations in volunteers' attitudes needs to rely more on the techniques of clinical psychology and anthropology: interviews and observation. In addition, researchers might find it profitable to sample former volunteers and even friends and family of volunteers to obtain a broader range of views. But, what is perhaps more important, the theories to be tested need to become more sophisticated in order to capture more adequately the actual complexity of volunteers' cognitive and affective reactions to their experiences.

SOCIAL NETWORK RECRUITING AND INTERPERSONAL CONTROL

This work has helped to highlight the important role played by social relations among volunteers. First, most volunteers are recruited through interpersonal networks. As was noted, this form of recruiting also plays a strong role in the recruitment of employees. Yet, despite its importance, we have virtually no systematic research on its effectiveness. Above it was argued that such recruitment practices helped to establish one of the most important social control mechanisms in volunteer-staffed organizations – interpersonal influence. When friends were also volunteers, the personal costs of negligent acts increased. Yet this contrasts with Young's (1987) argument that volunteers' close relationships interfered with their job performance. This study did not allow a more rigorous test of the causal effects of recruitment on the subsequent behavior of individual volunteers, but this would seem to be an area of promising research.

Certainly, in the studied organizations, interpersonal influence was the primary means by which volunteers organized behavior in their settings. No volunteers could be moved by threat of financial harm, nor did any of these organizations command high social status. These volunteers did things because a certain person asked them to do so. Yet, despite the potential power of this form of organizational influence, it remains little understood by theorists and practitioners alike. The direct application of interpersonal influence, then, would appear to be a valuable area for research. For example, it would be important to establish the boundaries of organizational interpersonal influence: which activities are legitimate targets, which not? Is interpersonal influence dissipated or strengthened with greater use? Which strategies are most effective?

CORE AND PERIPHERAL VOLUNTEERS

The research reported here forms the basis for an extension of the early observations of Michels (1959) concerning the tendency of voluntary associations to divide into an activist core and a more inactive periphery. It was argued that this metaphor of a core and periphery better describes the knowledge and control in volunteer-staffed organizations than does the bureaucratic pyramid. Volunteers gave no real authority to formal titles, but they did know "the leaders." The organization really worked best among the core members, who were knowledgeable and reliable and took an active part in the work of the organization. Certainly volunteer-staffed organizations with a large core membership (or ideally with all members in the core) would run most effectively.

Despite the fact that members of the studied organizations' core continuously sought to recruit new members from the periphery, they found it difficult to do so. Few of the periphery wanted to make the additional time commitment for rewards that were primarily ego-oriented. This may be less the case in volunteer-staffed organizations in which the members have a stronger interest in the policy direction of their organization, such as political action groups. Nevertheless, for many volunteer-staffed organizations, one of the most difficult management challenges seems to be the recruitment of volunteers into the core.

Why did certain volunteers join the core? Usually because they had a particular interest in the activities of the core, either because they liked to be in the center of activities (and so might assume leadership roles in many different voluntary associations) or because they were particularly dedicated to this organization's goals. These are personal preferences, hence are probably difficult to cultivate. However, from a practical perspective, the actual problem seemed to be the alienation of potential core members through exploitation.

It is common for a peripheral volunteer to "volunteer" for some extra task, and, in effect, make a tentative step toward joining the core. Yet, too often, over-worked and labor-starved members of the core respond to this step by seeking to pile even more tasks upon the prospective core member. Thus, a volunteer who does not want to spend a lot of time on a particular volunteer job will quickly learn "never to volunteer" and "never to attend a meeting" to avoid being saddled with burdensome demands. Many volunteer-staffed organizations face serious understaffing problems, and so this reaction to someone who seems to want to get involved is natural. Yet it exacerbates the understaffing problem, and can lead to resentment among volunteer co-workers and even to the collapse of the organization. One solution is to simply divide responsibilities into manageable pieces each year and then never ask an individual to do an extra job. This is a difficult discipline and may mean that the organization simply does not do some tasks in certain years, yet it is the only way to assure potential members of the core that they will not be exploited.

There was another way in which potential core members were discouraged: through forced turnover in the organization. There are some organizations, usually characterized as "training organizations" or staffed by students during their school tenure, that require volunteers to quit at a certain age or upon leaving school. This practice interfered with both recruitment to the core and the effectiveness of interpersonal influence. This is because one way members were recruited into the core was through simple longevity: the longer they stayed, the more they knew about the organization and fellow volunteers, thus drifting into core membership. Some members of the core in the studied organizations had over 20 years' seniority in their organizations. Since volunteers' work is a part-time activity, it can take them several years to become knowledgeable about the organization. Also, the longer they stay the more likely they are to develop friends in the organization, increasing the importance of interpersonal influence for more senior workers. Finally, the longer the average tenure of volunteers, the fewer the number of new recruits that need to be found each year. For these understaffed settings, the practical advantages of a senior, stable workforce would seem to be self-evident.

Certainly, as noted above, the poor reputation of student volunteers probably stems largely from the lack of meaningful social linkages they have with others in their volunteer-staffed organizations. Certainly, some organizations may be forced by their mission to maintain these policies of forced turnover (e.g. a college newspaper). Yet there may be other organizations that have limited volunteer tenure or targeted a population with a known finite tenure, perhaps for historical reasons. If the present analysis is correct, such organizations would not be able to draw as strongly on informal influence among volunteers. It is possible that many may find that they are well able to manage these constraints through more extensive formal surveillance, explicit job descriptions, and well established recruiting mechanisms (and probably a strong core paid staff). Those who are having more difficulties with volunteer irresponsibility may want to reconsider their forced turnover policy.

Systematic research could help with this important practice by describing the size and characteristics of the core membership in different kinds of volunteer-staffed organizations. It could test these exploratory hypotheses concerning the reasons why certain volunteers join the core and why others do not.

MARTYRED LEADERSHIP

In addition to direct interpersonal influence, these organizations were maintained by charismatic leaders who embodied the values of the organizations. These leaders assumed a mythic status: stories about the adversities they had overcome were told, and these leaders were praised by all. The two organizations that did not have these leaders, the student newspaper and gift shop, seemed to suffer much more severe disaffection and indirection. These leaders were vital to the effectiveness of their organizations for several reasons.

First, they personally kept the organizations functioning during difficult periods – by working long hours tirelessly, by rallying supporters to the cause, and by not becoming discouraged by adverse circumstances. These were individuals who were willing to "exploit themselves" to reach their organization's goals. Second, they were important embodiments of the goals and values of the organizations – they believed in the organization and sacrificed for it. They "led by example." Yet, these individuals were not distant heroes but continuously engaged with the other members, and volunteers who knew few others knew these leaders. Leaders who were not able to serve this personal emotional role for others, such as the editor-in-chief of the student newspaper (despite working tirelessly), were not able to pull the members together through critical periods. In fact, it is likely that the relatively trivial issue that precipitated the newspaper's collapse (a dispute over how to spend the small year-end surplus) arose as much from the volunteers' antagonism toward the editor-in-chief as from the substantive issue itself. He did not have the interpersonal skills or personal warmth to really bind the volunteers to his vision for the organization.

As a practical matter, how can these individuals be found or trained? To some extent these leaders create themselves from their own dedication to the organization's goals. They really do believe in what they are doing and this is infectious. If they need to charm others into joining the organization, they learn to be charming. No doubt there are probably some necessary interpersonal skills, such as sensitivity and empathy, that are not easily learned. Nevertheless, virtually all nonprofit organizations started from the zeal of at least one enthusiast.

There was another facet of the leadership of these organizations that merits discussion: the role of martyrdom. The successful studied organizations all had leaders who gave much more to the organization than did other volunteers. Thus these leaders incurred some degree of moral obligation on the part of other volunteers which could be called upon when action was needed. In the studied organizations, it was never overdone to the point of manipulation, although it is possible to imagine that this is a potential threat. It genuinely seemed to be a natural byproduct of organizations serving their communities and staffed by those sacrificing their free time to help others. Yet this aspect of volunteer leadership – and, in fact, any recognition of the emotional or symbolic component of volunteer leadership – remains unexamined. Particularly in small value-rational organizations this would seem to be one of the most important influences on volunteer organizational behavior and deserving of further attention.

EMPLOYEE–VOLUNTEER TENSION

The tension that can exist between volunteer and employee co-workers remains one of the unpleasant secrets of nonprofit organizations. The preceding discussion described how volunteers and employees, by the very nature of their different relationships to the organization, tend to undermine each other's legitimacy. Employees have higher professional and expertise-based status while undermining the legitimacy of volunteer "sacrifice" by taking salaries for their work. Volunteers give of themselves to the organization, yet undermine the professionalism of employees. One of the contributions of the present study is to bring this secret out into the open and begin to analyze how its destructive aspects can be reduced.

Among the studied organizations there was only one organization (out of the six volunteer-run organizations with employees) in which damaging levels of employee–volunteer conflict were observed. However, the discussion of the insubordination of the family planning volunteers suggested that there may have been difficulties in the larger family planning parent organization, which was outside the scope of the present study. As discussed in detail above, in those organizations with positive employee–volunteer relationships there was substantial "confounding" of volunteer–employee statuses, particularly with respect to the dedication and self-sacrifice (and underpayment) of the employees. None of these employees were alienated or merely working at a job for the money. They had become volunteer-like in their enthusiasm and dedication. They also outdid their volunteer colleagues in their praise of the charismatic leaders.

What this present study cannot provide are insights into how this relationship can be successfully managed in bureaucracies such as hospitals or museums, with their large and sometimes alienated employee workforce. It is possible that the converse of the processes in the studied volunteer-dominated organizations may also be true: relations are more successful when volunteers become more employee-like. If this analysis is correct, a strike at a hospital (which would emphasize the financial contracts between workers and the organization and lead to an airing of grievances) should prove to be emotionally disconcerting for volunteers. Are volunteers to assume that they are the only ones sacrificing for the organization? Are they really exploited? Certainly the relationships between volunteer and employee co-workers are complex and would seem to be a fruitful area for investigation.

VOLUNTEERS' JOB PERFORMANCE

As noted earlier, it is widely assumed that volunteers are less productive than employees, and certainly this study indicated that their organizations undertook less demanding tasks than their employee-staffed counterparts. Yet it is surprising that we do not really know in what ways, exactly, volunteer performance is less effective than that of employees. Is it that volunteers are more insubordinate or that they cannot be induced to complete the more tedious aspects of their work? Or is it that volunteers work fewer hours in a week and so coordination costs are higher? Or might it be, as Young (1987) implied, that volunteers do not exert the high levels of effort that can be obtained from contingently paid employees who fear being fired. This study indicated that the greater independence of volunteers did, indeed, constrain organizational performance, but it was manageable.

Volunteers' efforts can be effectively spurred and coordinated through either informal social controls *or* explicit bureaucratic ones. Volunteer-staffed organizations without either seem doomed to fail. Organizations can successfully manage volunteers with very informal procedures, but they must have strong interpersonal ties among a core group of volunteers of long standing. Similarly, effective organizations may be staffed by volunteers only peripherally involved in their volunteer organizations, but, if so, they must have clear job descriptions, a finite, undemanding, yet clearly worthwhile task, and work in a clear, legitimate hierarchical structure. Organizations certainly use both approaches (they would not appear to be mutually exclusive), yet no organization can be effective with neither one. It is simply too easy for volunteer-staffed organizations to cease to exist. Interpersonal ties and formal management practices can substitute for one another, but organized activity cannot exist in their absence.

We don't know what the particular effects of these different approaches are or which approach is "better." Close interpersonal ties would seem to create the supportive interpersonal climate that can be so attractive to volunteers, yet it may force the organization to retain only a narrowly homogeneous workforce. Highly structured relationships can be alienating, which would imply that volunteers may react negatively to a very structured environment. Certainly, many volunteers work for the opportunity to express important values, and these individuals may not remain long in a "rigid, business-like" workplace. Yet, we really do not know if this is the universal reaction to such structures. Experienced volunteers may welcome the chance to work in a well-organized effort, since they may have had bad experiences serving disorganized causes. Systematic research on the relative effectiveness of the two volunteer management approaches identified here would seem to promise rich returns.

THE MEANING OF VOLUNTEER WORK

As noted above, there is a great deal of uncertainty about the meaning and importance of volunteer work. It is both leisure and work, both giving to others and self-indulgent dilettantism. Those who work with volunteers need to clarify this uncertainty by emphasizing one or the other of these aspects of volunteer work. Yet, since volunteer organizational work is inherently *both*, each choice of emphasis has its advantages and disadvantages.

Volunteering is work

The advantage of emphasizing the "work" facet of volunteering is that it legitimizes the use of efficiency-oriented management practices. Volunteers' attention is focused on performance and client welfare. This approach should help the organization to make concrete contributions to its community and to its clients. However, this emphasis implies that volunteers receive "rewards" for their work, much like an employee receives pay.

This combination of assuming that volunteers must receive something they value from their work and uncertainty about exactly what these benefits might be creates certain practical management difficulties. The most obvious difficulty is that managers may strive to provide rewards that, in fact, have no appeal to their volunteers. An example, noted earlier, from the poverty relief agency provides an illustration of this common frustration. The dinner organized by the board to show its appreciation to its volunteers was a failure, since less than 10 percent of the volunteers attended. The organizers were frustrated and angry, muttering about "apathetic volunteers." The volunteers said they were reluctant to go to a gathering in which they wouldn't know anyone else and that they had volunteered for this organization because they wanted to make a small contribution in the fight against hunger, not to meet other people. Such experiences appear to be common among managers of volunteers, who must continually experiment to find something that "works as a reward" for at least some of their volunteers.

Another, less obvious, practical difficulty in emphasizing the work component of volunteering results from the fact that the kinds of rewards volunteers do value often are not directly under policy makers' control. Unlike pay, which can often be increased or terminated by supervisors happy or unhappy with their employees' performance, the benefits of volunteer work come from the work itself or from interactions with co-workers and cannot easily be altered by others in the organization. Thus, for control, volunteer-staffed organizations usually depend on interpersonal influence and respect for a valued leader, not on the administration of rewards and punishments.

Finally, in addition to the problems of uncertainty and the lack of control of salient rewards, certain kinds of volunteer rewards are "awarded" so early in a volunteer's tenure that organizations experience severe turnover problems. The best examples of organizations with this kind of work-reward problem are those staffed by high school and college students. The motives of student volunteers are, of course, mixed. Yet many of these young adults volunteer to learn a job skill or build up work experience ("resumé-building") for a post-graduation job or further education. Such benefits are clearly instrumental and as tangible as pay, but they can be obtained after a relatively short period of work – and sometimes simply from being listed as a volunteer without ever doing any work at all! Volunteer-staffed organizations that rely on resumé-building to attract, retain, and motivate face serious potential impediments to effectiveness.

In summary, there are a number of drawbacks to treating volunteering as a kind of work that is simply paid differently. The benefits obtained from volunteer work are often very unclear to all involved. Those rewards that seem to be most important are not under the control of the organization but derive from the participation itself. The organizations that try to substitute a nonmonetary tangible benefit, such as training, must rely on a sufficiently large population of potential volunteers who want that particular reward to compensate for the high turnover of those who have been trained. It is a very rare volunteer-staffed organization that can make any rewards, other than praise or respect, contingent on job performance. Yet these difficult problems associated with treating volunteers as workers are preferable to those which result from treating them as hobbyists.

Volunteering is leisure

Volunteering can be treated as a type of leisure activity rather than as a type of work. It differs from other forms of leisure by its requirement to work within a formal organization. However, part of the reason volunteering is enjoyable is the satisfaction that comes from social interaction or from contributing to a larger social good. Yet, like all leisure, it is done for the enjoyment of the activity and is something to be done when "in the mood" and only so long as it remains interesting. Certainly, this is characteristic, to some degree, of all organizational volunteering.

If volunteers expect their participation to be another hobby, they might reasonably be expected to treat it like any other leisure activity. Certainly, few people undertake hobbies that require the sustained discipline that usually characterizes organizational roles. Organizations which assume that volunteers are hobbyists must provide very short hours and be prepared for unreliable workers, or they must recruit only among that subculture of driven hobbyists. The practical difficulty created by this assumption is that what begins as a frank acknowledgement that the time volunteers will give is limited may become a reluctance to give volunteers any responsibility at all. The problems this practice caused for the newspaper and family planning clinic were detailed above.

The psychological importance of felt personal responsibility for job performance has been noted by those who study employees. Hackman and Oldham (1980) considered the psychological experience of personal responsibility for a task to be one of the major factors influencing employees' job satisfaction and internal work motivation. It is important to recognize that volunteers themselves often resent this form of indulgence, since it implies disrespect for their own contributions. The college newspaper student volunteer quoted at the beginning of Chapter 1 expresses great anger at this implicit denigration of her efforts.

It is in organizations treating their volunteers as hobbyists that we seem to find the most staff complaints about volunteers. Employees resent being told that their own "praise is in their paychecks" while volunteers are indulged and excused like small children. This management assumption can create two distinct "classes" of workers – the serious "professionals" and the volunteers doing the unimportant work – and cannot help but breed resentment.

Volunteering is, of course, a leisure activity, and this simply cannot be ignored. Yet the most successful of the studied organizations were those that communicated that their volunteers were serious (read: "important") workers. Approaches that emphasize the "working" component of volunteering are more likely to convey respect for volunteers' commitment of time and effort and to engender a reciprocal respect for the organization's need for reliable performance of responsibilities.

The paradox of volunteers is that they are paid nothing, yet they are working in organizational settings, performing work in the service of organizational objectives. That is, their activities look like the kinds of activities that people are paid to do (and are often done alongside co-workers who are paid). The fact that volunteers are willing to make these contributions without the expected inducements is somehow discomfiting. When confronted with behavior that does not fit neatly into the distinct categories of "work" or "leisure" but is an uneasy blend of the two, observers became perplexed. This unease with volunteering is reflected in the blame, described in Chapter 2, that has been attached to either the "employing" organization or to the volunteer.

Thus the practical management of volunteers entails the management of the meaning of their work. Perhaps this is why these organizations become so dependent on a visionary who can articulate the importance of the organization's mission. It may also be why the area in which there is the greatest growth in North American and Western European direct service volunteering is in self-help organizations (Kramer 1981). In these organizations the client-volunteers know why they are working.

CONCLUSIONS

This study is intended to focus attention on the organizational behavior of volunteers. Heretofore the management of volunteers has been something that practitioners have had to learn, virtually on their own, or through the assistance of the written experiences of one of their colleagues. Systematic research has tended to focus on surveys of volunteers' motives, to the virtual exclusion of attention to what volunteers actually do in organizations and how volunteers might more effectively work together. This exploratory work has served to identify several features of the organizational behavior of volunteers; however, it remains preliminary: it has identified and sought to explain, yet has not been able to test the relative importance of the many forces affecting volunteers. Its generalizations often have been presented in their starkest and most controversial form, in part in order to counterbalance the gentility or boosterism that characterizes much writing about the management of volunteer-staffed organizations. It is hoped that this work will spur attention – research as well as counter-argument – that will help volunteers to achieve their goals more effectively.

Appendix
Study methods

The information presented in this work is based on data collected by the author as well as available published research and theory reflecting on volunteer organizational behavior. In this Appendix, the systematic data collection in the 14 matched volunteer-staffed and employee-staffed organizations is described. These data form the basis for most of the ideas presented in the preceding chapters and so are described in detail. The material is organized in four sections. In the first, the sample selection and the data collection procedure in the organizations are described. This is followed by a brief description of each of the 14 organizations making up the sample. Next, an introduction to the measures reported in previous chapters is provided. Finally the Appendix concludes with a description of the manner in which these data are used in previous chapters.

SAMPLE

The research was designed to compare the organizational behavior of volunteer-staffed organizations with that of employee-staffed organizations doing comparable work. This allowed systematic comparison of volunteers with that group which forms the basis for organizational behavior – employees – while controlling as much as possible for the very powerful effects of the kind of work undertaken. It is important to sample all volunteer-staffed and all employee-staffed organizations because in most mixed volunteer–employee organizations the volunteers play ancillary roles. They do not do tasks comparable to those of their employee co-workers, nor do they exert meaningful control over the daily management of the work.

This sample selection does, however, result in a biased sample of volunteer-staffed organizations, since only those that could be matched on task to comparable organizations staffed by employees were studied. This effectively removed political advocacy groups, clubs, and other kinds of associations which exist primarily to express the values of their members.

Sample selection

Volunteer-staffed and employee-staffed service organizations that worked on the same or similar tasks were studied as a matched set. For purposes of matching, technology or organizational work was considered to be the organization's "primary task," which corresponds, according to Miller and Rice (1967), to the public definition of the identity and purpose of the institution. A volunteer-staffed organization must be both managed and staffed by volunteers with the allowance of at most two or three paid members. An employee-staffed organization must be both managed and staffed by employees. In the sampled volunteer-staffed organizations, the governing body and day-to-day managerial and work staff were volunteer, but several had decided that they needed the continuity provided by an employee putting in longer hours and having responsibility for the coordination of daily activities. These organizations remained volunteer-dominated and, therefore, did not seriously deviate from the sample criteria.

Organizations were selected for initial contact as follows: the entire population of volunteer-staffed organizations meeting the above criteria within a 70-mile radius of New Haven, Connecticut (which includes New York City), were identified through municipal and regional lists of community services, licensees, and telephone directories. They were matched with employee-staffed organizations that were as comparable on task and size as possible (e.g. only small community newspapers were matched to the volunteer-staffed newspaper). After these lists were compiled, the researcher began contacting organizations, stopping when a task-set pair was formed. That is, the sampling procedure was stopped when no more task-sets (matched volunteer–employee pairs) containing volunteer and employee-staffed organizations could be located. This procedure resulted in 26 initial contacts and 14 final study participants.

Descriptions of each of the sampled organizations follow.

THE SAMPLED ORGANIZATIONS

1(a) Volunteer-staffed day care center

Located in a medium-sized New England city, it cared for 25 children. The children ranged in age from a few months to four years. Those below two years of age were located in the "infant room," and those above two years of age in the "toddler room." The center was run as a cooperative with the parents of the children assuming maintenance, teaching, administrative, and governance tasks. Parent-assistants each worked a four-hour shift every week and attended monthly governance meetings. Two part-time teachers were hired for each room to provide "continuity and program development" for the children. The parents from each room elected their own chairperson, and each year the entire center elected a central coordinator and treasurer. The center was two years and six months old at entry. Its membership was composed of 46 men and women, with an average age of over 27. The turnover in the last year had been 13 percent of the membership, but since the center had a long waiting list, these individuals were easily replaced. Ten organization-sample interviews and 21 usable questionnaires were completed by members of the volunteer-staffed day care center.

1(b) Employee-staffed day care center

It was located in a medium-sized northeastern city and cared for 65 children. The children ranged in age from two and a half (toilet-trained only) to six years (a day-long kindergarten was part of the center). The children were divided into age-groups – two- to three-year-olds in one room, four-year-olds in another, and the five- to six-year-olds were divided into two kindergarten classrooms. The center was funded through an income-based sliding-scale fee and by a local social service agency. Hot lunches were provided by state and federal agencies. There were a director and an assistant director who completed administrative and governance tasks. There was comparatively more administrative work in the employee-staffed care center than in the volunteer-staffed center, in part due to a more complex funding structure. There was a head teacher for each of the four rooms; she supervised a staff of assistant teachers, day care aides, and occasional work-study students (all paid). All aides, teachers, and directors worked a standard 40-hour week. The center was just over six years old at entry and was composed of 20 women employees with an average age of just over 28 years. The turnover in the preceding year (excluding work-study students) had been 10 percent, but it had been much higher a few years earlier. This change reflected a dramatic improvement in salary and working conditions, according to the director. Six organization-sample interviews and seven usable questionnaires were completed by members of the employee-staffed day care center.

2(a) Volunteer-staffed weekly newspaper

This was a weekly student newspaper for a medium-sized private university located in a northeastern suburb. Each week 4,000 copies of the 10- to 12-page paper were distributed free on campus newsstands. The paper was entirely student-run. The editor-in-chief was appointed by the student council and received a partial scholarship. The editor-in-chief appointed the editors and managers, who in turn appointed their own staffs. Those who sold advertising space received a commission on the sale. The members wrote and laid out the paper each week. It was typeset and printed by a professional printer. The newspaper was funded primarily through the student council, but it also received advertising revenues. Work time varied greatly, based on the volunteer's own interest level; members worked on the paper from an hour or two a month to about 40 hours a week. It had been published (more or less) continuously for 30 years. The newspaper had a total staff of approximately 30 undergraduates. (Some participated sporadically, and no records were kept of the number of press cards in circulation.) There was a mix of men and women (again, precise information is not available). Turnover was hard to calculate in this organization – it was traditionally high, since students' interests continually changed. Moreover, while the researcher was finishing the organization-sample interviews, there was a rebellion by the editorial staff and all but one editor "went on strike" (or "were fired" by the editor-in-chief, depending on who was asked). The final two issues for the academic year were produced by the editor-in-chief and anyone he could find to help him. Since most of those who struck were graduating seniors anyway, the paper was expected to be functioning quite normally by the fall. Unfortunately, this event is reflected in the poor response rate on the structured instruments – only nine organization-sample interviews and six usable questionnaires were completed by the staff of the volunteer newspaper.

2(b) Employee-staffed weekly newspaper

This community-oriented newspaper was distributed free, once a week in apartment building lobbies and shops in a residential neighborhood of a large metropolitan city. Each week 50,000 copies of this 12-page paper were distributed. The paper was owned by the editor-and-publisher who hired all staff members. All staff were salaried (the advertising salespeople received an additional commission on sales) and worked a standard 40-hour week. The members wrote and laid out the paper, and then sent it to a professional printer to be typeset and printed. An independent group contracted to distribute the paper. The newspaper was published for profit; that is, the owner hoped to sell enough advertising space to cover costs and return a profit on his investment. The employee-staffed newspaper had been published for just under two years at entry. There was a staff of 13 men and women, with an average age of almost 26 years. The turnover in the last year had been 85 percent. In fact, the editorial staff was relatively stable, but the advertising salespeople had been turning over several times a year. There was "low morale" throughout this organization: the editorial and production staffs claimed to remain only because similar jobs in their fields are difficult to obtain, and the fact that the paper was operating at a deficit worried the owner. Eight organization-sample interviews and eight usable questionnaires were completed by members of this newspaper.

3(a) Volunteer-staffed poverty relief agency

This agency was a nondenominational Christian relief organization in a medium-sized northeastern city. Its primary task was the distribution of food to those who requested it (13,245 deliveries in the previous year), but it occasionally provided transportation to medical appointments as well. If clients wanted food, they called a telephone number that was monitored by an answering service. The answering service called the telephone volunteer on duty (two shifts a day, about four hours each) and left the clients' names and numbers. The telephone volunteer called the clients, collected information (address, number of people to be fed, whether or not on welfare, etc.), and told the clients what time to expect the deliveries. The telephone volunteer then called the driving volunteer, or, if the driver was already on a delivery, left the information at the central office. The central office was occupied by one of two part-time compensated coordinators. Drivers checked with the central office throughout their shift. About ten meals were delivered during an average day, although nearly 80 percent of their calls came in the few days before the twice-monthly welfare checks arrived. The organization was funded through a small foundation grant and individual donations of money and food. The volunteers elected a governing committee which hired the two coordinators. The coordinators handled the day-to-day administration of the service, working about 20 hours a week, and most volunteers worked one half-day shift a month. The agency had been serving the community for about nine and a half years at entry. About 180 women and men were members of the volunteer poverty relief agency; their average age was about 44 years. The turnover was 14 percent in the last year. Members of the agency continuously recruited new members, but their work had never been threatened by a lack of volunteers. Ten organization-sample interviews and 11 usable questionnaires were completed by members of the relief agency.

3(b) Employee-staffed poverty relief agency

This poverty relief agency was a municipal department of a medium-sized New England city that was statutorily required to provide emergency relief to those who did not qualify for any of the state or federal relief programs. In practice, most of their clients were chronic, usually men with drug- or alcohol-related problems. Clients needed to appear weekly to receive their checks from an assigned social worker. Unlike the volunteer poverty relief agency, this agency sought to rehabilitate its clients – work programs were instituted, and clients were required to attend counseling sessions before receiving their checks, etc. The administration of the department was the responsibility of a director and two assistant directors (all political appointees). One assistant director was responsible for the "professional staff" (social workers, case investigators, and their supervisors). The other assistant director was responsible for the "administrative staff" (clerk-typists, bookkeepers, a secretary, and their supervisors). All employees below the assistant directors' level were civil servants and members of a union; all worked a standard 35-hour week. The administrative costs of the agency were paid by the municipality, but the aid was provided by the state. In practice, the hard-pressed municipality continually searched for ways to reduce its costs. For example, permanent positions vacated through attrition were replaced with temporary, but federally funded, workers, and the case loads were more than double the legal maximum, leaving the social workers little time for counseling. The age of the organization was not precisely known. The New England municipalities (under Colonial British Elizabethan laws) were required to provide for their poor, and, therefore, this service has been provided for more than 300 years, although the present structure was developed during the late 1930s.

Fifty-three men and women, with an average age of just under 45 years, worked for the agency. Turnover was about 25 percent in the last year. It was particularly acute among the professional staff. (The most senior professional had only been working three years, and he claimed he was just earning money until he completed a professional degree program.) Furthermore, once an employee left, it could take up to a year to receive a replacement, since the municipal civil service commission had been defunct for several years. Ten organization-sample interviews and 13 usable questionnaires were completed by members of the employee-staffed poverty relief agency.

4(a) Volunteer-staffed symphonic orchestra

This orchestra provided a summer season of five weekly concerts. The concerts were sponsored by a state-supported college in a medium-sized New England city and were well attended in an auditorium with a capacity of approximately 1,000. The orchestra was run by the musical director, who was a college faculty member given a summer salary. He auditioned the musicians, determined the programs, and conducted most numbers. A few of the musicians helped him administer the orchestra. For example, the "manager" – one of the bass players – ran to the director's office to telephone missing musicians, leaving the director free to conduct the rehearsal. There was only one rehearsal, lasting about three hours, before each hour and a half concert. The college provided the auditorium, the musical director's salary, and had the programs printed in the campus print shop; each week members of a different local service group volunteered their services as ushers. The orchestra's fourth season was beginning at entry. The orchestra was composed of about 90 men and women. Their average age was just over 38 years, but they ranged from adolescents to individuals in their seventies. The orchestra lost a few members during the season (8 percent turnover). Ten organization-sample interviews and 47 usable questionnaires were completed by members of the volunteer-staffed symphonic orchestra.

4(b) Employee-staffed symphonic orchestra

The employee-staffed orchestra provided a winter season of five monthly concerts in a large eastern city. This orchestra began as a traditional patron-sponsored orchestra, but when its musical director left, the musicians formed a cooperative and hired a new musical director. The orchestra was funded through box office receipts, governmental matching funds, donations, and the income the orchestra earned performing outside their concert series. The musicians elected a governing committee which held a majority on the board of trustees. The trustees were responsible for governance, with the governing committee, a manager, a publicist, and an administrative assistant assuming administrative tasks. Unlike most orchestras, in this one the musical director assumed a modest role; seating and programs were determined by subcommittees of musicians. Each concert was held in a hall seating approximately 3,000, and there were three lengthy rehearsals before each concert. The office staff and a few governing committee members worked 40 hours a week throughout the year, but, on the average, most musicians worked much less than this. The musicians paid themselves "scale" (the lowest allowable by their union). At entry the orchestra had completed its fifth season as a cooperative. The orchestra was composed of 91 men and women with an average age of just under 39 years. There had been little turnover – an administrative assistant and one musician in the last year. Over 90 percent of the musicians were members before the cooperative was formed. Most musicians earned their primary income through other engagements and occasionally had to turn down more lucrative "gigs" in order to maintain their commitment to the orchestra. Seven organization-sample interviews and six usable questionnaires were completed by members.

5(a) Volunteer-staffed family planning clinic

The clinic provided gynecological, contraceptive, and related counseling services to women in a New England town. Their patient load at entry was 200 women. The office was open weekdays. Pregnancy testing was done in the office once a week, and clinics (for examinations) were held two evenings a month. The 14 volunteers elected a governing body and officers who hired the full-time compensated secretary. The secretary monitored the office, maintained the files, and conducted the billing. Income-based sliding-scale fees were charged, with state and federal bodies providing support for indigent clients. In addition, the clinic held an annual fundraising drive. All of these monies were deposited with the central state office, which provided the local clinics with the operating expenses they needed. Volunteers worked anywhere from four to five hours a month (clinic nights) to nearly 40 hours a week. New volunteers began by taking medical histories and were trained for sequentially more demanding tasks. The actual examinations were conducted by a nurse-practitioner, who was paid by the hour, although several volunteers were registered nurses and assisted with the examinations. This group had existed for over 50 years, although the clinic service had just recently begun again after a several year hiatus. Fourteen women with an average age of just over 34 years were members of this group. There had been no turnover in the last year. Seven organization-sample interviews and ten usable questionnaires were completed by members of this clinic.

5(b) Employee-staffed family planning clinic

This family planning clinic provided sex education, gynecological, contraceptive, and related counseling services to women in a large New England city. Its case load at entry was 4,000 women. Clinics were held four days and one evening a week. The clinic was a section of a municipal health department and was run by a director. At the next-lowest hierarchical level there was the community education supervisor; the fiscal officer who supervised the clerical staff; the clinic supervisor who supervised the counselors, lab technicians, and nurse's aides; and the nurse-practitioner who provided the in-house medical supervision. Several physicians were hired on an hourly basis to perform the examinations. All employees worked a standard 35-hour week and were unionized municipal civil servants. Patients paid an income-based sliding-scale fee, with federal and state programs providing support for indigent clients. All income was transferred to the municipality, which, in turn, provided the clinic's support. At entry the clinic had been serving the community for seven years. Twenty women and one man, with an average age of about 30 years, were employees of this family planning clinic. Turnover had been 10 percent in the preceding year. Ten organization-sample interviews and 16 usable questionnaires were completed by members of this clinic.

6(a) Volunteer-staffed gift shop

This gift shop sold gift items – fine table service, crystal, stationery, and knick-knacks – in the downtown district of a medium-sized northeastern city. The shop had approximately 288 square feet of floor (selling) space and was consistently profitable, relying predominantly on the patronage of long-time customers. The shop was open Tuesdays through Saturdays and was wholly owned (for fundraising) by a large community service volunteer group. The elected president of this group appointed a board to govern and administer the shop. All members of the service group were required to work six half-day shifts a year as sales clerks. The volunteer board hired a part-time paid bookkeeper and a full-time manager. This manager coordinated day-to-day activities and acted as head buyer. The membership of the board changed yearly, and the board members' involvement in the affairs of the shop varied with individual interests and talents. The shop was 49 years old at entry. There were 138 women members, with an average age of over 30 years. The only turnover in the last year resulted from those who had left the service group (4 percent) and, therefore, were no longer working in the shop. Nine organization-sample interviews and 26 usable questionnaires were completed by members of the volunteer-staffed gift shop.

6(b) Employee-staffed gift shop

This shop sold gift items, specializing in gourmet cookware. The shop consisted of approximately 864 square feet of floor (selling) space and was located in the downtown district of a medium-sized New England city. The store had been very profitable in the last few years, in large part due to growing interest in gourmet cooking. The store was open weekdays during the summer data collection period. It was founded by its current owner and was three and a half years old at entry. The owner hired the sales force, the buyer, and the bookkeeper. All worked a standard 40-hour week. The shop was composed of eight men and women, with an average age of more than 44 years. The turnover had been high (50 percent), but only among the sales clerks. Four organization-sample interviews and three usable questionnaires were completed by members of this gift shop.

7(a) Volunteer-staffed fire department

This fire department provided emergency medical technician, fire prevention, and fighting services to a rural New England town of approximately 15,000. They responded to approximately 500 alarms a year. In an emergency, the town dispatcher was called; she made an announcement through the radios and blasted a horn so others could go to their radios; next, the closest firefighter went to the station to take the apparatus (engine, hook and ladder, or ambulance) to the destination, while other members proceeded directly in their automobiles. The department was composed of four companies (three pump and one hook and ladder); the members seemed to encourage a lively competition among companies. Each company owned its own firehouse and elected a house administrative group and the "line" officers (lieutenants, captains, and deputy chiefs). The department as a whole elected the chief and two assistant chiefs in annual elections. The town purchased and maintained the equipment. In addition, the fire department held fundraising events. This department was celebrating its 125th year during the data collection period.

Each company was allowed 40 full members (all were men), and there was a waiting list for these positions. Firefighters were required to attend a certain percentage of activities (fundraisers, parades, Sunday morning drills, and, of course, fire calls) or they were dropped from full membership. Someone waiting for a full membership opening possessed all privileges, save voting and office-holding. Turnover was only 3 percent of full members in the preceding year. Eight organization-sample interviews and 31 usable questionnaires were completed by the fire department volunteers.

7(b) Employee-staffed fire department

This department provided fire prevention and fighting services to a New England suburb of 26,000. The department answered an average of 200 calls a month (there was a severe "arson problem" in this town). When a call was received at the emergency number, a loud buzzer sounded and the caller's voice was transmitted by the dispatcher throughout the firehouses. There were a central firehouse, in which five firefighters and the battalion chief were stationed, and two outlying stations with two firefighters each. There were four shifts working an average of 42 hours a week (two shifts a day, three days on, three days off). Also contained in the central station were the offices of the chief, assistant chief, drill instructor, and secretary. All appointments and promotions were made by the municipal fire commission. The positions were civil service, with the battalion chiefs and firefighters belonging to a union. The town directly funded the department, which was 77 years old at entry. The department was composed of 46 men (the one secretary was a woman) with an average age of just under 40 years. There had been no turnover in the previous year. However, there had been a bitter strike by the firefighters two years before, and a great deal of union–management (i.e. firefighter–chief) tension remained. Nine organization-sample interviews and 11 usable questionnaires were completed by members of the employee-staffed fire department.

Organizational comparisons

Tables A.1(a)–A.1(g) compare the volunteer- and employee-staffed organizations of each type, and Table A.1(h) contains a summary (mean differences) between organization types on the descriptive characteristics. The comparatively lower number of clients served by the volunteer-staffed organizations is analyzed in detail in Chapter 2. In addition, there was a significantly greater percentage of nonwhites in the employee-staffed organizations than

Table A.1(a) Comparison of volunteer- and employee-staffed day care centers

Descriptive characteristic	Volunteer	Employee
Organizational age (years)	2	6
Number of members	46	20
Previous year's turnover (percent)	13	10
Number of children served	25	65

Note: Numbers have been rounded to the nearest whole number.

Table A.1(b) Comparison of volunteer- and employee-staffed weekly newspapers

Descriptive characteristic	Volunteer	Employee
Organizational age (years)	30	2
Number of members	30	13
Previous year's turnover (percent)	67	85
Number of copies distributed	4000	50000

Note: Numbers have been rounded to the nearest whole number.

Table A.1(c) Comparison of volunteer- and employee-staffed poverty relief agencies

Descriptive characteristic	Volunteer	Employee
Organizational age (years)	9	300
Number of members	180	53
Previous year's turnover (percent)	14	25
Number of clients	13245[a]	23000

Note: Numbers have been rounded to the nearest whole number.
[a]Deliveries

Table A.1(d) Comparison of volunteer- and employee-staffed symphonic orchestras

Descriptive characteristic	Volunteer	Employee
Organizational age (years)	4	7
Number of members	90	91
Previous year's turnover (percent)	8	2
Number of concerts in season	5	5
Size of concert hall (approx.)	1000	3000

Note: Numbers have been rounded to the nearest whole number.

Table A.1(e) Comparison of volunteer- and employee-staffed family planning clinics

Descriptive characteristic	Volunteer	Employee
Organizational age (years)	50[a]	7
Number of members	14	21
Previous year's turnover (percent)	0	10
Number of patients	200	4000

Note: Numbers have been rounded to the nearest whole number.
[a]Clinic service resumed two years previously after a several year hiatus.

Table A.1(f) Comparison of volunteer- and employee-staffed gift shops

Descriptive characteristic	Volunteer	Employee
Organizational age (years)	49	3
Number of members	138	8
Previous year's turnover (percent)	4	50
Square feet of floor space (approx.)	288	864

Note: Numbers have been rounded to the nearest whole number.

Table A.1(g) Comparison of volunteer- and employee-staffed fire departments

Descriptive characteristic	Volunteer	Employee
Organizational age (years)	125	77
Number of members	160	46[a]
Previous year's turnover (percent)	3	0
Service area population	15000	26000
Alarms per year	500	2400

Note: Numbers have been rounded to the nearest whole number.
[a]The secretary was on temporary funds.

Table A.1(h) Mean differences between organization types on the descriptive
characteristics

Descriptive characteristic	$\bar{X}$ volunteer $n = 7$	$\bar{X}$ employee $n = 7$	F (1,12)
Organizational age (years)	40.31	62.59	.20 n.s.
Number of hierarchical levels	4.57	4.29	.10 n.s.
Number of clients	4822.57	12318.43	1193.27 **
Previous year's turnover (percent)	15.57	26.00	.50 n.s.
Respondent age (years)[a]	35.61	36.18	.03 n.s.
Nonwhite members (percent)[a]	3.17	14.81	5.18 *

Note: Calculations based on actual, not rounded, figures.
[a]Taken from organization-sample interview, n = 117, df = 1,115.
  * $p \leq .05$
 ** $p \leq .001$

in the volunteer-staffed organizations. As discussed below, all nonwhite volunteer-staffed organizations declined to participate and so are under-represented in this sample. It is unfortunate that the sample sizes in some organizations were so small. This resulted partially from the small size of the organizations and partially from the disinterest of many members. Participation was always completely voluntary, and the cultures in all of the organizations supported substantial member autonomy. However, the study was a combination of quantitative and qualitative methodologies, so undue reliance is not placed on any one measure.

THREATS TO SAMPLE REPRESENTATIVENESS

Sampling error

Sampling error is the degree to which the sample is unrepresentative of the population of interest. When a probability sample is drawn, sampling error is taken into consideration by the procedures of statistical inference; however, the present sample is not a probability one. In some ways the sample seems to be quite representative: the organizations were located in small rural towns, medium-sized cities, suburban areas, and very large metropolises. Three organizations were all-female; two were all-male. These organizations were managed by members ranging in age from 21 to early sixties. However, due to sampling error, there are two potential threats to the validity of the data.

First, there is the chance that the 14 organizations that agreed to participate differ in theoretically important ways from the 12 non-participating organizations. Unfortunately, it was not possible to collect the information necessary for comparisons of these groups from most of the non-participating organizations, since they withdrew after the first contact. There is, however, one difference between these groups that is worthy of note. Only three of the contacted organizations had nonwhites as leaders and all three decided against participation. Thus, white-run and white-staffed organizations are overrepresented in this sample.

Second, there may be general geographic differences that led this northeastern sample to be unrepresentative of other US and non-US samples. For example, many states do not distribute welfare through their municipalities; rural volunteer fire departments may be less common in the expansive west; certainly a part-time professional orchestra requires a large pool of freelance musicians that would be uncommon outside of large cities. However, it is probably the case that the differences between these matched task-sets are greater than the US geographic differences between northeastern and other organizations. For example, a large municipal welfare department probably isn't very different from a medium-sized county welfare department. Therefore, it can be reasonably argued that patterns in organizational structure, norms, and reactions found across these seven matched sets are representative of patterns in the population of US organizations.

The differences between these organizations and non-US ones are more difficult to address. Certainly all organizations are embedded in their own national and ethnic cultures, and volunteer-staffed organizations would be heavily influenced by cultural norms. The only feasible approach to this particular form of sampling error seems to be the provision of detailed descriptions of these organizations that allow readers to judge how far the sampled organizations differ from the non-US organizations of interest to them.

Respondents' alteration of research procedure

Although the researcher presented identical "packages" to each of the participating organizations, the relationship was altered in significant respects by members. Even though these alterations could be considered data in their own rights, the degree to which they introduced confounding factors that affect interpretations must be considered. There were two potentially confounding differences in the procedure between volunteer-staffed and employee-staffed organizations. First, although there are exceptions within types, volunteers were more likely to be interviewed in their own homes, while employees were more likely to be interviewed in their organizations. In addition, volunteers were more likely to be introduced to the study by the researcher, while employees were more likely to be introduced to it by a supervisor in their organization.

These type-specific differences in the evolution of the researcher–organization relationship may have influenced the validity of the data – that is, the researcher–respondent relationship in employing organizations was more likely to result in the gathering of mere presentational data in these organizations. Presentational data are those appearances that respondents strive to maintain in the eyes of supervisors, outsiders, and, sometimes, each other. In contrast, operational data are the running streams of spontaneous conversation and activities engaged in or observed by the researcher while in the field. In other words, since employees were interviewed in their offices and were introduced to the research by a supervisor, they might have been more likely to guard their responses, presenting information that would do them little harm if "spread around."

Fear that information they were providing might reach their supervisors did appear to be more common among employees. This was reflected in the refusal of the employees in the poverty relief agency and the fire department to place their completed (and anonymous) questionnaires in the box provided. When the researcher arrived to retrieve these questionnaires, these employees would unlock their desks or lockers, take out the questionnaires, and hand them to her personally. When asked about this practice, responses included, "everyone in this place knows my handwriting" or "they're all a bunch of lawyers around here." In contrast, volunteers frequently just dropped their completed questionnaires off with the chief officer, who, they thought, would see the researcher sooner. If there was any hesitation among volunteers, it appeared to come from disinterest, not fear. Therefore, it is probably best to assume that employees' reports might be more guarded than those of volunteers.

PROCEDURE

Data collection in each of the 14 organizations took place serially. The researcher was the only individual collecting data, and she could not collect data in all organizations simultaneously. Therefore, the two organizations in each matched set were studied concurrently, but the sets were studied serially. Data were collected from a matched set concurrently for four reasons. First, certain sections of the questionnaire were specific to a set, and all membership interviews in both organizations had to be completed before the task-specific items of the questionnaire could be constructed, that is, all interviews were completed in both organizations before questionnaires were distributed. Second, working in the matched set of organizations allowed the researcher to learn their specific technology as efficiently as possible. For example, what was learned about the deployment of hook and ladders or the layout and production of a newspaper in one organization could be compared with the practices in the other. Third, organizations in the set could be compared almost daily. Fourth, by sequencing sets, not organizations, there was no threat that, by chance, all organizations of one type would be studied before organizations of another type. The passage of time would not confound organization-type comparisons. Data collection in all 14 organizations was completed from January to September 1977.

Procedure in each organization

The data collection procedure followed in each organization was intended to be uniform across all organizations: the researcher presented the same proposal and tried to structure the relationship according to a general plan. Entry began with a telephone call to the organization's chief officer. The research purpose and requirements were introduced, and the offer of survey feedback was made in exchange for their assistance. This was followed by one or more site visits with one or more subgroups or individuals until the organization decided either to forego participation or to participate. Twelve of the 26 organizations contacted decided against participation. Next, the researcher scheduled an appointment with the chief officer for the "organization-leader interview." During this interview, descriptive information about the organization was obtained, including history, organizational structure, and the membership list.

Following the organization-leader interviews, ten or fewer "membership interviews" were scheduled with members by the researcher. A maximum of ten were scheduled due to time constraints; in some organizations it was not possible to schedule all ten. A random sample of members (stratified by rank) were selected for interviews; of those contacted, 9 percent of the volunteers and 9 percent of the employees refused to be interviewed. After all membership interviews were completed in both organizations in a matched set, questionnaires were distributed in both organizations. In smaller organizations, all members received questionnaires; in larger organizations, a random sample was drawn from the membership list. Those who participated in the membership interview received a number on their questionnaire so the researcher could match the instruments. Non-interviewed respondents were completely anonymous. Questionnaire distribution took the form of grouped questionnaire sessions (the researcher's requested format), personal distribution to members, mailed with a return envelope, or questionnaires and a return box left in the organization's offices. Two or more of these distribution formats were used in a single organization; therefore, there should be no organization-specific effects of different distribution formats. There was no significant difference in the questionnaire response rate of volunteers (61 percent) and employees (60 percent). After all questionnaires were returned, all members received survey feedback, targeted toward their individual interests.

Observational material was gathered throughout the data collection and feedback.

MEASURES

The data reported in this work consist of both qualitative and observational measures, as well as quantitative measures taken from organizational archives, questionnaires, and interviews.

Observational measures

The primary purpose of this study was theory-building rather than theory-testing. Therefore, qualitative observational data collection takes on an important role (Glaser and Strauss 1967). Systematic field notes were kept on all encounters with all individuals related to the research.

Wide-ranging information, both quantitative and qualitative, were collected; however, only those data directly relevant to the conclusions and analyses presented in this work are described.

Organizational characteristics

The quantitative measures reported here were taken from archival records (when they were available) or the "organization-leader interview." During this interview, the organization's chief officer was asked to provide organizational descriptive information, including the documents when they were available, and to make estimates if the information was not recorded. Because these measures were simply records of noncontroversial "facts," no attempt was made to gather reliability estimates of them.

Organizational age, number of clients, number of members, and number of hierarchical levels could all be taken from written documents; in the two cases where unavailable (volunteer-staffed newspaper and family planning clinic), estimates were made. The number of hierarchical levels variable was also taken from written documents or the organizational chart constructed during the organization-leader interview.

The remaining organizational variables required some judgment from the researcher. Previous year's turnover (percentage) was estimated by office-holders during the organization-leader interview, who were asked how many had left, with the researcher calculating the percentage. The nonwhite members (percentage) was estimated by the researcher, who, except in the volunteer-staffed newspaper, poverty relief agency, and fire department, saw all members of these small organizations. Officeholders were asked for their estimates in the other three organizations.

Respondents' self-reports

The following variables rely primarily on questionnaire self-reports, although in one case information from the organization-sample interviews was used as a test of cross-method measure convergence. All of the variables measured on the questionnaire are multi-item scales. Since most of the scales developed for this study had not been validated in prior samples, an extremely conservative procedure for scale construction was adopted to minimize the serious bias that results from single-sample scale construction that may capitalize on sample-specific variance (although, recall that this sample contains 14 separate organizations). Multi-item scales were constructed by examining the intercorrelation matrix, including items hypothesized to form a scale and all other nonscale items. Scales were constructed if all intrascale correlations were higher than all interscale correlations for that scale item. In no cases were the mean same-method interscale correlations of a scale item significantly greater than zero. In addition, when possible, cross-method correlations among scales measuring the same "trait" are analyzed.

For the membership interviews, a blind rater coded six randomly selected taped interviews. The percentage of scores on which the researcher and blind rater agreed are reported when available. Clearly, percentages based on such a small number are unstable; however, they do give some indication of interview variable reliability. Means, standard deviations, and intercorrelations among these study variables appear in Tables A.2, A.3, and A.4.

Table A.2 Means, standard deviations, and intercorrelations among the organizational-level variables

Variable	$\bar{X}$	s.d.	1	2	3	4	5	6
Organizational type[a]	–	–	–					
Organizational age (years)	51.45	90.51	–13	–				
Number of clients	8488.50	14182.87	–27	–06	–			
Number of members	65.07	57.81	52	09	–04	–		
Number of hierarchical levels	4.43	1.65	09	38	–03	35	–	
Previous year's turnover (percent)	21	27	–20	–09	48	–43	–45	–

n = 14; r = .36, p $\leq$ .10; r = .44, p $\leq$ .05.
[a]Nominal scale variable; measures of uncertainty are uncertainty coefficients.

Table A.3 Means, standard deviations, and intercorrelations among the organization-sample interview scales

Variable	$\bar{X}$	s.d.	1	2	3	4
1. Amount of face-to-face communication	3.98	1.10	–			
2. Amount of phone/written-only communication	.13	.47	–51	–		
3. How types differ[a]	–	–	14	06	–	
4. Respondent age (years)	35.74	12.68	02	10	22	–

n = 117; r = .15, p $\leq$ .05; r = .20, p $\leq$ .01.
[a]Nominal scale variable; measures are uncertainty coefficients.

Amount of face-to-face communication

In the membership interview interviewees were asked, "Now, some questions about communication patterns at [organization] .... By communication I mean any situation where someone is trying to tell someone else something. This can be group meetings, individual conversation, a telephone conversation, a written memo – any of these things," followed by requests to characterize communication with the interviewee's "supervisor" and with each of the other major organizational groups (identified *a priori* in the organization-leader interview). Since there were no differences in the number of groups identified across the 14 organizations, the number of groups with which the interviewee had face-to-face communication were summed. Scores ranged from zero to six groups with reported face-to-face contact. The interrater agreement for this scale was 80 percent.

Table A.4 Means, standard deviations, and intercorrelations among the pay status and questionnaire scales

Variables	X̄	s.d.	1	2	3	4	5	6	7	8	9	10	11
1. Pay status[a]	.63	—	—										
2. Material rewards/instrumental gain	5.48	1.45	16	(86)									
3. Material rewards/intrinsic value	5.36	1.08	08	44	(73)								
4. Symbolic rewards/service	5.49	1.06	−08	−01	18	(69)							
5. Symbolic rewards/social	5.36	.97	−06	20	18	29	(77)						
6. Hours per week	16.96	15.52	81	18	21	−13	−05	—					
7. Changing procedures	3.97	1.07	32	16	05	17	08	34	(78)				
8. Work demands	3.68	1.46	34	−01	12	06	03	37	30	(69)			
9. Work praiseworthiness	5.73	1.21	−11	07	04	15	16	−12	01	05	(63)		
10. Job satisfaction	5.87	1.11	−20	−23	19	17	18	−15	−01	−11	52	(73)	
11. Organizational commitment	3.97	1.57	−44	−01	09	22	16	−39	−21	−22	29	51	(81)

$n = 216$; $r = .11$, $p \leq .05$; $r = .16$, $p \leq .01$.
[a]Nominal scale variable. Mean is percentage volunteers; measures of association are uncertainty coefficients (positive, skewed to employees).

Amount of phone/written-only communication

This was computed in the same manner as the prior variable. The number of groups with whom the interviewee had solely phone or written contact was summed. Values ranged from zero to three groups, with an interrater agreement of 80 percent.

Material rewards/instrumental gain

This and the following three scales were developed in an earlier study reported in Pearce (1983b). Questionnaire respondents were asked to indicate on a seven-point Likert-format scale the extent to which each of several "organizational rewards" were important to them. This scale, which was composed of two items, "the chance to learn new skills" and "the opportunity to obtain more experience," had a coefficient alpha of .86.

Material rewards/intrinsic interest

Items from the above list of rewards comprised this scale: "doing tasks that hold my interest," "an interesting job," "enjoyment of just doing the work." The scale resulting from this seven-point Likert-type scale had a coefficient alpha of .73.

Symbolic rewards/service

The rewards that composed this scale were "the chance to further the goals of this organization," "a chance to make a real contribution," and "identification with the mission of the organization"; it had an alpha of .69.

Symbolic rewards/social

The final of the four scales composed from the list of rewards rated on a Likert-format seven-point scale as important or unimportant consisted of "enjoyment of the company of my co-workers," "working with people I like," and "associating with a good group of people." It had a coefficient alpha of .77 in this sample.

How types differ

Responses were coded from the interview questions: "Have you had any contact with [counterpart-type organizations]?" If yes, "how is their organization different from this one?" Or, if no, "do you have any idea what the differences might be?" The responses were coded into eight categories.

The interrater agreement for this variable was a low 25 percent, perhaps due in part to the numerous categories.

Hours worked per week (respondent report)

On the front page of the questionnaire, respondents were asked to report how many hours per week they worked.

Changing procedures

The questionnaire contained 18 exploratory statements about work rules and procedures. Intercorrelations among these items suggested four internally consistent scales. The changing procedures scale was constructed from eight statements rated on a seven-point Likert-format scale with 1 = strongly disagree and 7 = strongly agree: "it seems a new type of problem comes in every week"; "changes in the ways we do things or equipment are rare" (negatively scored); "the procedures often must be changed to maintain effectiveness"; "someone in this organization is always proposing a better way of doing things"; "most problems that come in are about the same and can be more quickly dealt with in a routine manner" (negatively scored); "there are frequent changes in the way we go about our work"; "each client or problem that comes in is different"; and "there have been many changes in the procedures or equipment we use in the last couple of years." It had a coefficient alpha of .78.

Work demands

The questionnaire contained a section in which the respondents were asked to characterize "this job in general" according to semantic-differential paired adjectives, with seven spaces separating the extreme pairs. Work demands was constructed of the following highly intercorrelated pairs: "difficult/easy" (negatively scored), "painless/painful," "challenging/dull" (negatively scored), "undemanding/demanding," and "relaxed/tense." It had a coefficient alpha of .69.

Work praiseworthiness

Similar to the above seven-space semantic differential scale, praiseworthiness, with a coefficient alpha of .63, this was composed of the following pairs: "praiseworthy/unpraiseworthy" (negatively scored) and "useful/useless" (negatively scored).

Job satisfaction

Finally, a third scale was constructed from the semantic-differential paired adjectives characterizing respondents' jobs: "unpleasant/pleasant," "boring/interesting," and "bad/good." It had a coefficient alpha of .73. In addition, an interview question which asked, "All in all, as of today, how much would you say you liked your job?" (rated from 1 = very dissatisfied to 5 = very satisfied), had an interrater agreement of 100 percent. The cross-method correlation coefficient for these two measures of satisfaction was .61. Because more individuals completed the questionnaire than completed the membership interview, the questionnaire measure of job satisfaction was used.

Organizational commitment

This scale is composed of three seven-point Likert-format items rated on agreement–disagreement: "I rarely think of quitting," "every now and then I think about leaving" (negatively scored), and "I frequently wonder if I would be better off at another organization" (negatively scored). It had a coefficient alpha of .81.

Volunteer/employee and core/peripheral statuses

During the organization-leader interview, a complete membership list was obtained including each member's pay status (volunteer or employee) and job title. Based on job title, all volunteer officeholders were classified as "core" members; all others were coded as "peripheral." Of course, many of the sampled volunteers were working as employees (elsewhere) and most employees had been or were volunteers (elsewhere). The few employees at the volunteer-staffed organizations had formerly been volunteers for their organizations, and most paid firefighters had been volunteer firefighters. No reliability information is available for data obtained from the organizations' archives.

USE OF DATA

The discussion in this volume of the organizational behavior of volunteers relies greatly on influences and speculations arising from the collection of the above-described observational and systematic data, as well as from subsequent reading across a wide array of social science disciplines. This work is intended to provide a broad understanding and a rich and vivid picture of volunteers in organizations, so it is not restricted to a conservative report of differences between volunteers and employees on the above variables. Some of the data lend themselves to computing numerical reliability and validity coefficients, but it would be misleading to imply that the survey findings therefore "prove" the causal statements made throughout this work. Rather all of the information gleaned about volunteer-staffed organizations is used to illustrate or buttress statements, and no formal hypothesis testing is reported. Those with rigorous scientific standards should consider this work to be the report of 14 case studies, informed by a comprehensive literature review. Furthermore, one purpose of this book is to stimulate further research; it is hoped that some of that research will be systematic and controlled and will permit more definitive conclusions about the causal statements offered here.

References

ACTION (1975). *Americans Volunteer: 1974*. Washington, DC.

Adams, Robert Lynn, and John Mogey (1967). "Marriage, Membership and Mobility in Church and Sect." *Sociological Analysis*, 28, 205–14.

Alderfer, Clayton P. (1972). *Existence, Relatedness, and Growth*. New York: Free Press.

Allen, Natalie, and William Rushton (1983). "Personality Characteristics of Community Mental Health Volunteers: A Review." *Journal of Voluntary Action Research*, 12, 36–49.

Allport, Gordon (1945). "The Psychology of Participation." *Psychological Review*, 53, 117–32.

Allport, Gordon (1952). "Why Do People Join?" *Adult Leadership*, 1, 10–12.

Almond, Gabriel, and Sidney Verba (1963). *The Civic Culture*. Princeton, NJ: Princeton University Press.

Anderson, John C., and Larry F. Moore (1978). "The Motivation to Volunteer." *Journal of Voluntary Action Research*, 7, 120–9.

Anderson, Robert T., and Barbara Gallatin Anderson (1965). *Bus Stop for Paris*. Garden City, NY: Doubleday.

Anderson, Walfred A. (1943). "The Family and Individual Social Participation." *American Sociological Review*, 8, 420–24.

Argyle, Michael (1959). *Religious Behavior*. Glencoe, IL: Free Press.

Argyris, Chris (1957). "The Individual and the Organization: Some Problems of Mutual Adjustment." *Administrative Science Quarterly*, 2, 1–24.

Arnold, Hugh J., and Daniel C. Feldman (1982). "A Multivariate Analysis of the Determinants of Job Turnover." *Journal of Applied Psychology*, 67, 350–60.

Babchuk, Nicholas (1965). "Primary Friends and Kin: A Study of the Associations of Middle-Class Couples." *Social Forces*, 43, 483–92.

Babchuk, Nicholas, and Alan Booth (1969). "Voluntary Association Membership: A Longitudinal Analysis." *American Sociological Review*, 34, 31–45.

Babchuk, Nicholas, and C. Wayne Gordon (1962). *The Voluntary Association in the Slum*. University of Nebraska Studies, New Series, No. 27. Lincoln: University of Nebraska Press.

Bales, R.F. (1950). *Interaction Process Analysis*. Cambridge, MA: Addison-Wesley.

Barber, Bernard (1950). "Participation and Mass Apathy in Associations." In Alvin W. Gouldner, ed., *Studies in Leadership*. New York: Harper, 477–524.

Barker, Roger G. (1968). *Ecological Psychology*. Stanford, CA: Stanford University Press.

Barker, Roger G., and Paul V. Gump (1964). *Big School, Small School*. Stanford, CA: Stanford University Press.

Barnard, Chester I. (1938). *The Functions of the Executive*. Cambridge, MA.: Harvard University Press.

Bass, B.M. (1985). *Leadership Performance beyond Expectations*. New York: Academic Press.

Batson, C. Daniel, and J.S. Coke (1978). "Altruism and Human Kindness: Internal and External Determinants of Helping Behavior." *Perspectives in International Psychology*. New York: Plenum Press.

Beal, George M. (1956). "Additional Hypotheses in Participation Research." *Rural Sociology*, 21, 249–56.

Bendix, Reinhardt (1974). *Work and Authority in Industry*. Berkeley: University of California Press.

Benét, M.K. (1972). *The Secretarial Ghetto*. New York: McGraw-Hill.

Billis, David (1987). "Some Puzzles and Models of Voluntary Organization." Presented at the Annual Meeting of the Association of Voluntary Action Scholars, Kansas City, MO, October.

Brief, Arthur P., and Steven J. Motowidlo (1986). "Prosocial Organizational Behaviors." *Academy of Management Review*, 11, 710–25.

Brown, Emory J. (1953). "The Self as Related to Formal Participation in Three Pennsylvania Rural Communities." *Rural Sociology*, 18, 313–20.

Buchanan, B. (1974). "Building Organizational Commitment: The Socialization of Managers in Work Organizations." *Administrative Science Quarterly*, 19, 533–46.

Bureau of Labor Statistics (1975). *Job Seeking Methods Used by American Workers*. Bulletin 1886. Washington, DC: US Department of Labor.

Bushee, Frederick A. (1945). "Social Organization of a Small City." *American Journal of Sociology*, 51, 217–26.

Chapman, Terry H. (1985). "Motivation in University Student Volunteering." In Larry F. Moore, ed., *Motivating Volunteers*, Vancouver, BC: Vancouver Volunteer Centre, 231–41.

Charms, R. de (1968). *Personal Causation: The Internal Affective Determinants of Behavior*. New York: Academic Press.

Clark, Peter B., and James Q. Wilson (1961). "Incentive Systems: A Theory of Organizations." *Administrative Science Quarterly*, 6, 129–66.

Conger, J.A. and Kanungo, R.N. (1987). "Toward a Behavioral Theory of Charismatic Leadership in Organizational Settings." *Academy of Management Review*, 12, 637–47.

Cousens, F.R. (1964). "Indigenous Leadership in Two Lower Class Neighborhood Organizations." In Arthur B. Shostak and William Gomberg, eds, *Blue Collar World*. Englewood Cliffs, NJ: Prentice-Hall.

Curtis, James (1971). "Voluntary Association Joining: A Cross-National Comparative Note." *American Sociological Review*, 36, 872–80.

Cyert, Richard M., and James G. March (1963). *A Behavioral Theory of the Firm*. Englewood Cliffs, NJ: Prentice-Hall.

Deci, Edward L. (1975). *Intrinsic Motivation*. New York: Plenum.

Dentler, R.A., and K.T. Erikson (1959). "The Functions of Deviance in Groups." *Social Problems*, 7, 98–107.

Dess, G.G., and D.W. Beard (1984). "Dimensions of Organizational Task Environments." *Administrative Science Quarterly*, 20, 613–29.

Dotson, Floyd (1953). "A Note on Participation in Voluntary Associations in a Mexican City." *American Sociological Review*, 18, 380–6.

Downing, Joseph (1957). "Factors Affecting the Selective Use of a Social Club for the Aged." *Journal of Gerontology*, 12, 81–4.

Dozier, J.B., and Miceli, M.P. (1985). "Potential Predictors of Whistle-Blowing: A Prosocial Behavior Perspective." *Academy of Management Review*, 10, 823–36.

Dubin, Robert, R. Alan Hedley, and Thomas C. Taveggia (1976). "Attachment to Work." In R. Dubin, ed., *Handbook of Work, Organization, and Society*. Chicago, IL: Rand McNally, 281–342.

Edwards, John, and Randall White (1980). "Predictors of Social Participation: Apparent or Real." *Journal of Voluntary Action Research*, 9 (1), 60–73.

Eisenhardt, Kathleen (1988). "Agency- and Institutional-Theory Explanations: The Case of Retail Sales Compensation." *Academy of Management Journal*, 31, 488–511.

Ellis, J., and K.H. Noyes (1978). *By the People*. Philadelphia, PA: Energize.

Erikson, Kai (1986). "On Work and Alienation." *American Sociological Review*, 51, 1–8.

Etzioni, Amitai (1975). *A Comparative Analysis of Complex Organizations* (revised edition). New York: Free Press.

Fayol, Henri (1949). *General and Industrial Management*. London: Pitman (first published in French in 1916).

Festinger, Leon (1961). "The Psychological Effects of Insufficient Rewards." *American Psychologist*, 16, 1–11.

Flashman, Robert, and Sam Quick (1985). "Altruism is Not Dead: A Specific Analysis of Volunteer Motivation." In Larry F. Moore, ed., *Motivating Volunteers*. Vancouver, BC: Vancouver Volunteer Centre, 154–70.

Fox, A. (1974). *Beyond Contract*. London: Faber & Faber.

Galbraith, Jay R. (1977). *Designing Complex Organizations*. Reading, MA: Addison-Wesley.

Gallagher, Orvoell R. (1957). "Voluntary Associations in France." *Social Forces*, 36 (December), 153–60.

Gallup Organization (1987). *The Gallup Study of Public Awareness and Involvement with Non-profit Organizations*. Princeton, NJ.

Gamson, William A. (1968). *Power and Discontent*. Homewood, IL: Dorsey Press.

Gidron, Benjamin (1977). "Volunteer Work and Its Rewards." *Volunteer Administration*, 11 (3), 18–32.

Glaser, Barney G., and Strauss, Anselm L. (1967). *The Discovery of Grounded Theory*. Chicago, IL: Aldine.

Gold, Doris B. (1971). "Women and Volunteerism." In Vivian Gornick and Barbara K. Moran, eds, *Woman in Sexist Society*. New York: Basic Books, 533–54.

Gold, Doris B. (1979). "Opposition to Volunteerism: An Annotated Bibliography." In Jean S. Gottlieb, ed., *Council of Planning Librarians Bibliographies, No. 8*. Chicago, IL.

Goodman, Paul S., and Johannes M. Pennings (1977). *New Perspectives on Organizational Effectiveness*. San Francisco, CA: Jossey-Bass.

Gottlieb, David (1974). "The Socialization and Politicization of VISTA Volunteers: Sex and Generational Differences." *Journal of Voluntary Action Research*, 3, 1–19.

Gough, Harrison G. (1952). "Predicting Social Participation." *Journal of Social Psychology*, 35, 227–33.

Greer, Scott A. (1955). *Social Organization*. New York: Random House.

Gulick, L.H., and L.F. Urwick, eds (1937). *Papers on the Sciences of Administration*. New York: Columbia University Press.

Hackman, J. Richard, and Greg R. Oldham (1980). *Work Redesign*. Reading, MA: Addison-Wesley.

Hackman, J. Richard, and J. Lloyd Suttle (1977). *Improving Life at Work*. Santa Monica, CA: Goodyear.

Hardee, J. Gilbert (1961). "The Social Structure and Participation in an Australian Rural Community." *Rural Sociology*, 26, 240–51.

Hausknecht, Murray (1962). *The Joiners*. New York: Bedminster Press.

Heckscher, Gunnar (1948). "Pluralistic Democracy: The Swedish Experience." *Social Research*, 15, 417–61.

Heinrich, Max (1977). "Change of Heart: A Test of Some Widely-Held Theories of Religious Conversion." *American Journal of Sociology*, 83, 653–80.

Herzberg, F., B. Mausner, and B.B. Snyderman (1959). *The Motivation to Work*. New York: Wiley.

House, Robert (1977). "A 1976 Theory of Charismatic Leadership." In J.G. Hunt and L.L. Larson, eds, *Leadership: The Cutting Edge*. Carbondale, IL: Southern Illinois University Press, 189–273.

House, Robert J., and Baetz, M.L. (1979). "Leadership: Some Empirical Generalizations and New Research Directions." *Research in Organizational Behavior*, 1, 399–401.

Hrebiniak, L.G., and J.A. Alutto (1972). "Personal and Role-Related Factors in the Development of Organizational Commitment." *Administrative Science Quarterly*, 17, 555–72.

Hyman, Herbert, and Charles Wright (1971). "Trends in Voluntary Association Memberships of American Adults: Replication Based on Secondary Analysis of National Sample Surveys." *American Sociological Review*, 36, 191–206.

Iaffaldano, M.T., and P.M. Muchinsky (1985). "Job Satisfaction and Job Performance: A Meta-analysis." *Psychological Bulletin*, 97, 251–73.

Independent Sector (1981). *Americans Volunteer: 1981*. Washington, DC.

Independent Sector (1986). *Americans Volunteer: 1985*. Washington, DC.

Jacoby, Arthur, and Nicholas Babchuk (1963). "Instrumental and Expressive Voluntary Associations." *Sociology and Social Research*, 47, 461–71.

Jenner, Jessica Reynolds (1981). "Volunteerism as an Aspect of Women's Work Lives." *Journal of Vocational Behavior*, 19, 302–14.

Jones, E.E., Kanouse, D.E., Kelley, H.H., Nisbett, R.E., Valins, S., and Weiner, B. (eds) (1972). *Attribution: Perceiving the Causes of Behavior*. Morristown, NJ: General Learning Press.

Kanter, Rosabeth Moss (1968). "Commitment and Social Organization: A Study of Commitment Mechanisms in Utopian Communities." *American Sociological Review*, 33, 499–517.

Kanter, Rosabeth Moss (1972). *Commitment and Community*. Cambridge, MA: Harvard University Press.

Katz, Daniel (1960). "The Functional Approach to the Study of Attitudes." *Public Opinion Quarterly*, 24, 163–76.

Kiesler, Charles A. (1971). *The Psychology of Commitment: Experiments Linking Behavior to Belief*. New York: Academic Press.

Knoke, David H., and David Mark Prensky (1982). "What Relevance Do Organization Theories Have for Voluntary Associations?" Presented at the 77th Annual Meeting of the American Sociological Association, San Francisco.

Knoke, David, and Christine Wright-Isak (1982). "Individual Motives and Organizational Incentive Systems." *Research in the Sociology of Organizations*, 1, 209–54.

Komarovsky, Mirra (1946). "The Voluntary Associations of Urban Dwellers." *American Sociological Review*, 11, 686–98.

Kouzes, James M., and Barry M. Posner (1987). *The Leadership Challenge*. San Francisco, CA: Jossey-Bass.

Krackhardt, David, and Lyman W. Porter (1985). "When Friends Leave: A Structural Analysis of the Relationship Between Turnover and Stayers' Attitudes." *Administrative Science Quarterly*, 30, 242–61.

Kramer, Ralph M. (1981). *Voluntary Agencies in the Welfare State*. Berkeley: University of California Press.

Lathram, Van M., and Cary M. Lichtman (1984). "Social Linkages and Organizational Commitment in Voluntary Organizations." *Social Behavior and Personality*, 12 (2), 165–70.

Lawler, Edward E., III (1971). *Pay and Organizational Effectiveness: A Psychological View*. New York: McGraw-Hill.

Lawler, Edward E., III, and John Grant Rhode (1976). *Information and Control in Organizations*. Santa Monica, CA: Goodyear.

Leat, D. (1977). *Towards a Definition of Voluntary Involvement*. London: Volunteer Centre.

Levine, F.M., ed. (1975). *Theoretical Readings in Motivation*. Chicago, IL: Rand McNally.

Levine, M., and A. Levine (1970). *A Social History of the Helping Services*. New York: Appleton-Century-Crofts.

Likert, Rensis (1961). *New Patterns of Management*. New York: McGraw-Hill.

Locke, Edwin A. (1976). "The Nature and Causes of Job Satisfaction." In Marvin D. Dunnette, ed., *Handbook of Industrial and Organizational Psychology*. Chicago: Rand McNally, 1297–349.

Lundberg, George A., Mirra Komarovsky, and Mary Alice McInery (1934). *Leisure*. New York: Columbia University Press.

Luthans, Fred, and R. Kreitner (1975). *Organizational Behavior Modification*. Glenview, IL: Scott, Foresman.

McGrath, Joseph E. (1976). *Stress and Behavior in Organizations*. In Marvin D. Dunnette, ed., *Handbook of Industrial and Organizational Psychology*. Chicago: Rand McNally, 1351–95.

McPherson, J.M., and W.G. Lockwood (1980). "The Longitudinal Study of Voluntary Association Membership – A Multivariable Analysis." *Journal of Voluntary Action Research*, 9, 74–84.

McPherson, J.M., and Lynn Smith-Lovin (1986). "Sex Segregation." *American Sociological Review*, 51 (1), 61–79.

Mahoney, Thomas A. (1979). *Compensation and Reward Perspectives*. Homewood, IL: Irwin.

March, James G., and Herbert A. Simon (1958). *Organizations*. New York: Wiley.

Mason, D.E. (1984). *Voluntary Nonprofit Enterprise Management*. New York: Plenum.

Mayo, Selz C. (1950). "Age Profiles of Participation in Rural Areas of Wake County, S.C." *Rural Sociology*, 15, 242–51.

Meillassoux, Claude (1968). *Urbanization of an African Community*. Seattle: University of Washington Press.

Meyer, John W., and Brian Rowan (1977). "Institutionalized Organizations: Formal Structure as Myth and Ceremony." *American Journal of Sociology*, 83, 340–63.

Meyer, Marshall W. (1979). "Organizational Structure as Signaling." *Pacific Sociological Review*, 22 (4), 481–500.

Michels, Robert (1959). *Political Parties*. New York: Dover (originally published in French in 1911).

Miller, E.J., and A.K. Rice (1967). *Systems of Organization*. London: Tavistock.

Milofsky, Carl, and Sandra H. Elion (1987). "The Love Life of an Alternative School." Presented at the Annual Meeting of the Association of Voluntary Action Scholars, Kansas City, MO, October.

Minnis, Mhyra S. (1952). "Cleavage in Women's Organizations: A Reflection of the Social Structure of a City." *American Sociological Review*, 18, 47–53.

Mintzberg, Henry (1979). *The Structuring of Organizations*. Englewood Cliffs, NJ: Prentice-Hall.

Mischel, W. (1983). *Personality and Assessment*. New York: Wiley.

Moore, Joan W. (1961). "Patterns of Women's Participation in Voluntary Associations." *American Journal of Sociology*, 66, 592–8.

Moore, Larry F., ed. (1985). *Motivating Volunteers*. Vancouver, BC: Vancouver Voluntary Action Centre.

Morris, Raymond N. (1965). "British and American Research on Voluntary Associations: A Comparison." *Sociological Inquiry*, 35, 186–200.

Mowday, Richard T., Lyman W. Porter, and Richard M. Steers (1982). *Employee–Organization Linkages*. New York: Academic Press.

Mulford, Charles L., Gerald E. Klonglan, George M. Beal, and Joe M. Bohlen (1968). "Selectivity, Socialization, and Role Performance." *Sociology and Social Research*, 53 (October), 68–77.

Nadler, David A., J. Richard Hackman, and Edward E. Lawler, III (1979). *Managing Organizational Behavior*. Boston, MA: Little, Brown.

Naylor, Harriet H. (1967). *Volunteers Today*. New York: Associated Press.

Olsen, Marvin (1970). "Social and Political Participation of Blacks." *American Sociological Review*, 35, 682–97.

Olson, Manacur, Jr (1965). *The Logic of Collective Action*. Cambridge, MA: Harvard University Press.

Organ, Dennis W. (1988). *Organizational Citizenship Behavior*. Lexington, MA: Lexington Books.

Orum, Anthony M. (1966). "A Reappraisal of the Social and Political Participation of Negroes." *American Journal of Sociology*, 72, 32–46.

Ouchi, William G. (1981). *Theory Z: How American Business Can Meet the Japanese Challenge*. Reading, MA: Addison-Wesley.

Ouchi, William G., and Michele Kremen Bolton (1988). "The Logic of Joint Research and Development." *California Management Review*, 30 (3), 9–33.

Pearce, Jone L. (1981). "Bringing Some Clarity to Role Ambiguity Research: Theoretical Integration." *Academy of Management Review*, 6, 665–74.

Pearce, Jone L. (1983a). "Attitude and Motivation Differences Between Volunteers and Employees from Comparable Organizations." *Journal of Applied Psychology*, 68, 646–52.

Pearce, J.L. (1983b). "Participation in Voluntary Associations: How Membership in Formal Organizations Changes the Rewards of Participation." In D.H. Smith and J. VanTil, eds, *International Perspectives on Voluntary Action Research*. Washington, DC: University Press of America, 148–56.

Pearce, Jone L. (1989). *More Symbol Than Substance: Actual Merit Pay Allocations*. Graduate School of Management: University of California, Irvine.

Pearce, Jone L., and James L. Perry (1983). "Federal Merit Pay: A Longitudinal Analysis." *Public Administration Review*, 43, 315–25.

Perrow, Charles (1970). "Members as Resources in Voluntary Organizations." In William R. Rosengren and Mark Lefton, eds, *Organizations and Clients*. Columbus, OH: Merrill Publishing, pp. 93–101.

Perrow, Charles (1979). *Complex Organizations: A Critical Essay* (2nd edition). Glenview, IL: Scott, Foresman.

Peters, Thomas J., and Robert H. Waterman (1982). *In Search of Excellence*. New York: Harper & Row.

Petty, M.M., G.W. McGee, and J.W. Cavender (1984). "A Meta-analysis of the Relationships between Individual Job Satisfaction and Individual Performance." *Academy of Management Review*, 9, 712–21.

Pfeffer, Jeffrey, and James N. Baron (1988). "Taking the Workers Back Out: Recent

Trends in the Structuring of Employment." *Research in Organizational Behavior*, 10, 257–303.

Phillips, Michael H. (1982). "Motivation and Expectation in Successful Volunteerism." *Journal of Voluntary Action Research*, 11, 118–25.

Pinder, Craig C. (1984). *Work Motivation*. Glenview, IL: Scott, Foresman.

Porter, Lyman W., W.J. Crampon and F.J. Smith (1976). "Organizational Commitment and Managerial Turnover: A Longitudinal Study." *Organizational Behavior and Human Performance*, 15, 87–98.

Porter, Lyman W., and Edward E. Lawler, III (1968). *Managerial Attitudes and Performance*. Homewood, IL: Irwin.

Porter, Lyman W., Richard M. Steers, Richard T. Mowday, and P.V. Boulian (1974) "Organizational Commitment, Job Satisfaction, and Turnover Among Psychiatric Technicians." *Journal of Applied Psychology*, 59, 603–9.

Puffer, Sheila M., and James R. Meindl (1987). "Altruism and Self-Interest in a Voluntary Organization: The Interactive Effect of Motives and Incentives on Volunteers' Attitudes and Performance." *Academy of Management Proceedings*. New Orleans, LA, 215–19.

Roethlisberger, Fritz J., and W.J. Dickson (1939). *Management and the Worker*. Cambridge, MA: Harvard University Press.

Rose, Arnold M. (1954). *Theory and Method in the Social Sciences*. Minneapolis: University of Minnesota Press.

Rose, Arnold, ed. (1958). *The Institutions of Advanced Societies*. Minneapolis: University of Minnesota Press.

Rothschild-Whitt, Joyce (1979). "The Collectivist Organization: An Alternative to Rational-Bureaucratic Models." *American Sociological Review*, 44, 509–27.

Rushton, J.P., and R.M. Sorrentino, eds (1981). *Altruism and Helping Behavior: Social, Personality and Developmental Perspectives*. Hillsdale, NJ: Erlbaum.

Salancik, Gerald R. (1977). "Commitment and Control of Organizational Behavior and Belief." In Barry M. Staw and Gerald R. Salancik, eds, *New Directions in Organizational Behavior*. Chicago, IL: St. Clair Press, 1–54.

Salancik, Gerald R., and Jeffrey Pfeffer (1978). "A Social Information Processing Approach to Job Attitudes and Task Design." *Administrative Science Quarterly*, 23, 224–53.

Schein, Edgar H. (1980). *Organizational Psychology* (3rd edition). Englewood Cliffs, NJ: Prentice-Hall.

Schindler-Rainman, Eva, and Ronald Lippitt (1971). *The Volunteer Community*. Washington, DC: Center for a Voluntary Society.

Schram, Vicki R. (1985). "Motivating Volunteers to Participate." In Larry F. Moore, ed., *Motivating Volunteers*. Vancouver, BC: Vancouver Volunteer Centre, 13–30.

Schwab, Donald P., Sara L. Rynes, and Ramon J. Aldag (1987). "Theories and Research on Job Search and Choice." *Research in Personnel and Human Resources Management*, 5, 129–66.

Scott, John C., Jr (1957). "Membership and Participation in Voluntary Associations." *American Sociological Review*, 22, 315–26.

Scott, William Abbott (1953). "Attitudes Toward Participation in Civil Defense." *Public Opinion Quarterly*, 17, 374–85.

Seltzer, Joseph, Lynn E. Miller, and Gary N. Powell (1988). "Turnover Among Volunteers in Nonprofit Organizations." Paper presented at the Annual Meeting of the Academy of Management, Anaheim, CA.

Selznick, Philip (1957). *Leadership in Administration*. New York: Harper & Row.

Shapiro, Susan P. (1987). "The Social Control of Impersonal Trust." *American Journal of Sociology*, 93, 623–58.

Sharp, Elaine B. (1978). "Citizen Organization in Policing Issues and Crime Prevention: Incentives for Participation." *Journal of Voluntary Action Research*, 7, 45–58.

Shaw, Marvin E. (1976). *Group Dynamics* (2nd edition). New York: McGraw-Hill.

Sheridan, J.E., M.D. Richards, and J.W. Slocum (1975). "Comparative Analysis of Expectancy and Heuristic Models of Decision Behavior." *Journal of Applied Psychology*, 60, 361–8.

Sills, David L. (1957). *The Volunteers: Means and Ends in a National Organization*. Glencoe, IL: Free Press, 1957.

Sills, David L. (1968). *Voluntary Associations*. In David L. Sills, ed., *International Encyclopedia of the Social Sciences: Vol. 16*. New York: Free Press, 357–79.

Simon, Herbert A. (1957). *Administrative Behavior* (2nd edition). New York: Free Press.

Smelser, Neil J. (1962). *Theory of Collective Behavior*. New York: Free Press.

Smith, C.G., and A.S. Tannenbaum (1963). "Organizational Control Structure." *Human Relations*, 16, 299–316.

Smith, Constance, and Annie Freedman (1972). *Voluntary Associations: Perspectives on the Literature*. Cambridge, MA: Harvard University Press.

Smith, David Horton (1966). "The Importance of Formal Voluntary Associations for Society." *Sociology and Social Research*, 50, 483–94.

Smith, David Horton, ed. (1973). *Voluntary Action Research: 1973*. Lexington, MA: Lexington Books.

Smith, David Horton (1981). "Altruism, Volunteers and Volunteerism." *Journal of Voluntary Action Research*, 10, 21–36.

Smith, David Horton, Jacqueline Macaulay, *et al.* (1980). *Participation in Social and Political Activities*. San Francisco, CA: Jossey-Bass.

Smith, David Horton, R.D. Reddy, and R. Baldwin, eds (1972). *Voluntary Action Research: 1972*. Lexington, MA: Lexington Books.

Snow, David A., Louis A. Zurcher, Jr, and Sheldon Ekland-Olson (1980). "Social Networks and Social Movements: A Microstructural Approach to Differential Recruitment." *American Sociological Review*, 45, 787–801.

Soelberg, P.O. (1967). "Unprogrammed Decision Making." *Industrial Management Review*, 8, 19–29.

Spinard, William (1960). "Correlates of Trade Union Participation: A Summary of the Literature." *American Sociological Review*, 25, 237–44.

Stark, Rodney, and William S. Bainbridge (1980). "Networks of Faith: Interpersonal Bonds and Recruitment to Cults and Sects." *American Journal of Sociology*, 85, 1376–95.

Staw, Barry M. (1976). *Intrinsic and Extrinsic Motivation*. Morristown, NJ: General Learning Press.

Staw, Barry M., and Jerry Ross (1985). "Stability in the Midst of Change: A Dispositional Approach to Job Attitudes." *Journal of Applied Psychology*, 70, 469–80.

Svalastoga, Kaare (1957). *Prestige, Class and Mobility*. London: William Heinemann (and the Scandanavian University Press).

Taylor, Fredrick W. (1967). *The Principles of Scientific Management*. New York: Norton (originally published in 1911).

Thompson, James D. (1967). *Organizations in Action*. New York: Free Press.

Thompson, Victor A. (1976). *Bureaucracy and the Modern World*. Morristown, NJ: General Learning Press.

Tocqueville, Alexis de (1968). *Democracy in America*. New York: Washington Square Press (first published in 1835–40).

Trendly, Mary Bosworth (1949). "Formal Organization and the Americanization

Process with Special Reference to the Greeks of Boston." *American Sociological Review*, 14, 44–53.

Trice, Harrison M. and Janice M. Beyer (1986). "Charisma and Its Routinization in Two Social Movement Organizations." *Research in Organizational Behavior*, 8, 113–64.

Van Maanen, John (1974). "Working the Streets: A Developmental View of Police Behavior." In H. Jacob, ed., *The Potential for Reform of Criminal Justice*. Beverly Hills, CA: Sage, 53–130.

Van Maanen, John, and Edgar Schein (1979). "Toward a Theory of Organizational Socialization." In Barry M. Staw, ed., *Research in Organizational Behavior: Vol. 1*. Greenwich, CT: JAI Press, 209–64.

Van Til, Jon (1985). "Mixed Motives: Residues of Altruism in an Age of Narcissism." In Larry F. Moore, ed., *Motivating Volunteers*. Vancouver, BC: Vancouver Volunteer Centre, 243–64.

Vroom, Victor H. (1964). *Work and Motivation*. New York: Wiley.

Vroom, Victor H., and Philip W. Yetton (1973). *Leadership and Decision-Making*. Pittsburgh, PA: University of Pittsburgh Press.

Walker, Charles R., and Robert H. Guest (1952). *The Man on the Assembly Line*. Cambridge, MA: Harvard University Press.

Wallace, M.J., and C.H. Fay (1983). *Compensation Theory and Practice*. Boston, MA: Kent.

Wallerstein, Immanuel (1965). "Voluntary Associations." In James C. Coleman and Carl G. Rosberg, Jr, eds, *Political Parties and National Integration in Tropical Africa*. Berkeley: University of California Press.

Wanous, John P. (1980). *Organizational Entry*, Reading, MA: Addison-Wesley.

Warner, W. Lloyd, *et al.* (1949). *Democracy in Jonesville*. New York: Harper.

Weber, Max (1968). *Economy and Society*. Guenther Roth and Claus Wittich, eds. New York: Bedminster Press (first English translation 1947).

Weiner, Yoash (1982). "Commitment in Organizations: A Normative View." *Academy of Management Review*, 7, 418–28.

Whyte, William F. (1955). *Money and Motivation*. New York: Harper.

Wilensky, Harold L. (1967). *Organizational Intelligence*. New York: Basic Books.

Williamson, Oliver E. (1967). "Hierarchical Control and Optimum Firm Size." *Journal of Political Economy*, 75, 123–38.

Williamson, Oliver E. (1975). *Markets and Hierarchies*. New York: Free Press.

Wilson, Kenneth, and Anthony M. Orum (1976). "Mobilizing People for Collective Political Action." *Journal of Political and Military Sociology*, 4, 187–202.

Wilson, Marlene (1976). *The Effective Management of Volunteer Programs*. Boulder, CO: Volunteer Management Associates.

Wood, James R. (1981). *Leadership in Voluntary Organizations*. New Brunswick, NJ: Rutgers University Press.

Wright, Charles R., and Herbert Hyman (1958). "Voluntary Association Membership of American Adults: Evidence From National Sample Surveys." *American Sociological Review*, 23, 284–93.

Young, Dennis R. (1987). "Executive Leadership in Nonprofit Organizations." In Walter W. Powell, ed., *The Nonprofit Sector*. New Haven, CT: Yale University Press, 180–94.

Zimmer, Basil G. (1955). "Participation of Migrants in Urban Structures." *American Sociological Review*, 20 (2), 218–24.

Zimmer, Basil G. (1956). "Farm Background and Urban Participation." *American Journal of Sociology*, 61, 470–5.

Name index

ACTION 64, 68
Adams, Robert Lynn 66
Aldag, Ramon J. 62
Alderfer, Clayton P. 156
Allen, Natalie 76
Allport, Gordon 70
Almond, Gabriel 65, 68, 69
Alutto, J.A. 95
Anderson, Barbara Gallatin 68
Anderson, John C. 71, 72, 73
Anderson, Robert T. 68
Anderson, Walfred A. 66
Argyle, Michael 68
Argyris, Chris 18
Arnold, Hugh J. 99

Babchuk, Nicholas 24, 26, 63, 65, 66,
    68, 71
Baetz, M.L. 131
Bainbridge, William S. 67
Bales, R.F. 139
Barber, Bernard 139
Barker, Roger G. 9, 42, 50–2, 55, 70,
    93, 94, 104, 164
Barnard, Chester I. 18, 119
Baron, James N. 155
Bass, B.M. 131
Batson, C. Daniel 76–7
Beal, George M. 89
Beard, D.W. 4
Bendix, Reinhardt 40
Benet, M.K. 44–5
Beyer, Janice M. 131
Billis, David 7, 29
Bohlen, Joe M. 89
Bolton, Michele Kremen 155
Booth, Alan 65, 68
Boulian, P.V. 98

Brief, Arthur P. 77
Brown, Emory J. 69
Buchanan, B. 95, 99
Bureau of Census, Current Population
    Survey 71–4
Bureau of Labor Statistics 159
Bushee, Frederick A. 71

Chapman, Terry H. 71
Charms, R. de 91
Clark, Peter B. 20, 24, 56, 66, 70, 75,
    77
Coke, J.S. 76–7
Conger, J.A. 131–2
Cousens, F.R. 66
Crampton, W.J. 98
Curtis, James 5, 65
Cyert, Richard M. 30

Deci, Edward L. 91
Dentler, R.A. 126
Dess, G.G. 4
Dickson, W.J. 86, 128, 162–3
Dotson, Floyd 6
Downing, Joseph 89
Dozier, J.B. 77
Dubin, Robert 48, 56

Edwards, John 64, 65
Eisenhardt, Kathleen 54
Elion, Sandra H. 123, 124, 132, 134,
    140, 146, 173
Ellis, J. 70
Erikson, Kai 105
Erikson, K.T. 126
Etzioni, Amitai 20–1, 22, 23, 70, 75–6,
    93, 94, 104, 105, 115–17, 120, 128

Fay, C.H. 166

Fayol, Henri 34
Feldman, Daniel C. 99
Festinger, Leon 91
Flashman, Robert 76–7
Fox, A. 41
Freedman, A. 25, 64

Galbraith, Jay R. 34, 47, 54, 113, 159
Gallagher, Orvoell R. 68
Gallup Organization 5, 65, 66, 67, 68,
    72–4, 77
Gamson, William A. 117–18
Gidron, Benjamin 76
Glaser, B.G. 199
Gold, Doris B. 27
Goodman, Paul S. 166
Gordon, C. Wayne 24, 26, 63, 71
Gottlieb, David 71
Gough, Harrison G. 69
Greer, Scott A. 115
Guest, Robert H. 105
Gulick, L.H. 34
Gump, Paul V. 9, 50–1, 70

Hackman, J. Richard 44, 62, 87, 88, 181
Hardee, J. Gilbert 65
Hausknecht, Murray 63, 68, 69
Hawthorne Studies 86
Heckscher, Gunnar 6
Heinrich, Max 67
Herzberg, F. 8
House, Robert J. 131, 136
Hrebiniak, L.G. 95
Hyman, Herbert 65, 68

Iaffaldano, M.T. 86
Independent Sector 5, 6, 67, 72–4

Jacoby, Arthur 24
Jenner, Jessica Reynolds 100, 101, 107
Jones, E.E. 90, 93

Kanter, Rosabeth Moss 94, 102–3, 106
Kanungo, R.N. 131–2
Katz, Daniel 85
Kiesler, Charles A. 95–6, 164
Klonglan, Gerald E. 89
Knoke, David H. 22, 24, 30, 67, 82, 93,
    94
Komarovsky, Mirra 68
Kouzes, James M. 162
Krackhardt, David 163
Kramer, Ralph M. 17, 182

Kreitner, R. 62

Lathram, Van M. 98
Lawler, Edward E., III 86, 113, 167
Leat, D. 70
Levine, A. 28
Levine, F.M. 61
Levine, M. 28
Lichtman, Cary M. 98
Likert, Rensis 88, 153, 203
Lippitt, Ronald 63, 70
Locke, Edwin A. 87
Lockwood, W.G. 65
Los Angeles Times 167
Lundberg, George A. 66, 68, 71
Luthans, Fred 62

McGrath, Joseph E. 51–2
McPherson, J.M. 4, 27, 65
Mahoney, Thomas A. 41
March, James G. 30, 62
Mason, D.E. 117, 124
Mausner, B. 8
Mayo, Selz C. 68
Meillassoux, Claude 78
Meindl, James R. 83
Meyer, John W. 52, 54, 172
Meyer, Marshall W. 52, 54
Miceli, M.P. 77
Michels, Robert 47, 137, 174
Miller, E.J. 185
Miller, Lynn E. 100
Milofsky, Carl 123, 124, 132, 134, 140,
    146, 173
Minnis, Mhyra S. 25, 66, 74, 78
Mintzberg, Henry 34, 159
Mischel, W. 88
Mogey, John 66
Moore, Joan W. 24–5
Moore, Larry F. 62, 71, 72, 73
Morris, Raymond N. 27
Motowidlo, Steven J. 77
Mowday, Richard T. 86–7, 97–8,
    99–100, 105
Muchinsky, P.M. 86
Mulford, Charles L. 89

Nadler, David A. 123, 125, 128
Naylor, Harriet H. 70
Noyes, K.H. 70

Oldham, Greg R. 44, 62, 87, 181
Olsen, Marvin 68

Olson, Manacur, Jr. 22, 76, 82
Organ, Dennis W. 87, 106, 113
Orum, Anthony M. 67, 68
Ouchi, William G. 153, 155, 167

Pearce, Jone L. 55, 77, 78, 87, 92, 166, 167, 203
Pennings, Johannes M. 166
Perrow, Charles 18, 22–4, 34, 84, 151, 159
Perry, James L. 87, 166
Peters, Thomas J. 119, 153
Petty, M.M. 86
Pfeffer, Jeffrey 87, 155
Phillips, Michael H. 77–8
Pinder, Craig C. 56, 61
Porter, Lyman W. 86, 98, 163
Posner, Barry M. 162
Powell, Gary N. 100
Prensky, David Mark 22, 30, 82, 93, 94
Puffer, Sheila M. 83

Quick, Sam 76–7

Rhode, John Grant 113
Rice, A.K. 185
Richards, M.D. 62
Roethlisberger, Fritz J. 86, 128, 162–3
Rose, Arnold M. 5, 68, 137
Ross, Jerry 85
Rothschild-Whitt, Joyce 25–6, 29, 30, 115, 122
Rowan, Brian 52, 54, 172
Rushton, J.P. 77
Rushton, William 76
Rynes, Sara L. 62

Salancik, Gerald R. 87, 95–7, 104
Schein, Edgar H. 42, 166
Schindler-Rainman, Eva 63, 70
Schram, Vicki R. 5, 71–2
Schwab, Donald P. 62
Scott, John C., Jr. 67
Scott, William Abbott 89
Seltzer, Joseph 100
Selznick, Philip 119
Shapiro, Susan P. 113
Sharp, Elaine B. 75, 78
Shaw, Marvin E. 123, 126
Sheridan, J.E. 62
Sills, David L. 23, 25, 27, 30, 48, 50, 67, 74–5, 77, 78, 80, 81, 90, 127, 137, 139, 151

Simon, Herbert A. 18, 47, 62, 109, 166
Slocum, J.W. 62
Smelser, Neil J. 79–80, 93, 136
Smith, C. 25, 64
Smith, C.G. 114, 120–1
Smith, David Horton 15, 23, 63, 64, 69, 74, 76, 89
Smith, F.J. 98
Smith-Lovin, Lynn 4, 27
Snow, David A. 67
Snyderman, B.B. 8
Soelberg, P.O. 62
Sorrentino, R.M. 77
Spinard, William 67
Stark, Rodney 67
Staw, Barry M. 85, 91–2, 140, 164
Steers, Richard M. 98
Strauss, A. 199
Suttle, J. Lloyd 87
Svalastoga, Kaare 6, 65

Tannenbaum, A.S. 114, 120–1
Taylor, Frederick W. 45
Thompson, James D. 18, 34, 45, 47–8, 52–3, 113
Thompson, Victor A. 18, 19, 29
Tocqueville, Alexis de 4
Trendly, Mary Bosworth 78
Trice, Harrison M. 131

Urwick, L. F. 34

Van Maanen, John 42, 164
Van Til, Jon 77
Verba, Sidney 65, 68, 69
Vroom, Victor H. 56, 86, 156

Walker, Charles R. 105
Wall Street Journal 161
Wallace, M.J. 166
Wallerstein, Immanuel 6
Wanous, John P. 62, 82, 159
Warner, W. Lloyd 25
Waterman, Robert H. 119, 153
Weber, Max 30, 50, 115, 131
Weiner, Yoash 105, 163
White, Randall 64, 65
Whyte, William F. 128, 157
Wilensky, Harold L. 134
Williamson, Oliver E. 53, 155
Wilson, James Q. 20, 24, 56, 66, 70, 75, 77

Wilson, Kenneth 67
Wilson, Marlene 79
Wood, James R. 118–19, 129
Wright, Charles R. 65, 68
Wright-Isak, Christine 67

Yetton, Philip W. 156
Young, Dennis R. 28, 79, 83, 84, 106,
    109, 112, 174, 178–9

Zimmer, Basil G. 67

Subject index

absenteeism 100, 111–12
Africa, voluntary associations 6, 78
age: relationship with volunteering 68, 69
altruism 11, 70, 76–8
apathy 137, 139
associations 22–3; definition 18
attitudes 85; of employees 11, 86–8; of volunteers 11, 87–103, 173–4; *see also* job satisfaction; organizational commitment
attributions 11
Australia: socioeconomic status of volunteers 65

"behavior settings" 9, 50–1
behavioral commitment 95–7, 163–4
behavioral demands 55

Canada: high levels of volunteer membership 5; motives for volunteering 71, 73; socioeconomic status of volunteers 65
charismatic leadership 131–6
charities 16–17
Chile: attitudes of volunteers 89; personality traits of volunteers 69
co-workers: friendship 162–3
cohesion commitment 102–3, 106
cohesive groups 122–8
commitment 102–7, 163–4
communication 37–8, 201, 203
compensation: effects on work design 158–9; symbolic role 165–8; *see also* pay
continuance commitment 102–3
control commitment 102–3
control of volunteers 12, 111–30

coordination 37–8, 52–3, 157
coordinators 45–7
core membership 10, 47–50, 205; altruism 134; exploitation 154–5; incentives 56; interpersonal influence 122–4, 170; recruitment 136–41, 174–6
crystallized norms 126–7

day care center (employee-staffed) 186
day care center (volunteer-staffed) 185–6; control of volunteers 127; coordination 46; employee–volunteer relations 143, 145; employees 142; individual dominance 132–3; mixed "professional" and "cause" character 80–1; officeholders 137; organizational commitment 99; ownership 19; restriction to limited tasks 129
day care centers 7, 194; hours of work 36; job satisfaction 90–1; support staff 44
decision-making: attractiveness 156
Denmark: high levels of volunteer membership 6; socioeconomic status of volunteers 65
differential labor costs 53–4

effort 101; devalued 164–5
egalitarianism 55–6
employee-staffed organizations, definition 185
employee-volunteer relations 141–7, 170, 177–8
employees: competition with volunteers 27–8; motivation 61–2;

organizational behavior 5;
professional status 143–4
esteem 115–17
explicitness of the act of volunteering
96–7

family planning clinic (employee-
staffed) 44, 191
family planning clinic (volunteer-
staffed) 190–1; coordination 46;
election of officeholders 137;
employee–volunteer relations 144;
employees 142; freedom of
volunteers 111–12, 132; ideological
characteristics 26; individual
dominance 132–4; mixed
"professional" and "cause" character
80–1; motives of volunteers 74;
organizational commitment 99;
ownership 19; problems of size 127;
professional credentials of volunteers
35, 49, 143, 144
family planning clinics 7, 194; hours of
work 36; job satisfaction 91
fire department (employee-staffed) 51,
121, 193
fire department (volunteer-staffed)
192–3; charismatic leader 132;
control of volunteers 127;
coordination 46; employee–volunteer
relations 143; employees 142;
"exchanges" with non-members 18;
membership list 154; motives of
volunteers 26, 35, 74; organizational
commitment 99, 171; ownership 19;
performance 18–19, 129; prestige of
offices 50; professional credentials of
volunteers 48–9, 143, 144;
professional standards 80–1; staffing
levels 51
fire departments 7, 195; hours of work
36–7; job satisfaction 91
food distribution agency see poverty
relief agency
France: levels of volunteer membership
5, 68
freedom of action 4, 112
friendship with co-workers 162–3

gender: relationship with volunteering
68
Germany: socioeconomic status of
volunteers 65

gift shop (employee-staffed) 121, 192
gift shop (volunteer-staffed) 191–2;
employee–volunteer relations 19,
125, 143–4, 153; employees 142; lack
of charismatic leadership 134–6, 176;
motives of volunteers 26, 74;
organizational commitment 99;
ownership 19, 20; problems of size
127; reliance on direct interpersonal
ties 81
gift shops 7, 195; hours of work 36; job
satisfaction 91
"Good Citizens" 74–5, 77
governmental volunteers 16–17
Great Britain: demographic
characteristics of volunteers 68;
socioeconomic status of volunteers
27, 65; volunteers in social welfare
service organizations 17
groups, cohesive 122–8

hours of work 36–7, 202, 204
"Humanitarians" 74–5

indifference 137, 139
information exchange 37–8
instrumental gain 202, 203
insufficient justification effect 91–2
interpersonal influence 12, 114, 120–3,
128, 129, 131–47, 174
interpersonal networks see social
networks
intrinsic interest 202, 203
irrevocability 96–7; see also revocability
Israel: volunteers in social welfare
service organizations 17

job design 33–6; effect on job
satisfaction 87–8
job duties 41–2
job performance see performance
job satisfaction 85, 90–1, 202, 205
"Joiners" 74–5

leadership 160–3; charismatic 131–6;
control of values 118–19; effect on
job satisfaction 87–8; external
scrutiny 121–2; martyred 162, 170,
176–7
League of Women Voters 120
legal-rational settings 30–1
leisure 10, 171, 181–2

"managerial work": attractiveness 156
"martyred leaders" 162, 170, 176–7
material rewards 202, 203
membership: apathy 137, 139;
    bifurcated 56; uncertainty 42–3,
    154–5; see also core membership;
    peripheral membership
Mexico: demographic characteristics of
    volunteers 68; high levels of
    volunteer membership 6;
    socioeconomic status of volunteers
    65
money see pay
motivation 11, 25, 61–84
motives 20, 70–6, 173–4

National Foundation for Infantile
    Paralysis 127; motives of volunteers
    74–5
Netherlands: volunteers in social
    welfare service organizations 17
newspaper (employee-staffed) 187
newspaper (volunteer-staffed) 186–7;
    coordination 46, 46–7; employees
    142; "exchanges" with non-members
    18; lack of charismatic leadership
    134–5, 176; motivation 74;
    organizational commitment 98–9;
    ownership 19; performance 18–19;
    personal animosities 153;
    professional credentials of volunteers
    49, 143; professional standards 80–1;
    punishment of volunteers 140–1;
    recruitment 51
newspapers 7, 194; hours of work 36;
    job satisfaction 91
nondependent workers 160–3
nonprofit nongovernmental
    organizations 16–17
normative commitment 163–4
normative power 115–17
norms 126–7

officeholders 136–7
orchestra (employee-staffed) 121, 190
orchestra (volunteer-staffed) 189–90;
    charismatic leader 132–3;
    employee–volunteer relations 145;
    employees 142; motives of
    volunteers 26, 74; organizational
    commitment 99; ownership 19;
    performance 51, 129; professional

credentials of volunteers 143;
    professional standards 80–1
orchestras 7, 194; hours of work 36, 37;
    job satisfaction 91; performance 51
organizational commitment 93–106,
    202, 205
organizational control see control of
    volunteers
organizational design 52–4
organizational goals 30, 80–1
organizational roles 29, 151–3
organizations 6, 16–17; ownership
    18–20; typologies 20–4; see also
    voluntary organizations

part-time workforce 157–8
pay: defining features 8–9; delivery
    systems 87–8; equal 40; see also
    compensation
Peace Corps 17
performance 83–4, 170–1, 178–9;
    expectations 56–7; levels 51
peripheral membership 10, 47–50, 205;
    assumption of core roles 170, 174–6;
    interpersonal influence 122–4;
    isolation 154–5; lack of interest 56
personal leadership 131–6
personal networks see social networks
Polio Veterans 74–5, 80
poverty relief agencies 7, 194; hours of
    work 36; job satisfaction 91
poverty relief agency (employee-
    staffed) 121, 188–9
poverty relief agency (volunteer-
    staffed) 188; absence of strong social
    ties 125–6; charismatic leader 132–3;
    election of officeholders 137;
    employee–volunteer relations 143,
    144–5; employees 142; formal
    procedures 41–2, 51, 171; freedom of
    volunteers 111, 132; mixed
    "professional" and "cause" character
    80–1; motives of volunteers 26, 74;
    organizational commitment 99;
    ownership 19; performance 51;
    problems of size 127; professional
    credentials of volunteers 35, 49;
    restriction to limited tasks 129
primary tasks 35
profit-making organizations: number
    of volunteers 16–17
proximity of co-workers 52–3
public nature of volunteering 96–7

"real-time" informal coordination 37–8
reasons for volunteering 20, 70–6,
    173–4
recruitment 159–60, 174
reliability 100, 111–12
remuneration see pay
retention of volunteers 82–3
revocability 104–6; see also
    irrevocability
roles 29, 151–3

secretaries 44–5
self-interest 70
separation of "work life" from
    "personal life" 38–40
service motives 76–8
service rewards 202, 203
shops see gift shops
social contacts 11, 39–40
social incentives for volunteering 78–80
social networks 159–60; importance for
    recruitment 66–8, 174
social power 116, 122–4
social rewards 202, 203
social welfare service organizations 17
socioeconomic status of volunteers
    65–6
support staff 44–5
Sweden: high levels of volunteer
    membership 6
symbolic rewards 202, 203
symphony orchestra see orchestra

task performance see performance
task-sets 35

uncertainty 3–4, 9, 55; in formal
    organizational roles 151–3; of

membership 10–11, 42–3; of
    membership boundaries 154–5; of
    roles 112–13, 169–73; of volunteer
    motivation 11
understaffing 50–2, 154
United States: demographic
    characteristics of volunteers 68;
    Farmers' Cooperatives 89; motives of
    volunteers 71–4; participation rates
    of volunteers 5–6; socioeconomic
    status of volunteers 65; volunteers in
    social welfare service organizations
    17
unreliability 109, 117, 126–7, 129

value of volunteer work 9–10, 26–8, 31
value-rational settings 30–1
values 115, 118–19
VISTA 17, 71
volition 96–7, 104–6
voluntary organizations 15–26;
    definition 185
volunteer–employee relations 141–7,
    170, 177–8
volunteers: demographic characteristics
    68–9; governmental 16–17;
    importance 161–2; individual goals
    30; personality 69–70; professional
    status 143–4; socioeconomic status
    65–6

wages see pay
work 171, 180–1
work attitudes see attitudes
work demands 202, 204
work praiseworthiness 202, 204
work procedures 202, 204
work settings 7–8
working hours 36–7, 202, 204
workplace attitudes see attitudes